THE OTHER SIDE OF VIRTUE

Where our virtues came from,
what they really mean,
and where they might be taking us.

First published by O-Books, 2008
O-Books is an imprint of John Hunt Publishing Ltd., Laurel House, Station Approach,
Alresford, Hants, SO24 9JH, UK
office1@o-books.net
www.o-books.com

For distributor details and how to order please visit the 'Ordering' section on our website.

Text copyright: Brendan Myers 2008

ISBN: 978 1 84694 115 3

A CIP catalogue record for this book is available from the British Library.

Design: Stuart Davies

Printed in the UK by CPI Antony Rowe
Printed in the USA by Offset Paperback Mfrs, Inc

We operate a distinctive and ethical publishing philosophy in all
areas of our business, from our global network of authors to
production and worldwide distribution.

THE OTHER SIDE OF VIRTUE

Where our virtues came from,
what they really mean,
and where they might be taking us.

Brendan Myers, Ph.D

BOOKS

Winchester, UK
Washington, USA

CONTENTS

ACKNOWLEDGEMENTS

In the summer of 2004, a friend of mine and I were exploring the forested countryside near a village in Hessen, in Germany. We found a landscape of gently rolling low hills, majestic hardwood trees that made the paths seem like cathedrals, and just the right amount of open meadow in between. Towns and settlements seemed to merge with the contour and character of the landscape. Flowers decked almost every house, in window boxes and hanging planters, and pictures of flowers were carved and painted onto the timbres, some of them more than five hundred years old. When we started out the day was sunny, clear, and beautiful. We ate from wild cherry trees that grew on the slopes of the hills. Within two hours we were caught in a vicious thunderstorm, and had to be rescued by a local farmer in his truck. Nonetheless, we still felt good. The sudden downpour only added to the beauty of the day. This experience got me thinking, and soon after that it got me writing.

'The Calling of the Immensity' was written in Germany and in Ireland. The other movements were written later, after moving back to Canada. I owe thanks to Philip Carr-Gomm and the Mount Haemus project for spurring me to turn some jumbled notes into an essay, and to turn an essay into a book. In the spring and summer of 2006 I presented what had been written so far at several conferences and community events. I wish to thank the organisers of these events for giving me the opportunity to share my ideas. I'm also grateful to the many people who attended my presentations for their valuable criticisms and suggestions.

There are some personal friends of mine whose advice, conversation, and help was so valuable that they must be named. Foremost among them are Laura Jackson, Tom Webb, Jennifer Gibson, and Amy Taylor. In different ways they all helped to clarify many things. And I am deeply grateful to Natasha Bertrand, who provided in-depth comments on the final manuscript, and showed me how my burdens were not so heavy as I imagined them to be. I also owe special thanks to my long-time friends Austin Lawrence and Maryanne Pearce. They introduced me to new research resources, and helped to shore up my confidence. But most of all, they welcomed me into their home like a family member for a whole summer, and they gave me the great gift of blessed time and space to write. I feel most fortunate to have all of these people as friends, and I often felt that while writing this book, I was writing for them.

Brendan Myers
Elora, Ontario, Canada
July 2007

I dedicate this one to
Maryanne Pearce and Austin Lawrence, and to their children
Kadri and Joven.
Blessed be!

OVERTURE: STORYTELLING AND FIRE

This book is meant to be read by candlelight. Go to a silent place, or as quiet a place as you can find. Seat yourself near a window with an interesting view, and open the curtains. Disable the ringer on your telephone. Have something to drink at hand. Arrange a pillow to support your neck and head. Take a moment to feel your breath. When you are still and at rest, the ceremony will begin.

* * *

Imagine a house. It is a simple house, yet comfortable and elegant, perhaps made of timber-frame, perhaps of brick or stone. The time of day is around the middle of the afternoon. The sky is partly cloudy, the air is warm, the trees and flowers still glistening from an early morning rain. In this house, someone lights the fire in the hearth. For a gathering of the clann is about to begin! Soon after the fire is lit, the guests start to arrive, in twos and threes and fours. As each guest passes under the arch of the door she is offered a welcoming hug, a cup of wine, and a seat by the fire. When the sun has almost set, someone lays a table for a feast. Three, four, perhaps five courses are prepared. Grandparents are served first, and then the smallest of the children, and then the rest. Stories cross the table back and forth, throughout the meal. Each guest takes her turn to recount a strange happening or new development in life, or a joke or a tall tale, or a fragment of personal history, or something else altogether. There may even be a debate or an argument, but it is friendly, as no one is trying to defeat anyone. When the feasting is finished, those who didn't help with the preparation clean off the table and put everything away. The gathering moves back to the circle around the fire, and then the storytelling continues. More wine is poured out. Musical instruments appear. Old songs and new songs pass through the fire. Everyone, or almost everyone, takes a turn, and sings along to their favourite ones. As children start passing into sleep, their guardians bring them to bed. Then the stories and songs grow more ribald and risky, and then after that, more subtle and sad.

Stars wheel overhead, and the moon passes into the west. The fire burns lower, until there are more embers than flames. Couples start to drift away, to light their own little fires in the privacy of each other's hearts. And when all the songs are sung and all the stories are told, then the last of the revelers kiss and hug each other, and pat each other's shoulders and wish each other well, and set out for home. Perhaps some of them look east, to see if a new morning is about to break. They pause for a moment to take in the sight, and to remember the reasons why life is good.

This story could have happened three thousand years ago. Yet it could have happened yesterday. For feasting and storytelling around a fire is the most ancient of humanity's rituals. To speak of a circle of people round a fire as the essence of community and social coherence is not to say anything new. But to speak of it as the essence of *humanity* is to call the mind back to mythology. It is to suggest that the distinctiveness of humanity is like that fire: something energetic, something in constant motion, something that shines brightly in the darkness, and even something that sometimes consumes and destroys what it touches. To sit in a circle with one's closest intimates, sharing the heat and light of a fire, sharing food, sharing music and stories and knowledge, is to share things to do with the body, the passions, the mind, and the heart—which all together, perhaps, constitute the spirit. I submit that this ancient ceremony, this original activity of love and pleasure, is the very birthplace and cradle of Virtue.

* * *

Did I really say *Virtue*?

Among fashionable people the notion of Virtue is an object of ridicule and contempt. It implies a style of life in which people aim to keep up an appearance of moral purity or perfection, even if such purity is secretly admitted to be unattainable in practice. The very word reminds us too much of Sunday school as a child. You had to dress in your best-looking clothes. Then you had to sit in a circle of uncomfortable chairs while a middle-aged woman with horn-rimmed glasses and a beehive hairdo told you how important it is to be clean, polite, friendly, helpful, obedient to grown-ups, and self-consciously *nice* to everybody. It is no wonder that to most people, Virtue means the same thing as unbearable pretentiousness.

More seriously, the idea of Virtue that most people find familiar comes from early Christian sources, especially writers like Aquinas and Augustine. The virtues they listed were generally *passive* qualities: that is, qualities which in some way or another depend on some kind of social or theological authority. In the 4th century St. Augustine upheld *docilitas*, or 'to be docile', as the most important Christian virtue. The word *docilitas* is etymologically derived from the Latin word *docere*, meaning 'a teaching'. Modern words like 'doctor' or 'doctrine' come from the same source. To be docile, therefore, is 'to be able to be taught', that is, to have the disposition to accept authority. Six centuries after Augustine, St. Thomas Aquinas made a list of seven special virtues, which he thought were essential for every Christian. Three of them, the 'theological' virtues of Faith, Hope, and Charity, require the virtuous person to give himself to others, even to the point of total self denial. The other four, the 'cardinal' virtues of Courage, Prudence, Temperance, and Justice, are active virtues, requiring initiative and will. But they were borrowed from the pre-Christian tradition that begins with Plato and Aristotle. Chastity, best known as the Christian virtue of sexual abstinence, is actually a special form of temperance. Its role is to regulate anything that might stir up the passions, whether sexual or otherwise. Therefore Chastity also requires dull clothing, inoffensive speech, and restraint in the enjoyment of music, dance, food, and material comfort. Passive virtues like these do involve willpower and strength, as counter-intuitive as that may seem. But this strength serves to police the passions, and prevent anything from stirring up the delicate serenity of *docilitas*. In general, passive and self-denying qualities like these are what most people understand as Virtue itself.

But there are problems here. You could be successfully Virtuous this way without exploring much of the world, without discovering your full potential, without accomplishing anything of significance (even to yourself), and without even being *happy*. Of course, the effect of the successful development of this kind of virtue is that one may not even *want* any of these things. But it seems to me that a restrained life is also an *incomplete* life—it would miss out on so much of what makes life interesting, enjoyable, and worthwhile, and so much of what it is to be fully human. The story of Christian virtue also begins with the story of Moses, the holy man who climbed the holy mountain to receive the Law. Like any system of ethics based on law, it was intended to separate right from wrong as clearly as possible. This is why most of them begin with 'thou shall not'. Of course, the law forbids things that nearly everyone would agree do not belong in a civil society: thievery and murder, for instance. So on the face of it, there can be no objection. But we should be very cautious about taking up such a gift and accepting it without question. Such pre-packaged gifts are sometimes like the Trojan Horse. They often conceal all sorts of other problems and complications. In the case of the Ten Commandments, the problem is this: if you accept it, you effectively hand over to God the responsibility for determining what is right and wrong. Your only choice in life is whether to obey or to rebel—precisely the choice made by Eve, in the Garden of Eden. It might be explained that human beings are not qualified, not intelligent or knowledgeable enough, or simply not *entitled* to make such determinations on their own. In that presupposition one can see a very un-flattering picture of what it is to be human. I find that lack of confidence in humanity disturbing.

Fortunately, we also have *other stories* to turn to, which are not Christian, but which express and define many ethical and social ideas which we still take to be important today. We have *Beowulf* from Anglo-Saxon Britain, the *Illiad* and *Odyssey* from ancient Greece, the *Eddas* and the many sagas of the Scandinavian world, Germany's *Nibelungenlied*, Ireland's *Táin Bo Cuailnge* and *Caith Maigh Tuireadh*, just to name a few. In the ancient world such stories were recited by semi-professional storytellers as after-dinner entertainment in the feasting-hall, often to musical accompaniment. They were not always the simple and child-friendly faerie tales we find familiar. Sometimes the main heroes are rough and violent, or even excessively cruel. Sometimes there are scenes of explicit sexuality. Not in spite of, but precisely because of such scenes, those stories are *honest* in their representation of human relations. In that honesty there are strong moral messages being expressed. They show how a good person acts, and they show the consequences of wickedness and vice. Furthermore, in mythology the gods do not tell anyone what to do, except for when they initiate heroic quests. Nor do they do any of the hero's work for him. Indeed some heroes deliberately challenge the supremacy of the gods, and try to usurp their place. This makes the role of the supernatural very different indeed. And sometimes the gifts the gods gave us were not pre-packaged and ready-made like the Ten Commandments. Prometheus gave us the gift of fire. Demeter, Adonis, Gaia, and others give us their own bodies for food. The Tuatha de Dannan of Ireland gave us the Four Hallows: a spear, a sword, a cauldron, and a stone, objects associated with the sovereignty of the land. Other gods gave us knowledge for hunting, agriculture, metallurgy, weaving, spinning, musicianship, even language and literacy, and more things besides. These are gifts of a different nature. What they essentially *are* frequently depends upon what we *do* with them. And while most ancient mythologies describe an afterlife for the soul, that afterlife was not the reward for living virtuously. Rather, living a good life, here on Earth, was its own reward. The afterlife, if there was one, would be a continuation of your mortal life; and anyway, it would take care of itself.

The original idea of Virtue had nothing to do with Christianity. In Europe, it is older than the Gospels by more than six hundred years. Consider the origin of the word itself. It comes from two sources. The first is the Latin 'Virtus', itself rooted in the word 'Vir', meaning 'man'. From this direction, Virtue means something like 'manliness', and implies 'macho' qualities like toughness and aggression. The other source is the Greek word 'Arête', which is sometimes directly translated as 'Virtue', but can also mean 'Excellence'. Excellence is what happens when some quality or talent is perfected, completed, rendered praiseworthy and beautiful. It is what makes someone or something stand out as special, a cut or two above the ordinary, and deserving of special admiration. There is nothing passive about Excellence. Instead of modesty or humility, the logic of *arête* calls for active qualities like initiative, honour, and intelligence. It also implies a few half-moral, half-aesthetic qualities like nobility, strength, proper pride, beauty, and grace. And it implies various social qualities, like friendship, generosity, honesty, truthfulness, and love. Virtue ethics could be more properly called 'Arêteology', meaning an account (*logos*) of what is excellent (*arête*) in human affairs. This account describes not only the things someone does, but also the kind of person she is. And it had almost nothing to do with obeying laws. Laws were meant for the ordering of society; *being a good person* was something else. The questions of ethics, in the ancient world, would never have been: What laws or rules should I follow? Which of my choices creates the least harm, or the most benefit, for those it affects? Who am I to obey, and what gives him his authority? To a Virtuous person of the ancient world, those would have been the wrong questions. The right questions were what kind of person should I be? What kind of life should I live? What is an excellent human being like? What must I do to be happy? The general answer to questions like these went like this. You have to produce within yourself a set of habits and dispositions, something like a 'second nature', which would give you full command over your powers and potentials. In other words, you have to transform your *character*. The 'familiar' side of virtue has to do with a predisposition to follow laws and commandments. The 'other side' asserts that *who you are* is much more important than the rules you follow, and at least as important as the things you do, when it comes to doing the right thing, and finding the worth of your life.

The term 'character' has many meanings. Aristotle defined it as "that by reason of which we say that the personages are of such and such a quality" (*Poetics*, 5084). Here I shall take it to mean the sum total of all one's habits. But that may not be all. Character stands at the intersection between your own, internal, first-person experience of the world, and the various ways that other people recognise you. Character has to do with your values and choices, desires and interests, feelings and emotions, expectations and perceptions, even your conflicts and problems. It especially concerns how those things are consistently sustained over time. It thus encompasses your whole sense of being a 'self', being a 'person', being *who you are*. A "virtuous" character, in the original sense of the idea, was not simply a good or kind personality, nor simply the kind of person who regularly helped others. She was also someone in full possession of herself. Her actions expressed her sense of self-worth, her dignity, and her pride—indeed her actions expressed her *spirit*. Were someone like that to appear today, we might be inclined to admire her integrity, or else find her a little bit intimidating. And in both cases this response would be surprisingly close to the original meaning.

This book is about that original idea, and how it is intimately connected with what it is to be human, and what it means to live a worthwhile life. I shall show how it appeared in the heroic and classical cultures of ancient Europe. Then I shall show how it appeared again in various different historical movements that revived or patterned themselves after those ancient cultures. The Italian Renaissance, Romanticism in High Germany and in Merry Old England, are only the most well known examples. There are also contemporary movements afoot, such as modern-day Druidry and Wicca, which embody the original idea of Virtue in various eclectic ways. What all of these different movements seem to have in common is that in their own way they all expressed one or more of the following three primary ideas.

1. First and foremost, life involves inevitable encounters with events that seem, at least at first, to impose themselves upon you. Fortune, nature, other people, and death itself, are among them.

2. Second, these events also invite us to respond. The response generally involves the development of various human potentials and resources. Some of these are social, such as one's family and friendship ties, and some are personal and internal, like courage and integrity.

3. And third, that if we respond to these imposing events with excellence, and if the excellent response becomes *habitual*, they can be transformed into sources of spiritual meaning and fulfillment. This transformation opens the way to a worthwhile and flourishing life.

There are a few others, but these ones are the most important. If I had to gather them into one sentence, this is what I would say: Virtue is the ancient idea that excellence in human affairs is the foundation of ethics, spirituality, self-knowledge, and especially the worthwhile life.

*   *   *

Three mottos were inscribed over the entrance to the temple of the Oracle of Delphi: "Know Yourself", "Everything in moderation and nothing in excess", and "Thou Art." Why are these mottos important? What do they have to do with Virtue? I believe the first one, the requirement to Know Yourself, is how the source of ethics originally appeared to ancient people. It is what Socrates referred to when he said that "the unexamined life is not worth living." Questions of character, selfhood, and identity took precedence over utilitarian or legalistic questions of right and wrong for nearly all ancient European poets and philosophers. Frequently the problem took the form of the question of what is humankind's purpose, function, destiny, and place in the universe. Before philosophy attempted to interpret the world in a systematic way, artists and mystics interpreted the world mythologically — often doing so in ways that deliberately inter-mixed cosmological speculation with moral teaching and artistic expression. When the ancient storytellers recited the heroic tales of Beowulf, or Cu Chullain, or Seigfreid, or Odysseus, they were getting more than just their after-dinner entertainment. They were also getting a fairly substantial moral education. Portraits of excellent human beings were being painted for them. People would learn about the virtues, and the vices, what they would be praised for, and how they would be judged, through the characters in the stories. And more than that: they learned what to do to lead flourishing, worthwhile, and meaningful lives.

One might expect, therefore, that a society like ours which prizes individualism would also generally uphold an ethic of self-knowledge. As the Canadian philosopher Charles Taylor defined it, contemporary individualism is the idea that:

...everyone has a right to develop their own form of life, grounded on their own sense of what is really important or of value. People are called upon to be true to themselves and to seek their own self-fulfillment. What this consists of, each must, in the last instance, determine for him- or herself. No one else can or should try to dictate its content.[1]

It's now rather unusual to hear the qualities of passive self-denial, like humility, being promoted as positive and necessary qualities for all. Instead we uphold values like personal freedom, limited only by minimal requirements to refrain from interfering in anyone else's freedom. But let us be honest: is this really all that one can expect from someone who has attained a mature individuality? When asked "who are you?" most people give the most mundane sort of answer: they give their name, or a job description. A few might answer with a paradoxical non-sequitor that reflects the absurdity of the question, like "I am who I am." The deeper ethical and metaphysical problem is rarely addressed. What kind of being can give an answer, of any kind, to that question? "An individual", is a common answer today. But what an empty and banal answer it is! As I see it, self-knowledge is not a casual stroll in a garden. It is a climb on a rugged mountain; it is a deep dive in a cave. The call to "Know Yourself" presents selfhood and identity as *a problem to be resolved*, not something given to you like a finished product. It presents selfhood and identity as if it were an unknown quantity: as if the news of who and what we are is still traveling to us from the distant reaches of outer space. To pose selfhood and identity as a problem is to pose your eyes and ears, your skin and flesh, your teeth and bones, even your own mind, as a problem. It is to pose everything in your life as a problem, even the very presentation of the problem itself. And that, it seems to me, is something many people utterly fail to grasp.

Is my judgement too harsh? I think not. Western civilisation is one of the wealthiest, most technologically advanced, most knowledgeable societies the world has ever known. Its people enjoy great personal and political freedom. So why is there so much *unhappiness* in our society? A California psychologist found that teenagers today are much more self-centered and rebellious than teens of 50 years ago. But they are also more prone to anxiety and depression. Another study undertaken by researchers at Florida State University found that compared to 20 years ago, high-school students have increasingly unrealistic expectations for their own futures, and less and less real motivation and drive to make those expectations happen. They would rather demand things than work for them. A researcher at Columbia University in New York found that "while affluence provides a plethora of opportunities, it seems to do little for upper-middle-class kids' sense of self... they have higher rates of depression, anxiety and substance abuse than the general population."[2] Alan Bloom, author of *The Closing of the American Mind*, observed how the ethic of individualism has produced not mature self-knowledge, but immature self-centeredness. This self-centeredness has bred an insidious relativism, which leads his students to be apathetic about major social, political, environmental, and cultural problems. As he says:

> The great majority of students, although they as much as anyone want to think well of themselves, are aware that they are busy with their own careers and relationships. There is a certain rhetoric of self-fulfillment that gives a patina of glamour to this life, but they can see that there is nothing particularly noble about it. Survivalism has taken the place of heroism as the admired quality. This turning in on themselves is not, as some would have it, a return to normalcy after the hectic fever of the sixties, nor is it preternatural selfishness. It is a new degree of isolation that leaves young people with no alternative to looking inward. The things that almost naturally elicit attention to broader concerns are simply not present.[3]

I observed this trend among many of my own students at three different universities where I taught undergraduate courses in philosophy, as did most of my colleagues. The most common answers that students gave to principled questions concerning the right and the good were evasive statements like, "That depends on your point of view", or "I can see both sides of the argument", or "that's just my opinion", or "Your mileage may vary".

One of my most articulate students, when asked what things make life meaningful, said: "Oh, whatever people want, so long as we're not harming or judging anyone." I understand why my students spoke this way. They do not wish to create controversy or conflict; they do not wish to appear dogmatic or closed-minded. Nonetheless, these answers are varieties of deliberate non-thinking. They are public declarations of an unwillingness to commit to anything, and an unwillingness to make serious choices about the value and meaning of their own lives. Indeed I began to doubt whether they believed anything substantial at all.

If apathy and relativism do not seem obviously problematic, since they might harm no one, then what about addiction? The personal and social effects of addiction to gambling, alcohol, tobacco, drugs, pornography, junk food, shopping, even video games, are profound, and often destructive. Observe how so many people believe that having a good time with friends means "getting wasted". If addiction isn't enough, then what about yob culture? A 'yob' is a British term for someone who regularly performs criminal acts, ranging from petty theft and vandalism, up to arson, assault, sexual violence, and occasionally even murder. But they do these things not for economic gain, nor for power. They do them to stave off boredom. 'Yob culture' is criminality for the sake of entertainment. Witnesses reported, for example, that the shooters at Littleton "whooped and hollered like it was a game", as they spread terror on their school.[4]

What about the way our economic and political systems, our public debates in the mass media, and even legal proceedings in our courtrooms, are full of competition and aggression? One of capitalism's central principles, for instance, is 'competitive advantage'. In the race for wealth, prestige, success, and even justice, those who attack others and put others down are rewarded more than those who lift themselves up. We congratulate bigots and slanderers for their toughness, their purity of intention, their powers of observation, especially if they are politicians, lawyers, religious leaders, television hosts, or journalists. Perhaps we are glad we were not targeted by them, or we are secretly afraid to be targeted next.

Canadian philosopher Charles Taylor called this situation 'The Malaise of Modernity'. As he described it, this malaise has three parts. The first is 'atomistic individualism', which gives people enormous personal freedom while at the same time cutting people off from each other. People no longer see their social relations as inherently valuable. Rather, people see others as burdens, or as instruments for their own personal gain. Friendships are sustained only as long as each individual finds personal gain in the relationship: hence they are almost infinitely interchangeable, and even disposable. The second part of modern malaise is 'instrumental reason'. This form of reasoning calculates one's personal economic interests very precisely, but at the cost of stripping away much of the magic, the mystery, and wonder of the world. Instrumental reason turns everything into a factor in a cost-benefit analysis. The third part of the Malaise, according to Taylor, is the way our politicians act more like managers than like leaders. The summary result, as he describes it, is that the values of modernity *cannot offer anything of value beyond the self to live for.* As Taylor says, "individualism involves a centering on the self and a concomitant shutting out, or even unawareness, of the greater issues or concerns that transcend the self, be they religious, political, historical."[5] By its very logic, individualism is categorically unable to recognise the independent significance of history, politics, the environment, social justice, art and culture, friendship, honour, family life, even love. It offers only 'self-interest' as the reason why people should care about their relationships and communities, the natural world, and themselves. It therefore cannot offer people anything unambiguously meaningful beyond themselves to strive for. It gives people no reason not to waste their lives as couch potatoes if that is what they have individually chosen to do.

Most of the aforementioned researchers pointed to economic or social explanations: the movement of industrial jobs to third-world countries, the dumbing-down of public education, the breakdown of the traditional nuclear family, the glamorization of 'slacker culture' in films like *Failure to Launch* and *Clerks*. But I suspect these problems may also be products of something deeper, something that strikes both rich and poor alike, something like *nihilism*. This is the condition of someone who perceives her life to have no meaning, no purpose, or nothing genuinely worthwhile to live for. Perhaps many people engage in addictions, or yob culture, or worse acts of violence, because they are unable to see anything better, or perhaps anything *else*, to live for. Perhaps many people do these things in order to have their very existence noticed and acknowledged as *something* rather than nothing, even if that something is self-destructive, or criminally insane. Instead of a model of a genuinely good and beautiful life, we are presented with unlimited material consumerism: in the form of reality television, celebrity fashion and lifestyle, other forms of escapist pop-culture entertainment, and the "rat race" of "the 24/7 lifestyle" in which everyone must "keep up with the Joneses". These things distract our attention away from the crisis of meaning in our lives: hence why they are so popular. But the kind of life these things offer is fitting only for zombies, not human beings. They merely project the superficial appearance of living well. The mantra of pop culture, "Live life to the fullest", in my judgement has lost its meaning. Perhaps it never had a meaning, except as a marketing slogan. At any rate, it has become the new banality.

* * *

These are two of the main paradigms of value that contemporary 'Western' culture supports. The first is the model of Christian ethics. It has the advantage of being simple and easy to grasp, and it tends to produce good social consequences. But its divine-command model of ethics requires passive obedience to authority, and the suppression of certain healthy human passions, especially those associated with sexuality. The other paradigm of life is modern individualism. It offers enormous personal and political freedom, perhaps more freedom than any other model of social life ever adopted by any people in history. But it has a secret nihilism in its heart. It doesn't offer a substantial reason or purpose to live. It doesn't tell us *what* our freedom is *for*. That empty space could be filled with something noble. But it could just as easily be filled with material consumerism, substance abuse, or criminal violence. Of the two, I therefore see nihilism as the bigger danger. But both of these models, in different ways and for different reasons, fail to deliver what they promise, namely, *genuine self-knowledge*. They therefore cannot be the basis of a genuinely worthwhile and flourishing life.

How do you even begin to find that self-knowledge? In this book I will *not* be saying that the worthwhile life is merely a matter of always 'seeing the bright side' or 'learning the lesson' of every difficult situation. Although I talk about Spirit, I will *not* be talking about 'channeling positive energy'. These popular proverbs simply do not do the job: they only offer short-term distractions. They do not offer any genuine self-knowledge since they do not pose any serious and deep questions, nor do they put any of your powers and potentials to the test. And they often distract from the problems that they are supposed to solve, since they assert that a change in attitude or point-of-view, or even the mere repetition of a positive affirmation, is all one needs to do to be happy. No engagement with the world or with other people is asked for. But 'positive thinking' alone will not tell you who you are. Nor will it cure cancer, nor will it prevent global warming, nor eradicate poverty, nor will it help you grieve the death of a loved one. Some situations do not go away no matter what your attitude is. In fact the attitude-based prescription for happiness tends to create an infantile self-centeredness which recognizes nothing of value beyond the self. It therefore fails to create the genuine sense of meaning that it promises. Instead it just tires people out, and often leaves them less happy than when they began. Hence why its believers end up spending more money on the next motivational training event, the next life-coaching session, the next neuro-linguistic programming treatment, or the next afternoon of retail therapy—or, even worse, the next Virginia Tech shooting.

My suggestion for an answer will not be a modification of either Christianity, or modern individualism. Rather, I believe we should assert something like this. The good life involves each person finding within herself the purpose and worth of life. But this activity of self-exploration must not cut people off from sources of meaning beyond themselves. It must not lead the way to nihilism, relativism, apathy, and empty self-centeredness. Similarly, we should assert that some values really are 'out there', beyond the self, and are not a matter of personal opinions and preferences. But we must find a way to assert this without falling back on old models of conformity and obedience. That is the philosophical task I've set for myself in this book. It's not as easy a task as it may sound, and in some ways my solution will be only partial, and incomplete. I'll not pretend that I have all the answers. The first movement introduces the matter through poetry. Movements two, three, and four describe the historical origin and development of the idea of virtue, and of the worthwhile life. In the fifth movement, I look at its logical structure. Throughout the book, I ask questions like, How should *we* conceive Virtue? Are there any genuine sources of meaning that justify it? What, if anything, makes for a worthwhile life?

Interestingly, these crucial questions can only be asked after a break from the original problematic situation has already begun. To ask, 'Where does the worthwhile life begin?' is already to embark on the worthwhile life. This may seem paradoxical. But it is the key to the answer. To think philosophically or spiritually is to think in a way that breaks from the previous non-philosophical, non-spiritual way of thinking. To even ask how to begin to think differently is already to think differently. The process is normally initiated by an experience that cuts into the structure of one's ordinary routine, as if from outside. Something must happen that cannot be accommodated by an auto-pilot. Self-knowledge is found, perhaps only found, with an event or a situation that *calls one's life into question*.

This thought-opera is a sustained exploration of that central, definitive, and transformative moment, the moment in which a person responds to something that questions her life. It is also about the response, in which a person discovers who she is. We shall explore fragments of literature, storytelling, and history from before the advent of Christian virtue, and before the rise of modern malaise. From there, we shall ask questions about what excellence is, how we flourish as human beings, and what things make life worth while. These are ethical questions, for they are questions concerning how we ought to live. Of all questions, surely they are among the most important that anyone will face in their lives. Anything else we know, or think that we know, suspends itself whenever the central ethical question appears. Self-knowledge blossoms first and foremost with adventurous transformations of our way of being in the world. The Immensity, as I shall call it, is the situation that calls upon us to make the choices which create those transformations. It is a situation that *changes* us. But since our choices are involved, this is the change that also *configures* us, *creates* us, and so *makes* us who we are. To answer the call to Know Yourself is not only to discover who and what you are, but also to *become* that which you discover yourself to be.

FIRST MOVEMENT:
GATHERING THE FRAGMENTS

1. People! Why do you busy yourselves so? Why all this flutter and flurry? Why the toiling, the fighting, the building up and tearing down? What are you doing? Where are you going? And—why the costumes and why the masks? Who are you? Who *were* you—before you went mad? If you can still remember at all?

2. The life work of the noble soul is this: to fashion Beauty and The Good as one.

3. Wyrd, Urverly, and Skuld: ignore these grey goddesses at your own risk. Any young man who scorns them will die. Actually, the truth is that even if you court them and earn their love, they will still kill you—but it will be a brilliant ride!

4. The semi-magical energy of life flows all over the world. It is neither created nor destroyed, but constantly changes shape, from the green mantle of the earth, to fur and feather, and scale and skin. Even now it has been gathered for you, from all over the world, and put into your hands. Who knows what great things were accomplished by the heroes of the past with that self-same energy! And what new potentials will you create with it, and bequeath to the world?

5. Dancing, singing, feasting, making music, and love—these are the sacraments of *my* temple. For to share them at all, one must hold certain virtues in common—like the ability to affirm that life is good. That affirmation can bless and make sacred the ground that you walk on.

6. It's amazing—you think you know someone well for a long time, and then one small unexpected thing happens and she becomes a complete

stranger. But it is usually the case that the ways in which other people are strange and different are also the ways they are *interesting*. Indeed it is when we discover something new and wonderful about them, when we least expect it, that we love them the most.

7. Mediaeval astrologers assigned virtues to the seven spheres of sun, moon, and planets, and to each of the twelve signs of the Zodiac. The idea was to make certain qualities appear part of the very fabric of nature and the cosmos itself. To fight against them was to fight against nature; an ultimately futile and self-destructive thing to do. We enlightened moderns, who know better than to believe in magic, enforce our virtues with the invisible hand of economics and technological progress.

8. Just about every choice you ever make in life creates new tracks of inevitability, and projects them forward to the future. Especially the choices which are *irreversible*, the choices which entail no going back to un-do what was done. These choices create a new *destiny* for you, and sometimes also for the world. Let us pass a judgement upon our destinies, as we do upon our choices.

9. The Great Queen visited me one long and lonely night, and said: "You shall be my representative and my chief ambassador on Earth." Naturally I accepted. How could I refuse? Yet I could not help but think that She offers this job to almost everybody.

10. When the foundation of ethics is duty and law, it will usually be the case that the law will command things that are contrary to our inclinations, habits, and desires. Indeed it is likely that the law will assume that people are naturally predisposed to do exactly the *opposite* of what the laws require them to do.

11. "It is the eleventh hour, and we stand at the turning-point in history"— don't we always?

12. The greatest achievement of spirit: the ability to transform nearly anything—even our suffering and tragedy—into *art*.

13. The gods and heroes of mythology fought with dragons, giants, fell beasts and monsters: the children of the primordial chaos from which the world was won. The new monsters threatening the world today were born not of chaos, but of *apathy*. The quest to find and to fight them will take a hero to foreign lands, just as the adventures of mythology took the heroes of ancient times to the Otherworld. But the final battle for the meaning of your life will be fought within your mind.

14. Do we really know that the virtues of the past would be good for the present? What would be the *reason* that ancient values are good for us, and where would we find that reason? Not simply 'because they are ancient', for that would lead us back to circular arguments. How about from the simple wish to Know Yourself, and have a good and beautiful life? If that is the animal we are tracking, then our hunting ground could be the whole field of history. For the age of an idea is not the ground of its truth.

15. Virtue in unexpected places: even a deck of Tarot cards promotes Justice, Strength, and Temperance. It has models of Virtuous people, like kings, queens, priests, lovers, and fools. Of course, it also has that other fellow—

16. See humankind at its best and its worst, and say to yourself the magic words "Thou Art." For everything that others have done—dwells also as potential in you.

17. The strength, or the health, or the fragility, of your sense of self worth can often be revealed by which star in the sky you wish upon.

18. Perhaps the reason for all the taboos and moral warnings about sex is because in sexuality we discover so much about who and what we really are.

19. A beautiful moment is celebrated by everything in the world.

20. We hear so much talk about survival—given the threats of global warming, attacks by foreign terrorists, or the depletion of the world's petroleum and other strategic resources. The threats are very real—but the talk of survival is all so much flappery. Survival is not an end in itself. *Life* is. And there is so much more to life than mere survival.

21. If your deity dwells within the circles of the world, and not in some separate, transcendental realm, it will follow that people or things which are exemplars of excellence, any kind of excellence, will embody the divine image more perfectly—whether they are paragons of goodness and beauty, or of wickedness and vice. But it will also be the case that *illumination* and *enlightenment* itself may be found in the wonder of the earth, the voice and the touch of a lover, and the integrity of one's own soul.

22. Another person is another world.

23. To be receptive need not mean the same as to be passive. To be receptive takes preparation, and perhaps a bit of work and effort as well, involved in the act of *pulling something in.*

24. The worst thing in the world is a person with no passion.

25. For us, spirit is not something to be waited for. Nor is it something to 'have' in your heart or mind. Nor is it the spirit which 'has' a body. It simply doesn't fit the case to use the language of *possession* to talk about spirit. We should, to be more accurate about it, use the language of *activity.* For us, spirit is something to *do.*

26. The world is not a refugee camp, nor is it a prison, nor a cave of shadows—unless we treat it that way. The world is our home and place, our castle and our garden—but again, only if we make it so.

27. You are what you do. Therefore do that which will transform you into the person you wish to be.

28. To some, Death makes the shadows deepen and grow. It makes the work we must do in life seem empty and less worth doing. But Death can also make the beauties and wonders of the world become all the more precious, and the injustices of the world all the more outrageous. It can force people to make the most of what they have in front of them.

29. Antoine de Saint-Exupery said "Man discovers himself when he measures himself against the obstacle." He wrote this in a novel about flying single-seat reconnaissance aircraft; his obstacles were gravity, and the earth beneath his wings. Surely he was right: sometimes we discover our own power when encountering something that *stands in its way*.

30. The worthwhile life gives to itself its own morality. Its very logic produces its own laws, and inside itself it separates right from wrong. The quest for the good life creates for itself its own destiny.

31. The call to Know Yourself permits no self deception. It calls for an acknowledgement of both the fire of the divine within us, and also the earth of mortality upon us.

32. In any disaster or catastrophe, when great losses and tragedies are about to happen, or have happened, the only answer that is truly spiritual is the one which has *confidence in humanity*, and trusts in humanity's ability to solve its own problems. Any other answer is misanthropy.

33. People flourish best when they live not just for their own sake, but mainly for the sake of life itself—their own life, the life of others, and the world, all together. Those who live only for their own sakes end up with small and limited lives.

34. At the end of the eleventh century, the Pope threatened to excommu-

nicate anyone who had long hair, and ordered that such people were not to be prayed for when dead. Anselm, Archbishop of Canterbury, threatened the same, even during the reign of King Henry I, who wore ringlets. I wonder what the pope and the saint were afraid of. Were they worried that care for the body would lead to a neglect for the things of the soul? Was long hair a symbol of strength, pride, beauty, or even *virility*? Were they afraid that a fashion for it would trigger—a resurgence of paganism?

35. Sometimes the only choices open to us are absurd choices, reflecting an absurd situation. But that is no reason *not to choose*.

36. Whether the gods exist or whether they do not exist, whether magic and prayer really works or whether they are just forms of therapy, whether or not we have a soul and whether it is immortal, whether or not there is a heaven and a hell awaiting us after death—nevertheless we must still discover how to live. For if I possess all the knowledge of metaphysics and cosmology, or all the important occult secrets old and new, even the wisdom of the gods themselves, and yet did not know how to live, then I will have failed as a human being.

37. The priestess of Delphi says, "Know Yourself". The very statement, whether a request or a demand, presupposes that people do not intrinsically or automatically know themselves. But how can this be? Are you a stranger to your own soul? In fact the answer is often Yes—for often you find your own actions *surprising to yourself.*

38. What a sorcerer is the Bard! How by the magic power of *storytelling* she can order the heavens, raise the dead, and teach us who we are.

39. If one believes that God is up there in heaven, separate from the world, and is preparing a reward for you in the next life, the belief can have the result of making people accept their fate, however hard and unjust, and be less willing to change it. But for us, who find illumination in the mortal world, the situation is this: Where poverty, oppression, or pollution has

taken root, and made the world less fit for the flourishing of life, there we find *work to do.*

40. Kant said that practicing virtue will not make you happy, but only "worthy of happiness". Yet one should always be suspicious when someone says doing the right thing is serious business. Why should the beautiful life be put in opposition to the good life? Only to make life more bearable for those who have lost the taste for it. Indeed the Golden Rule is usually preached with great gusto by those who have lost the spontaneous talent to love their neighbors.

41. You say it is blasphemy to find salvation here on Earth, in the material world? I say it is a crime against life to deny its power to illuminate you! One should never let theology or metaphysics draw your attention away from the colours of the trees in the autumn, and the warmth of the sunlight, and the twinkle in your lover's eye—

42. "Back to traditional values! Back to the way things were!"—but conservatives still put a limit on *how far back* they want to go. This is a sign that something else is at work in their thinking.

43. A passive virtue is a paradox. By being modest, humble, obedient, faithful, and chaste, one is in effect using the will to suppress the exercise of the will.

44. The state enforcement of family values will lead to the destruction of those values. It will make those values arise from duty and obligation— not from spontaneous love.

45. Still, the world of the noble soul is not without law and order. There are things to be done, things not to be done, and many more things in between. But a law is not a command from a sovereign. To a noble soul, a law is *a representation of a relationship.* The noble soul sees her laws moving and changing each day, just as relationships do. And she follows

her laws by doing the things that sustain and enrich her relationships.

46. A new definition of sin: to squander, to hoard, or to waste the gifts that Fortune gives you.

47. What's so great about spirituality? "It will change your life". Well that's obvious: but it is not so obvious that the change would *necessarily* be for the better.

48. "Is it not the case that sometimes we must encounter *resistance* in order to know the extent of our possibilities? Is it not through struggle, sometimes, that we know we are alive at all?" Yes it is—but this does not mean that we must become hard. The problems that call our lives into question also put us into new relationships with things. Rather than attack the questioner, then, wouldn't it be better to *answer* her?

49. Our favourite characters in our best loved stories are not always the ones who are predictable in their goodness, but are often the ones that are transformed by their circumstances and their actions and so achieve new self-knowledge—whether they find themselves more noble or more wretched than before.

50. "But what about the next life? What if you stake everything in this mortal world, but it turns out to be only a tiny part of your whole existence, and there is an afterlife where we continue on?" I see that Pascal's Wager has hypnotized you. Let me help you come back to your *senses*. I say that you should stake everything in this world, right before your eyes, and do all that one may to live a worthwhile life, and to create a world worth living in. For a good life in this world is its own reward. If there is no afterlife then we will have lost nothing. And if there is an afterlife, it will be an added bonus. In either case, the worthwhile life in this world, here and now, is what matters; and if you continue to insist on "what if?", then the burden of proof rests on *you*.

51. Corporate free trade? The global market? International investment? I might prefer for my country to be invaded by an army. There is something unambiguous, and even *honest*, about being shot at.

52. We have learned that a house "marks the man" as surely as the clothes. Some day we shall find that it is the same for the world we live in.

53. Yogananda said that the social environment is stronger than the will. By contrast, Freud said that despite the power of our unconscious drives, the voice of reason always gains a hearing. Civilisation itself may some day hang upon which of them was right.

54. "We are made in the image of God." Yes we are—but is it so obvious *which one?*

55. Beware the healers who prescribe constant cleansing and prevention. Ask yourself how many of the ailments and afflictions they talk about were in fact *invented by them*, so that they could be in a position to provide the cure.

56. It is not the appearance of the sacred in our lives which makes us spiritual. Rather, we become spiritual by responding to it. For every appearance of something sacred, there is a response. Yet it is also the response to things which makes the sacredness in them apparent. "Where did that begin then?" I don't know, my friend. I didn't start this fire; I'm just taking my turn to carry it.

57. Most problems in life stem not from people who do wrong, but from people whose sense of entitlement is so strong that think themselves incapable of doing wrong. The man who takes no personal responsibility, who blames others for all things, may be worse than the man who wants to do what he knows to be wrong, even if the first fellow causes less harm.

58. The mind craves order. It would rather have an absurd reason, a poor

reason, a stupid reason, or even a demonstrably false reason—than no reason at all.

59. There is no need to court controversy over small things. It is often prudent and energy-efficient to keep your opinions on small things under your hat. But it is often a mark of a substantial character to court controversy over the big things.

60. Americans think that the Berlin Wall was pulled down in 1989 by Ronald Regan. Europeans believe that it was pulled down by Michael Gorbachev. But they are both wrong. It was pulled down in July of 1985 by Bob Geldoff.

61. True and lasting happiness comes from a place potentially terrible.

62. Too many walls in this world! Not enough windows, open doors, and bridges. But that does not mean we should not have gate houses on our bridges or locks on our doors.

63. A Great Soul's three most treasured possessions, never to be traded or sacrificed for anything: her intelligence, her dignity, her spirit.

64. A story can be beautiful and poetic even if it does not have a stereotypically happy ending.

65. Consider life in Biosphere-2. Wouldn't the human spirit eventually reject it for being too sanitized, too predictable, too *safe?* We need an environment that challenges us; we excel through exploring the unknown.

66. Love and Peace are diametrically opposed. Love is an activity: it is an energy in motion, directed toward some person or object, in oneself or in the world. Peace is rest, stillness, silence, *inactivity*. Love is therefore never at peace—and we should not want it to be.

67. Treat things, and people, as if they are what they appear to be—and then let them surprise you.

68. The whole of the universe has been preparing itself for you, and the life you are living, and indeed this very moment, right now. Shouldn't you be in a perpetual state of amazement and wonder? Or are you still worried about what you are 'supposed' to do about it?

69. "A friend is a second self" said Aristotle. I think that not quite right— other people, no matter how close, remain other people. But the souls of two intimate friends do seem to overlap each other. And the love they offer each other takes them higher and deeper than anyone can go alone.

70. Life responds to initiative; life responds to *audacity*—life has no patience for indecisive hesitation.

71. Those who disrespect intellectuals, the sciences, the arts, philosophical thought or higher education—end up consigning themselves to the violent ignorance of blind fanaticism.

72. For any heroic adventure: the transformation of character is as much a part of the victory as the rescue of any princess or the slaying of any dragon.

73. Religious people often say that in the absence of God and the afterlife promised to us by God, we will all be at a loss, unable to know right from wrong, unable to find meaning in our lives. But I reject the claim that the only alternative to nihilism is religious faith, or that the only alternative to faith is nihilism. As additional alternatives, I offer a forest at dawn, a rainbow after a storm, a kiss from someone who loves you. Spirituality is very simple. The values that configure a meaningful life need only transcend the individual self to be spiritual. They need not transcend the whole world.

74. Gift-giving and charity as a form of parasitism: when the purpose of giving the gift is to show off your ability to give, and to put the recipient in debt.

75. Peace and tranquility as experiences that *disturb* you: for we do not trust easily enough, and we fear that something may be hiding behind it.

76. Not death, but *immortality*, confers absurdity and meaninglessness. There is nothing an immortal could do, or build, or achieve, that would outlast him.

77. Death is what guarantees that the world will always be *interesting*— for it guarantees that no one will be able to explore all of it in a single lifetime.

78. It may be uncharitable of me to admit it, but it is consistent with the logic of Virtue that there are some people who are leading wasted, worthless lives; that there are *failed human beings*. The all-important, subtle difference, however, is that such people are being punished not by some judge or law-giver, but by their own actions and choices. But let us not blame the victim. For it is also part of the logic of Virtue that a successful life is a collaborative affair. If there are failed lives among us, then let us ask ourselves how we, too, have failed.

79. Once you set out on an adventure, there is no going home again until it is over.

80. The highest kinds of spiritual fulfillment are found in the beauty of the land, sea, and sky; the togetherness of family and friendship and love; and the integrity of one's own spirit.

81. Behold the prophets and mystics of the future: they climb their holy mountains and return not with new tables of the law, but with poems, stories, and *songs*—

SECOND MOVEMENT:
THE HEROIC

§ 82. Heroic Societies

The Heroic societies of ancient Europe include the Celts of Ireland, Britain, and Western Europe, Germanic and Scandinavian people, the Greeks of the time of Homer, as well as the Macedonians. Going further east, we find the Heroic spirit among the Persians, in the Hindu culture that produced the Vedas and the Mahabarata, in feudal Japan and China, and many other places. If the only thing missing is iron-age technology, then some Aboriginal societies of North America would qualify—the Haida people of Canada's Pacific coast, for instance. Heroic society persisted in Europe from the early Bronze age well into that period we sometimes call the Dark Ages. Anthropologically speaking, most Heroic societies were chiefdoms. They were more complex, larger, and more organised than tribes or bands. Yet they did not have the centralization and bureaucracy of state-level kingdoms, theocracies, and republics. The main political unit was an extended family called a clann or a tribe, consisting of around two or three thousand people. The leaders were the heads of these families, and they had to earn their titles through a combination of diplomacy, warfare, and sheer charismatic appeal. Complex legal codes often existed, such as the *Brehon* law of Celtic Ireland. In fact heroic-age Icelanders created the world's first modern-style representative parliament: an annual two-week gathering of the island's 39 chiefs, and other influential people, known as the *Althing*. There was a 'Lawspeaker', who had various administrative and ceremonial duties, such as job of proclaiming the decisions of the Althing from the Law Rock. But in most Heroic societies leadership was invested in outstanding people, not in an institutional office from which the person himself was theoretically separated. As Tacitus, the Roman historian, says of the Germans,

The power of the king is not absolute or arbitrary. The commanders rely on example rather than on the authority of their rank—on the admiration they win by showing conspicuous energy and courage and by pressing forward in front of their own troops.[6]

Heroic societies were also technologically advanced: most possessed the knowledge of bronze or iron working, and many knew how to make steel. They built huge feasting halls where the chief would hold court, plan battles, dispense justice, bestow honours, and re-distribute the wealth of the tribe. Similarly, they built great mounds of earth and stone in which to bury their dead. Some of the warriors got what is now known as a 'Viking Funeral', in which the bodies are set adrift on boats which are then lit on fire. Heroic societies often had an educated class in their social order, responsible for religious and legal affairs, as well as for the arts. Among the Celts, for instance, these people were called Druids. In language, while the written word was being used for things like monuments, property boundary markers, and graves, the spoken word still had primary authority. It had legal power, for instance in the swearing of oaths. It also had supernatural power, as in the recitation of magical chants or the invocation of deities by name. Histories, genealogies, laws, and legends were communicated mainly by word of mouth. With the use of poetic devices like rhyme and meter, and with regular 'conferences' where the content of stories could be agreed upon by the senior poets, long epics could be memorized and kept mostly unchanged for decades, or even centuries.

I wish to emphasize that a heroic society is distinguished not simply by its developmental level, but mainly by certain values unique to it. As a general rule, Heroic societies are societies in which warriors and fighting-men are the biggest stars of the show. And on top of that, just about everybody is one. The 'rite of passage' by which young boys were recognised as adult men was the grant of weapons by the chief of the tribe. Most of the time people worked as farmers or craftsmen, but nearly anyone could be called upon to take up a spear and head into battle, at nearly any time. The chief of a tribe or a local king might keep a few full-time fighters in his personal retinue, but large standing armies were almost unheard-of, because they were not necessary. Nearly everybody was already a warrior. Successful or famous warriors were entitled to the biggest share of the best-quality resources and luxury goods, and were given responsibility for lawmaking, judicial arbitration, wealth distribution, and the like. But to earn these benefits, you had to fight actual battles and earn personal glory for your victories. Then, as now, no one can boast about things not yet done.

Luckily, or perhaps unluckily, heroic societies had a custom which provided a ready-made excuse to go to war: the "blood feud". If someone committed a crime, the usual response was for the victim's family to seek some sort of vengeance. If the crime was murder, then the family of the deceased would seek justice by attempting to assassinate the killer. Whole tribes could be locked into mutual murderous enmity for generations. The story of *Beowulf*, which gives a detailed picture of Anglo-Saxon heroic culture, ends with a blood feud flaring to life after a fragile peace had been declared. Despite the ravages of the supernatural monsters which feature in the story so prominently, it is the human disaster of the blood feud which ultimately causes the downfall of the heroes. Because of this custom, the killing of a family member was seen as particularly heinous since no one could avenge it. On his death-bed, Beowulf expresses thanks that during his life he was never responsible for the murder of a kinsman.

There were, of course, other classes besides the warriors able to earn prestige and power in heroic societies. Seers, prophets, and magic-users of all kinds could become socially prominent, for they had the job of descrying the future and so helping people prepare. They also had the job of performing sacrifices to the gods in order to court their favour, or to put it another way, to bribe the gods into bestowing boons and preventing disasters. Women were accorded special respect for supernatural affairs and for possessing a special connection with all things magical and divine. Tacitus wrote that the Germans "believe that there resides in women an element of holiness and a gift of prophesy; and so they do not scorn to ask their advice, or lightly disregard their replies."[7] Skalds, bards, musicians, storytellers, and poets of all kinds could earn respect as well. In many cases, however, their function was to shore up the renown of the warriors, for instance by retelling the stories of great battles.

Feasting and storytelling in the hall of a great chief was the central cultural activity in most Heroic societies, and indeed the very birthplace of Virtue. The reason for this becomes clear when we look at this custom in detail. First of all, Virtue is borne of storytelling because of the nature of storytelling itself. Storytelling is one of the ways we both discover, and also create, who we are, because storytelling is a representation of the world and of life. To represent something is to 're-present it'; to present it again, a second time. In *The Poetics*, Aristotle defined tragic drama as "essentially an imitation not of persons but of actions and life". (*Poetics* 50a16.) Several contemporary philosophers, such as Paul Ricoeur and Alasdair MacIntyre, have made similar observations. One might make this representation of life for the sake of entertainment, or for the sake of artistic appreciation. But the purpose of *mythological* storytelling is more than that. A mythology is a story with the force of *logos* (hence myth–*ology*), the Greek philosophical concept referring to the rational account of the universe. Mythology has the function of re-presenting the world as having a meaningful order, and of helping us find a place in that order. It therefore describes events like the creation of the world, the activities of the gods, the origin of the human race, and perhaps the ultimate destiny of things. It presents models of both good and bad human lives, in which the listeners could recognise themselves, and learn. It holds life up to critical scrutiny, to examine it, to draw special attention to certain aspects of it, to pose questions, and test possible answers. In good storytelling we recognise ourselves: we find examples of how we live and how we think and feel, at our best and our worst occasions. In optimistic or hopeful moments, we can recognise ourselves not as we are but as we wish to be: that is, we find representations of our higher selves, noble, wise, brave, and good; or somehow we see our more *realised* selves, the people we *aspire* to be. The stories told by the bards and skalds in the feasting halls of their lords might have been of any kind: news, anecdotes, jokes, tall tales and fables, accounts of recent happenings or of historical events, and so on. But with mythology, they transformed their view of the world. It became not just the place where ancient people collected their food and other material needs. It became their *home*. They could feel that they belong to the world, and could make a place for themselves in it, feel safe while at rest, find life within it to be enjoyable, and indeed find it to be beautiful. This did not make the world any less dangerous: people still had to contend with storms, floods, droughts, wild animals, and other dangers. But they could place these problems within their world view, and so understand them, and be ready for them.

Furthermore, a story is not just a group of words and fine phrases. It is a *social event*, an occasion when someone is speaking and someone else is listening, and both of them together are thinking. Storytelling is an event which brings people together, for to share a story is also to share many more things necessary for the storytelling event to happen. The people involved must also share a conception of what a story *is*, as well as a language in which to tell it. As part of their language they must share a stock inventory of metaphors and symbols, although this does not prevent the use of symbols in new ways, or the creation of new symbols. Already this presupposes that for two or more people to share a story, *they must have some ideas in common; they must have an understanding of each other*. They must be able to trust that when one speaks the other understands. This opens the possibility that they may be able to share more things with each other: material goods and services, for instance, or help in collaborative projects, or emotional support, or even love. Indeed, for someone to tell a story she must have made an ethical decision: that the listeners deserve the benefit that this story may give them. Similarly, the listeners have made an ethical decision too: that the teller deserves a hearing. This in turn opens the possibility for people to have respect for each other: to become companions, or even friends.

The second aspect of the culture of the feasting hall is, of course, the feast. For millennia, it was the case that to share food also meant to share time and labour, agricultural land, and living space. This sharing of material goods calls for communication, co-operation and friendship, and ultimately for the holding-in-common of ideas and values. Indeed, so many of the world's religious customs have their origins in food production. We find this in the *potlatch* of the Canadian West Coast native tribes, the community meals of the Sikhs, the *tarb-feis* ("bull-feast") of ancient Celts, mediaeval European harvest festivals and mummer's plays, the "blessing of wine and cakes" in Wicca, and even the Catholic sacrament of the Eucharist where the Last Supper of Christ is re-enacted. To treat food as a gift from a god, and the sharing of food as a re-dramatisation of an act of a god, is to affirm the sacredness of our embodied being in the world. 'Sacredness' can be understood broadly here, as that hard-to-define quality which renders something important, significant, out of the ordinary. It might be attached to special customs or traditions, or even apparently irrational taboos. It will certainly be attached to various special responses like a reverent manner, a serious tone, a requirement to give thanks.

The sacredness of the feast may not be so easy for modern people to see. Agriculture now depends on machines and chemicals more than on manual labour. We also import food from around the world, and are not limited to eating 'locally'. But for ancient people, a successful harvest or hunt was a life-and-death issue. So it was natural to have community celebrations on the occasions when food becomes available in greater than usual quantities. The feast is still a part of modern day weddings, birthdays, graduations, and holidays both religious and secular. It appears again in formal occasions like conference receptions, business meetings, political summits and affairs of state. Even occasions of sadness are marked with feasts: funerals, for instance. And each of these occasions are tied to storytelling as well. At a funeral we re-tell stories of the life of the deceased. At marriage receptions, we recount the lives of the newlywed couple and how they met. At graduations, we reminisce yet again. Even after going to a movie or a hockey game we head to the bar to talk about what we had just seen over a few drinks. We feast and tell stories together when we want to affirm friendship, and life.

Finally, but briefly, we can look at the hall itself, the building in which the feasting and storytelling took place. Obviously, building a feasting hall is a collaborative affair. It requires people to pool their time and labour, and to co-operate with each other, just as feasting and storytelling does. But there is more to it than that. As observed by philosopher Karsten

Harries, what separates a human home from an animal's shelter is that the human home addresses spiritual needs. Foremost among them, he says, is our need to *belong* somewhere.[8] Ancient people therefore designed many of their buildings in ways that drew down a cosmic order to the human level. They were round, in imitation of the horizon and the dome of the sky, for instance. Or they had solar and stellar alignments in their design, as in the case of temples like Stonehenge and Newgrange. These architectural practices made people feel as if they had a home, that they belonged to the universe.

Virtue, I wish to suggest, began in three heroic-age customs: the telling of stories, the production and sharing of food, and the construction of homes and public buildings where people may gather for feasting and storytelling. These activities are all necessary for survival. But they are also the necessary means to philosophical and spiritual discovery. For all of them open new ways for people to meet each other and to create lives together that are desirable and good. Let us turn now from the nature and logic of Heroic-age storytelling, to its actual content. For it is in the literature of the Heroic age that the original notion of Virtue takes shape: virtue as excellence, nobility, even greatness; virtue as that which enables mere mortals to surpass themselves, and rise to the level of the gods.

§ 83. Fortune

Heroic-age people saw the world as a constantly changing, turbulent, often dangerous place. The seas, forests, high mountains, and remote places were the abodes of unknown creatures and inexplicable forces. Death could carry you off at just about any time. To illustrate this, here are the words of The Venerable Bede, an 8th century chronicler recounting a discussion between a British tribal king named Edwin and his priests and advisors on whether to convert to Christianity. One of the priests says something which sums up the pre-Christian point of view most elegantly:

> Your Majesty, when we compare the present life of man on earth with that time of which we have no knowledge, it seems to me like the swift flight of a single sparrow through the banqueting-hall where you are

sitting at dinner on a winter's day with your theigns and counselors. In the midst there is a comforting fire to warm the hall; outside, the storms of winter rain or snow are raging. This sparrow flies swiftly in through one door of the hall, and out through another. While he is inside, he is safe from the winter storms; but after a few moments of comfort, he vanishes from sight into the wintry world from which he came. Even so, man appears on earth for a little while; but of what went before this life or of what follows, we know nothing.[9]

This passage is a wonderful representation of what people from the pre-Christian heroic society of Britain believed about their world. As it comes directly from the mouth of one of them, it is a clear line of sight into the minds of ancient people, even if only a brief one. But more than that, it is a profound philosophical statement of the place and the existential condition of humankind in reference to the great immensities of birth and death. As a visual image it is immediately clear what the speaker is intending, for it is not hard to imagine a bird flying into the room in which you are sitting, flittering about for a while, and then streaking out again. Where it has been before entering the room, and where it goes afterward, are great unknowns. The metaphor holds that human life on earth is much like the flight of the sparrow: transient and fleeting, short and quick, and bounded at both ends, before birth and after death, by mysteries. This is not the unsophisticated opinion of a barbarian. One of the beginning-places of wisdom and maturity is the honest acknowledgement of what we do *not* know. Such an acknowledgement is a recognition of something that clearly configures human life, even if its nature escapes our under-standing—in other words, a spiritual or philosophical mystery.

But Heroic-age people wanted not just to *describe* the way of the world: they also wanted to *understand* it. In their view, the mysterious and sometimes tragic transformations of the world are apparently controlled by an unseen force or power that is always slightly beyond human knowledge. In Anglo-Saxon this mysterious force is called 'Wyrd', in Greek 'Daimon', in Old Irish 'Fál', and in modern English, 'fortune', 'destiny', or 'fate'. The Anglo-Saxon term originally meant 'what happens' or what is someone's 'lot' in life. Fate is the cosmic order behind the chaos: it decrees in advance that certain events or situations *must* or *must not* come to be, no matter what we mere mortals do. To Anglo-Saxon Britons, the basic truth of the nature of the world was summed up in the saying, *Wyrd bid ful araed*, 'fate is everything'.

This is not to say that fate was a malevolent force: fate is just 'what happens'. And this did not mean that life is without any redeeming qualities. Rather, it is to say that these are the terms in which people of the time understood the world they lived in. Any projects, wishes, desires, or plans for life anyone may have must be pursued in confrontation with, or at any rate in reference to, the transience of things. "Much love, much hate, must he endure who thinks to live long here in this world, in our days of strife," says the unknown poet of *Beowulf*.[10] When about to undertake the search for the monster called Grendel, Beowulf tells his friends how to distribute his belongings should he be killed, for although he is confident in his power to succeed in the battle, it is not for him to boast of great deeds not yet done. The outcome is something which, as he says, "fate will go as it must."[11] The literature of heroic societies is full of similar affirmations.

The notion of Fate is also bound up with the notion of *transience*. This is, very simply, the idea that things are mysterious because they are constantly changing and moving, and we don't know how or why. We can attempt to understand the mystery of things by trying to discern whether there is a process or a pattern that tends to guide or reveal itself in all the changes that go on. The most well known expressions of transience to come from European heroic societies are the various fragments of the Greek philosopher Heraclitus, for instance:

- We step into and we do not step into the same rivers. We are and we are not.
- The same thing is both living and dead, and the waking and the sleeping, and young and old, for these things transformed are those, and those transformed back again are these.
- The cosmos, the same for all, none of the gods nor of humans has

made, but it was always, and is, and shall be: an ever-living fire being kindled in measures and being extinguished in measures.
• Changing, it rests.[12]

The last of these fragments is my favourite. On the surface it reads like a logical paradox, a contradiction in terms. Changing is an activity; resting is the relaxation or cessation of activity. But I think Heraclitus is making an astute observation here, and what appears like a paradox is but his characteristic style of expression. His point is that the natural and normal condition of things is to be on the move.

Transience is an elementary idea. It can occur to anyone who takes a direct and honest look at the way things are. It should be unsurprising, then, that it appears in other cultures far removed in time and space from European heroic societies. For instance, Crowfoot, a spokesperson for the Blackfoot Nation of what is now Alberta, Canada, affirmed it in his dying words.

What is life? It is the flash of a firefly in the night. It is the breath of a buffalo in the winter time. It is the little shadow which runs across the grass and loses itself in the sunset.[13]

Crowfoot spoke these words in 1890, many centuries and an entire ocean away from Heraclitus. But he has surely said very nearly the same thing.

Within this turbulent, unpredictable world, what are people to do? What, if anything, can be done do protect ourselves against the slings and arrows of outrageous fortune? First of all, it must be noted that we cannot rely on the gods to save us. In heroic societies, the gods were not lawmakers or judges. Rather, they were controllers of natural forces. They had power over the fertility of plants, the weather, the movements of animals, and so on. They were also divine ancestors, and the progenitors of human tribes. As such they had influence in politics, military affairs, and even the psychological drives of the heart and mind. One can think of the gods as personifications of these forces (which, by the way, does not confirm or deny that they exist). But they too were subject to fate, just as we mortals are. Even the Oracle of Delphi once declared: "not God himself could escape destiny."[14] And the mythologies describe the gods with many of the same flaws and failings that we have. This understanding of the role of the gods implies that we cannot look to them for salvation or enlightenment. They are models of ourselves from whom we can learn; indeed their similarity to us makes them excellent teachers. But they are not going to 'save' us from fate, or death, or anything else. Nor do they 'purify' anyone of sin or evil. If people were to overcome such things, they had to do it on their own.

But we are not at a loss. There are several ways that stand out in the literature of heroic societies. In the next few sections, I shall describe the most important among them.

§ 84. Friendship
Your first line of defense against fortune and fate is your social relations, especially *friendship*. Heroic literature has many instances of great friends who live, fight, and die together: Beowulf and Wiglaf, Achilles and Patroclus, Cu Chullain and Ferdiad. A famous Icelandic epic called *Njáil's Saga* tells the story of two farmers, Njáill Thorgeirsson and his friend Gunnar, whose friendship proved unbreakable despite blood-feuds raging between their families. One could add the great friendship between Robin Hood and Little John to the list here; their stories represent a little pocket of Heroic culture in an emerging 'modern' world. The *Hávamál*, a 12th century collection of wisdom-poems from Iceland and Scandinavia, says of friendship:

> Young was I once, and went alone,
> And wandering lost my way;
> When a friend I found I felt me rich:
> Man is cheered by man.[15]

The idea appears to be that our friends make life valuable and meaningful, and that the things we do together with friends is our most important source of happiness.

In heroic mythology, friendships are often forged from a situation of adversity and conflict. Gilgamesh met his great friend Enkidu as he attempted to enter a bridal-house. Enkidu sought to prevent him, and a titanic wrestling match followed. Although Gilgamesh won, he declared that "there is not another like you in the world".[16] They embraced each other and their friendship began. Similarly, in the Irish story of the Coming of the Tuatha de Dannan, the Gods and the Fomorians send out one champion each to act as both scout and ambassador. They met at the centre of a field, and as soon as they discovered that they were speaking the same language the tension eased. They traded information about their families and customs, examined each other's weapons, and passed on the messages from their commanders. Then they promised each other that "whatever might happen in the future, they themselves would be friends."[17] Friendships in heroic societies can be formed on the basis of mutual honour, not just admiration for fighting ability, and these friendships are often able to withstand the hardest tests and trials.

In the *Illiad*, whenever Patroclus is mentioned, it is always added that he is the 'great friend' of Achilles. The two are almost impossible to separate. When Patroclus is killed by Hector, Achilles' grief is nearly boundless. He refuses to wash his battle-wounds until after Patroclus is cremated. Later on, the ghost of Patroclus himself appears to Achilles and makes a final request:

> Never bury my bones apart from yours, Achilles,
> Let them lie together
> Just as we grew up in your house…
> So now let a single urn, the gold two-handled urn
> Your noble mother gave you, hold our bones—together![18]

When a friend is lost, the survivor feels as if a large part of himself has died too. In the *Táin Bo Cuailnge*, the friendship of Ferdiad and Cu Chullain is put to the greatest test that the heroic mind can conceive: the two are compelled to fight each other to the death. Ferdiad and Cu Chullain had known and loved each other since childhood. They fought each other for three days, and they were so evenly matched that neither could get an upper hand. At the end of each day they embraced each other, staunched each other's wounds with their own hands, sent food and medicine to each other, quartered their horses in the same paddock, and camped their charioteers by the same fire. Cu Chullain eventually emerged the winner, but he was inconsolable afterward. When his enemies came upon him after the fight with Ferdiad was done, he refused to defend himself.[19]

The Heroic model of friendship is something we may need to re-learn. Today, we often use the language of technology to describe our personal relations. We say things like "let's hook up", or "we connected". We no longer have circles of friends: we now have 'networks' of 'contacts'. People are not machines, so we should not use the vocabulary of machine function to describe our relationships. Furthermore, as Charles Taylor observed, social relationships of all kinds, from acquaintances and neigh-bours to marriage partners, are now defined in a context of individualism, personal freedom, and self-fulfillment. This context makes people value others only as instruments of their own self-fulfillment.[20] This, he claims, is basically narcissistic, as well as ultimately unsatisfying. This is exactly the situation Aristotle warned against in the 3rd century BCE: a friendship based on what each partner gains from the other is a shallow and false friendship, easily ended.[21] In a heroic society, by contrast, a person's social relations are all-important: they help constitute his very identity. Friendship is more than a matter of survival expediency, although it does grant large survival advantages. In times of accident or calamity, one will need friends for help or rescue. One earns the right to call upon this help by being there for others in their time of need. It is in one's interest, then, to be respectful and cooperative. But the spirit of heroic friendship is intrinsically valuable as well: it is the friendship of those who find in each other *a second self*. In Aristotle's words:

The perfect form of friendship is that between the good, and those who resemble each other in virtue. For these friends wish each alike the other's good in respect of their goodness, and they are good in themselves; but it is those who wish the good of their friends for their friends' sake who are friends in the fullest sense, since they love each other for themselves and not accidentally...[22]

True friendship, in this account from Aristotle, is the friendship of those 'who resemble each other in virtue'. There is no distinction being made here between the interests of the self and that of the friend. So there is no question of balancing or prioritizing those interests. The language of 'interests' simply doesn't fit the case. The point is that friendship breaks down the barriers between people. Friends desire each other's existence the same way they desire their own. As Aristotle says, "good men will be friends for each other's own sake since they are alike in being good".[23] True friends, being 'alike in goodness', share the same higher-order qualities and so are able to share in each other's happiness. They love each other for who they are, not for what pleasure or benefit they can gain from each other. Thus the friendship is 'not accidental'. Yet virtuous friendship is still pleasurable, and the friends do benefit from each other. And finally, true friendship is an indispensable part of the virtuous life. "For no one would choose to live without friends, but possessing all other good things."[24]

In heroic society, not only friendship but social bonds of all kinds were inextricably tied to ethical norms and principles, and indeed to personal identity. A person's social place and function *is* his identity. Take away someone's standing as a farmer, a blacksmith, an artist, a father or mother, or whatever, and there would be nothing left. A personal identity, in a heroic society, is a social identity. Each person understood what he owed others, and what others owed him, in terms of his role in society. And the most intimate and important of his social roles is that of the friend. As observed by the contemporary philosopher Alasdair MacIntyre:

...morality and the social structure are in fact one and the same in heroic society. There is only one set of social bonds. Morality as something distinct does not yet exist. Evaluative questions *are* questions of social fact. It is for this reason that Homer speaks always of *knowledge* of what to do and how to judge. Nor are such questions difficult to answer, except in exceptional cases... Without such a place in the social order, a man would not only be incapable of receiving recognition and response from others; not only would others not know, but he would not himself know who he was.[25]

By the way, if you combine this social definition of identity with the culture of the feasting hall, and the tribal solidarity of the blood feud, then you get Heroic age 'family values'!

But clearly, this social model of personal identity clashes with some important and widespread modern values, especially modern individualism. While it has benefited people enormously, individualism also has troubling social and political consequences. In Heroic society, it is clear that history, culture, friendship, family solidarity, and the like, were things of values that transcended the self. Yet we would not understand the Heroic point of view properly if we thought Heroic people believed in some kind of polar opposite to modern individualism. Most of the characters of heroic mythology were obsessed with honour and renown. As we shall soon see, their highest goal in life was a particular form of personal glory called 'apotheosis'. This obsession with honour could be interpreted as an example of individualism. But the Heroic view of an individual's worth is radically different from our own. Honour was a *public* good. Its significance flowed from *shared* values, not from privately chosen values. Even personal identity was a public good: your identity, even your standing as a human being, is configured by your place and your role among those with whom you live. Thus the heroic person views his friends, loves, and family relations as positive assets, not purely as instruments for his own personal happiness, and certainly not as limitations or burdens. Not that a heroic person's whole sense of identity and personhood is entirely socially constructed, of course. A heroic individual still knows who he is, and has his own goals and values. But it is the case that the heroic person looks to his various social roles to know what his interests are. Similarly, he looks to others to know just what qualities someone in his position is expected to have, as well as to confirm that he has them. When MacIntyre says that morality and the social structure are the same in heroic societies, this means that the moral system does not judge people as human beings *simpliciter*, but rather it judges people in terms of their social place, for instance as farmers, as landlords, as blacksmiths or craftspeople, as artists, as fathers or mothers or children, and so on. As noted by Alasdair MacIntyre, heroic individuals "can certainly be said always to act in their own interests as they understand them, but the interests of an individual is always his or her interests *qua* wife or *qua* host or qua some other role."[26] Each person understood what he owed others, and what others owed him, in terms of his role in his social world. But the most intimate and important of his social roles is that of the friend.

There is a strong difference, clearly, between the ancient understanding of individuality, and our own. Philosopher Charles Taylor aimed to resolve this tension by claiming that "Even the sense that the significance of my life comes from its being chosen... depends on the understanding that *independent of my will* there is something noble, courageous, and hence significant in giving shape to my own life."[27] In other words, the very notion that people should guide their lives by their own choices depends on an understanding of values that dwell apart from individual choices. I must put off to later my suggestion for what things contribute to that understanding. Let it suffice for the moment to say merely this. Friendship, and love, and family life, and social bonds of all kinds, form a horizon of independent and shared value that the worthwhile life cannot do without. We may therefore need to re-learn how to have Heroic friendship and love again. Yet we must re-learn this value without falling back on old forms of docile obedience, or passive acquiescence to authority. The reason to cultivate friendship, as ancient Heroic people knew, is not just because you can benefit from having friends, but because *having friends is a way to understand who you are.*

§ 85. Honour

If there is one singular quality that appears to govern or underlie all human life in heroic societies, it is the quality of *honour*. Aristotle upheld Honour as the greatest of all possible possessions.[28] To him it is second only to wisdom as the most important part of the good life. I believe that honour is the highest virtue for Heroic societies because it is the one virtue that the hero is prepared to die for. Hector, the Trojan hero of the *Illiad*, tells his wife Andromache, "I would die of shame to face the men of Troy and the Trojan women trailing their long robes if I would shrink from battle now, a coward."[29] Similarly, when Beowulf was fighting Grendel's mother, and found that his sword was useless, he carried on fighting. To give up would bring shame and dishonour upon him, and that would be worse than death. The poet of Beowulf says:

> Still he was resolute, not slow in courage,
> Remembered his fame, the kinsman of Hygelac.
> The angry champion threw away his sword,
> Bejeweled, ring-patterned; it lay on the ground,
> Strong, bright-edged. His own strength he trusted,
> The strength of his hand-grip. So must a man,
> If he thinks at battle to gain any name,
> A long-lived fame, care nothing for his life.[30]

Later in the story, when Beowulf has been killed by the dragon, his friend Wiglaf tells a group of cowardly deserters that "Death is better for any warrior than a shameful life!"[31]

Most Heroic literature defines Honour as a social quality. The Nordic word for honour is *troth*, which also means trust, and loyalty, and is related to the English word 'truth'. The idea appears to be that an honourable person is someone who is loyal, trustworthy, reliable, honest, and so on, in his relations with others. In Irish the word for honour is *enech,* or *oineach*, which also means 'good name', 'reputation', or 'face', and can also mean generosity. In both languages the concept is already a public one, and already related to a particular way of being present to others and relating to them. The contemporary philosopher John Casey says that the idea of the Noble is "an idea of being-in-the-world, of one's self being fulfilled in a social role or function, and of an identification of oneself with the public world which is revealed in feeling and action."[32] The heroic character may feel in himself a sense of being an honourable person, but he looks to his friends and his kin, to verify that sense. Honour is bound up with a gainful reputation. Furthermore, Honour is something that can be 'given' to others. It is in this sense like respect. Ordinary respect is accorded to someone for the reason that she is in the same tribe, or holds a particularly prestigious social place, or simply is a fellow human being. But Honour is a special, peculiar kind of respect, above and beyond ordinary respect. It is accorded to those who consistently demonstrate various particularly praiseworthy qualities. Thus it is more like admiration or great praise. Finally, honour is something given to perception. If someone is honourable then her entitlement to admiration and respect is visible in the pride in her gaze, the strength of her posture, the confidence instilled in those around her. As Casey said, "Nobility is something that can be presented directly to the eye."[33] Indeed, one sign of a dis-honourable person is the way he demands the respect he feels is owed to him. A truly honourable person doesn't have to make any demands. His honour is plain for all to see.

How does someone become an honourable person? Primarily, it is through actions, especially sustained and habitual actions, for which his friends and associates are likely to praise him. A person 'has' honour, or 'is honourable', if others 'do honour to' her; which means, at the most basic level, that they speak well of her. To 'do honour to' someone can also mean to give that person a prestigious or otherwise highly visible place, or other unusual privilege, often symbolic, but sometimes more than symbolic. It can mean giving someone a special gift like the 'Hero's Portion' (a special cut of meat at a feast, described in Celtic mythology), or like the prestigious weapons which King Hrothgar gave to Beowulf. It can mean composing songs and stories about the person's life, or erecting monuments and memorials in the person's memory. A person earns the praise of others by being, for instance, a generous and magnanimous gift-giver. When helping those who ask for help the honourable person is as selfless as he can be. He refrains from giving scorn and insults, and from making fun of people—he especially avoids uttering so-called 'friendly' insults, which are often more hurtful than insults from enemies. The honourable person keeps his promises and tells the truth. Even in the

English language, 'honour' is related to 'honesty', with its attendant connotations of truth-telling and fair dealing. Above all he must uphold the reputation of others—for his own sake as well as for theirs. His social bonds are constructed such that a dishonour he brings upon himself would be reflected on his friends and family as well. Thus in heroic societies there were strong social pressures which reinforced and rewarded mutual cooperation and respect. As Tacitus says of the Germans, although not without irony: "Good morality is as effective in Germany as good laws are elsewhere"[34]

The literature of heroic societies often contains explicit statements of what is praiseworthy, and what is not. For instance, here is a passage from a 7th century Irish work called *The Testament of Morann*, my favourite heroic-age wisdom text.

Tell him [the newly proclaimed ruler], let him be merciful, just, impartial, conscientious, firm, generous, hospitable, honourable, stable, beneficent, capable, honest, well-spoken, steady, [and] true judging. For there are ten things which extinguish the injustice of every ruler... rule and worth, fame and victory, progeny and kindred, peace and long life, good fortune and tribes.[35]

The Testament of Morann is from a genre of literature modeled on the ceremonial speeches delivered by the Druids or other religious functionaries on the occasion of the inauguration of a king, to instruct the new king how to rule well. Notice once more that the expressions of ethical principle come in the form of a list of desirable character qualities. It was not just the case that a person's social position assigned to him his status. It also assigned a more-or-less definite list of personal qualities expected from anyone holding that position. This list served as a means of judging whether a person was properly fulfilling the requirements of that position, and whether he was earning its benefits and privileges. His qualities of character, rather than his specific actions, are being judged here. Given the way the warriors were obsessed with fame and glory, it might be surprising that the qualities which the Testament of Morann emphasizes have to do with the intellect, with social cooperation, and with charitable giving. Militaristic qualities are not absent, of course. But most of the qualities on this list have to do with how well he supports and benefits those who are close to him.

Here is another example called the *Instructions of Cormac*, a 9th century Irish text which offers something resembling a 'middle path':

'O grandson of Conn, O Cormac', said Carbre, 'I desire to know how I shall behave among the wise and the foolish, among friends and strangers, among the old and the young, among the innocent and the wicked.

'Not hard to tell', said Cormac.

'Be not too wise, be not too foolish,
be not too conceited, be not too diffident,
be not too haughty, be not too humble,
be not too talkative, be not too silent,
be not too harsh, be not too feeble.
If you be too wise, one will expect (too much) of you;
If you be too foolish, you will be deceived;
If you be too conceited, you will be thought vexatious;
If you be too humble, you will be without honour;
If you be too talkative, you will not be heeded;
If you be too silent, you will not be regarded;
If you be too harsh, you will be broken;
If you be too feeble, you will be crushed.'[36]

These words always struck me as remarkably thoughtful. A list of character qualities is given in response to the broad question from Carbre, on how to act no matter what the situation. In the section quoted here, honour appears like a strong notion of balance. Each named quality is paired off with what appears to be a natural opposite, and Carbre is encouraged to possess them all, but never to excess. One can have too much of a good quality, and so act wrongly.

Two critical observations arise here. What we have seen of Honour so far leaves the way open to interpret the quality as nothing more than a sophisticated form of self-interest. We might act honourably only because we want to receive the praise of others, and not because acting honourably is an inherently good thing to do. But the fact that heroes are prepared to die rather than incur shame implies that it has high intrinsic value, apart from whatever material or social advantages it can produce. For one thing, the maintenance of honour even in the face of death signifies that the reasons for acting honourably need not be connected to egotistical self-gain. Even when death is not on the line, most heroic literature treats honour as something social, not something personal. It is the quality that disposes one to act in ways that earn the praise of others. The source of its significance is in communities and friendships, not individual desire. As a social quality, it serves to strengthen and reinforce the social bonds which, as we have seen, are at the foundation of all ethical norms in Heroic societies, and even the foundation of personal identity itself.

This leads to the second critical observation. While honour is deeply social, it is also deeply *hierarchical*: for this kind of honour to be valuable, some people must have more than others. It is the province of special, successful, outstanding people, and it is also closely associated with social status and prestige. In the ancient world, as Casey observed, "to be 'honourable' is to possess a certain rank, and 'dishonourable behaviour' might be thought of in the first place as behaviour not suitable to a senator, or to a feudal lord."[37] To do something that is 'beneath' you originally meant to do something that is fitting for someone of lesser rank. In our culture today, we do not normally think of honour as such a public thing, nor do we like the elitist connotation. In the 1995 film *Rob Roy*, the personal and private definition that we find more familiar today is expressed: "Honour is a gift a man gives to himself". We tend to think of honour as something more like dignity, or personal integrity, something that can belong to everyone. There is nothing like a one-to-one correspondence between the ancient principle of Honour and the contemporary idea of Integrity.

But there are important similarities that we can learn from. Both Honour and Integrity are qualities which enables someone to want to do something right and just, not because of the good consequences that may entail, and not because the act fulfils the requirements of some moral law. Rather, a person's own sense of purpose and worth motivates her. One who has honour can hold herself high, and carry herself with pride, grace, dignity, assertiveness, and even nobility. Honour is related to friendship in more than just the way that an honourable person can call upon others for help or rescue, and a dishonourable person usually can't. A person can have friends *only if she deems herself worthy of having friends*. In this respect a person's sense of self-worth is an inherent part of all her social relations. The true friend is someone who believes she has a role to play in the world, and can make a difference in people's lives. A person could not have friendship or love without this sense of her own possibilities. It is a healthy sense of honour that gives her this sense. Indeed an honourable person is able to benefit and love others, and change the world for the better, precisely because she deems herself both capable, and *worthy*, of doing so. Someone without much self-esteem may feel unable to do so. He might think that anything he tries to do will be futile, and destined for failure. He may be mistaken about what honour is, or he might not care that he hasn't got any. Such people usually find their lives rather bitter and hard. But the honourable person, by contrast, is able to unreservedly participate in the world. She can fully value her friends and treasure her time with them, and indeed thoroughly enjoy her life.

§ 86. How to be a Heroic Chieftain

The chieftain was the most prestigious person in a Heroic-age tribe. He or she (usually *he*) was the re-distributor of the tribe's goods, especially the prestige items like weapons and jewels. He was also the supreme justice in matters of law, and the commander on the battlefield. Warriors were expected to show unwavering loyalty to the chief. They fight for the chief's honour as well as for their own: as Tacitus says of Germanic warriors, "the chiefs fight for victory, the followers for their chief."[38] In most cases, the members of a war-band would be related to each other: they would be part of the same tribe or clan. Family bonds would lend extra force to their loyalty. But to be a warrior also meant, in large measure, to have sworn allegiance to a battle chieftain, and to have sworn to protect him with your life. That loyalty is the quasi-political side of friendship and honour. One may well ask, then, what does it take to become a chieftain? How do you earn the kind of honour that would motivate others to fight for you, even to the death?

The main things a prospective chieftain had to do was be unflinchingly courageous in battle, and be a liberal and magnanimous gift-giver. In return for his retainers' loyalty the chief owed them his unreserved generosity. Tacitus observed that the members of a war-band "are always making demands on the generosity of their chief." It was the custom among the Norse and Anglo-Saxons to give gifts of gold or silver arm-rings as rewards for great deeds. Warriors would wear them as a public symbol of the honour they had earned by the things they did. Arm-rings could also be traded for commodities and services, like money. King Hrothgar, one of the main characters in the story of *Beowulf*, has the nickname of "Ring-Giver". And the story opens with the funeral of a king named Sceaf, whose generosity is upheld as a model for others to follow:

> So ought a [young] man, in his father's household,
> Treasure up the future by his goods and goodness,
> By splendid bestowals, so that later in life
> His chosen men stand by him in turn,
> His retainers serve him when war comes.
> By such generosity any man prospers.[39]

The chieftain's relationship to his retainers therefore was a bit like a contract: the retainers owed loyalty, the chief owed generosity in return. But a good chief also owed generosity to everyone, even to complete strangers. Tacitus wrote of the Germans that "it is accounted a sin to turn any man away from your door", and that "no distinction is ever made between acquaintance and stranger as far as the right to hospitality is concerned."[40]

Note that a chieftain's power flows mainly from honourable qualities of character, like courage, generosity, and hospitality. Even if his position was hereditary, it carried no authority of its own. The chieftain had to be an admirable and praiseworthy man: the kind of man whom others would want to freely offer their loyalty. And he had to be this kind of man by his own merits. If anyone obeyed the commands of the chief, it would not be because they were afraid of him, or because they thought that his office carried some kind of special political or divine authority. As Tacitus says of the decision-making assemblies of the Germans, "such hearing is given to the king or state-chief as his age, rank, military distinction, or eloquence can secure—more because his advice carries weight than because he has the power to command."[41]

Generosity and hospitality are two of the foremost qualities of the honourable person, and aside from fighting prowess they are the qualities most likely to earn the praise of others. The *Hávamál* introduces hospitality like this:

All hail to the givers! A guest hath come.
Say where shall he sit?
In haste is he to the hall who cometh,
To find a place by the fire.[42]

The next three strophes go on to describe that a seat by a warm fire, and something to drink, and good conversation, are owed to the visitor. Similarly, the *Hávamál* praises generosity as that which holds friendships together:

He who giveth gladly a goodly life leadeth,
  And seldom hath he sorrow;
But the churlish wight is chary of all,
And grudgingly parts with his gifts.[43]

A similar Irish custom requires that when a guest comes to call, he or she must be provided with a cup of tea, if not a warm meal as well, and a place by the fire, before he is asked his business.

In these qualities you have something like a primer on Heroic-age political science. If you want to be a great chieftain, first you must build a feasting hall. Then, invite all your friends to come and have a big drinking party. Give them loads of food, clothing, weapons and armour, jewelry, and other gifts. Praise their exploits. Hire a bard to praise your own exploits. Then, of course, go out and do some exploiting. Raid your neighbour's cattle, steal their land, fight and kill their warriors, or at least drive them off in fear. Use their treasure to pay for the next big drinking party, and for the next round of gifts to give to your friends. Then go out and do some more exploiting, and encourage your friends to bring more friends with them. Keep doing this over and over again until you hear people say that you are a great chieftain. Don't ever stop, not even when the next contender for the job takes up a sword, which you gave him as a gift last year, and runs you through. After all, he will organize a decadent state funeral for you, and raise a mighty burial mound over your grave.

Now that I think about it, has politics changed all that much in two thousand years?

§ 87. Courage, Trust, and Hope

Honour, loyalty, generosity, friendship, and the like, are what people owe to each other (and to their lord) in heroic society. These qualities are largely social in nature. This may lead some readers to ask, are there any individual qualities? Is there some defense against fate which an individual can invoke for himself alone, and not with others? Yes there is: and to describe it, here is a story. Around the year 900 a Norwegian chieftain named Thorolf Mostur-Beard, leader of one of the first colonies of Iceland, chose the location of his first settlement by throwing two carved wooden posts, the high-seat pillars from his temple, into the sea. He then declared his intention to settle where they landed. Part of the reason for this was practical. He needed to know how the currents moved, and where they would take someone who got lost at sea. But he was also, in his mind, allowing nature and the gods to guide him. This action was therefore, in effect, an expression of confidence in the workings of the world, and trust that the world would lead him where he needed to go to accomplish his purpose. The site is still in use today: it is in the centre of

Reykjavik, Iceland's capital city. This form of 'defense' against fate, illustrated in this story, is personal. It involves *placing trust* in Fate.

The reason I say 'place trust' and not 'have faith' is because the act of placing trust in Fate is an act of courage. The courageous person wants to make something happen. She does not want to wait and react: she wants to be the cause of things. So she must develop the qualities which enable her to take action *despite* whatever unknown or tragic consequences may come. Not only courage, but also forthright determination, perseverance, bravery, decisiveness, strength, and initiative, could be included here. The first three lines of *Beowulf* tell the listeners right away that it is a story about courage, and that in the character of Beowulf they have a model of a courageous man.

> *Hwaet!* [Listen!] We have heard of the glory of the Spear-Danes
> In the old days, the kings of tribes—
> How noble princes showed great courage![44]

In many places in the story, various reasons are presented for why courage is valuable; and not the least of which is that it changes one's relationship to fate. One memorable line reads: "So fate often saves an un-doomed man when his courage holds."[45] In other words, as we say today, "Fortune favours the bold". The idea is that Fate is likely to benefit those who are decisive, who take initiative, and who do not shirk from an opportunity to act, even if the outcome is uncertain.

Courage has a social dimension that must be mentioned. It was essential to a person's honour. Manifesting strength, especially in the service of a great cause, would almost always earn the praise and admiration of others. It was a sign that the person could be counted on and trusted, and so it re-affirmed solidarity with others. As seen, it was one of the ways a chief impressed his followers and earned their loyalty. To be hesitant or indecisive was often taken as a sign of shame, and would likely result in the destruction of one's reputation under a flurry of satire and scorn. And as seen in the *Instructions of Cormac*, a humble person may end up with no honour. But I think the more important dimension of courage is its link to a certain attitude toward the world: an attitude which trusts that things are working out as they are meant to, and that one's own actions can contribute meaningfully to the world. It trusts that one's actions are not, at the end of the day, ultimately futile.

The very notion of Fate is the notion that events and forces in the world are driving toward some inevitable, unavoidable conclusion—even if that conclusion is beyond our field of view. By placing trust in it, and being courageous in the pursuit of your goals, you are expressing hope that fate will favour you. Placing trust in fate means expressing the hope that all events will eventually result in the best of all possible outcomes, and indeed in the creation of the best of all possible worlds. In a future that us unknown and unknowable, both catastrophe and triumph are equal possibilities. It is therefore always possible to have hope. Fate is neither malevolent nor benign; it has the potential to be both. It is thus always possible for the hero to carry on, no matter what the burden, the obstacle, or the opposition. It is in this way that we can see Fate itself in a new light. Pessimism becomes akin to irrationality. To be meek or cowardly is to have a false idea of what Fate is ultimately about. Courage, by contrast, helps people face the uncertainties and challenges of life. It is tied to a disposition to see the world as full of opportunities. It also helps us to accept the painful sides of life, and carry on after a tragedy. However much Fate makes the world seem strange and full of uncertainty, it stirs up our courage, calls it forth, and puts it to the test. To a Hero of the mythological age, Fate is thus a life-affirming principle.

§ 88. Magic.

In most of the heroic literature, people attempt to respond to fate with magic: they might make religious sacrifices or spells to influence fate, or they may try to predict the future. The outcome of the *Cath Maigh Tuireadh* is magically predicted in advance by a Druid named Figol mac Mámois. Similarly, Maeve of Cruachan consulted a Druidess named Fedelm, to ask how she sees the condition of her army in the near future. "I see it crimson, I see it red," says Fedelm, finding in favour of Maeve's adversaries, Cu Chullain and the army of Ulster. In the *Orkneyinga Saga* there is a short story called "Hakon Consults a Soothsayer". It story begins with a negotiation between the client, Hakon Paulson, and the seer he wishes to consult, to determine their mutual trustworthiness. The seer tells Hakon many things about his life to come, starting with the biggest news: "You'll end up as sole ruler of Orkney, though you'll most likely think you've waited long enough for it." The seer also says that Hakon will commit some kind of nearly unforgivable crime, and spend much of his life atoning for it. When Hakon tells the soothsayer that his life will turn out better, the soothsayer answers by saying he can believe whatever he likes, but everything would happen as predicted anyway.[46] The sooth-sayer's almost comic flippancy is a wonderful instance of how ancient people were able to trust that things will work out the way they are hoped for, or at any rate, the way they are expected to, for good or ill.

Aside from the warriors, Heroic society also had an important place for the priest who gives sacrifices to the gods. A sacrifice is a ritual intended to sway fate in one's favour, for instance by placating the cthonic and/or dangerous deities into leaving you alone, or else by bribing the friendly deities into providing blessings and benefits. The Venerable Bede describes how Saint Alban was captured by the soldiers of a pagan king, and told "If you want to enjoy eternal life, sacrifice at once to the great gods."[47] The *Orkneyinga Saga* mentions a Christian King of Sweden whose efforts to put down paganism were so stringent that the nobility deposed him, and in his place they set up a pagan king named Svein the Sacrificer.[48] One can only guess how he came about this name.

Here's another example of magic use from the *Táin Bo Cuailnge*. Just before Maeve's army is about to advance on Ulster:

Four of the provinces of Ireland gathered there at Cruachan Ai. Their sages and druids delayed them for a fortnight waiting for a sign. The day they finally set out Medb said to her charioteer:

'Everyone leaving a lover or a friend today will curse me', she said. 'This army is gathered for me.'

'Wait a minute', the charioteer said, 'until I turn the chariot around to the right, with the sun, to draw down the power of the sign for our safe return.' [49]

What we see happening here is a group of Druids, the magic-wielders and wisdom-keepers of the Celts, holding up the departure of the army until they received an omen. The omen would reveal the moment that fate has favoured for the beginning of their enterprise. This too is part of the social function of the seer: not just the descrying of the future, but also the divining of 'propitious moments' for important undertakings, and hence a form of bravely trusting fate.

When the Druids give the go-ahead, Maeve's charioteer performs a little magic of his own. He turns his chariot right-hand-wise, as we saw, to "draw down the power of the sign." Here we have an example of a general magical correspondence in which clockwise is beneficial, and counter-clockwise is baneful. We also have a rationale for this correspondence explained right in the story. The turning motion is 'with the sun'; it is a repetition of the motion of the powers being invoked. Clockwise is the direction of the passage of the sun over the sky (if you are in the northern hemisphere). The action of turning the chariot right-hand-wise "draws down the power of the sign", which presumably is the omen that the Druids had been waiting for. With this act, the charioteer influences fate in his favour. Magical actions in a warrior society are normally based on repetitions of the actions of natural or supernatural powers, and especially of events from the mythological origin of the world. As we have seen in the research of Eliade, in this repetitive magical act the original creative powers of the world are brought to the present, and put to the work of influencing events according to the invoker's wishes.

The trouble with magic is that it is often just as unpredictable and dangerous as the world it attempts to control, for Fate is itself one of those original creative powers that magic calls upon. Therefore it doesn't always work quite as one expects. And sometimes one's enemies are rather good at doing magic as well. (Those who believe in magic normally also believe in a range of excuses like that one for why it doesn't appear to work all the time.) When Christian missionaries came to Britain, they did not assert that magic was unreal or blasphemous. Instead they asserted the more pragmatic claim that Christian magic simply works better than Pagan magic. Bede's *Ecclesiastical History of the English People* is full of accounts of successful Christian miracles and failed Pagan spell-craft. But it is not just in Christian history that magic is coming to be seen as an unreliable or problematic. In ancient Greece, around the same time as the foundation of philosophy, and while the heroic age was not yet over, the playwright Aeschylus put into his *Agamemnon* a tough-minded criticism of the seers and priests of his time:

> And, truly, what of good
> Ever have prophets brought to men?
> Craft of many words,
> Only through evil your message speaks.
> Seers bring aye terror, so to keep men afraid.[50]

The idea appears to be that prophets are constantly forecasting doom and gloom, keeping people afraid. (And probably keeping themselves rich: since they often claimed to be able to persuade the gods to change the course of fate—for a price!) Magic, therefore, isn't always the best shield against fate. Sometimes, indeed, magic makes it worse. But I have described it here at some length for a reason. Whenever heroic literature describes magic, it is usually the case that there is a certain belief about the future in play, and that belief has an interesting implication. However much one may think that magic can reveal part of the future it will always be the case that the whole future remains unknowable. In the Greek tragic drama Oedipus Rex, which is all about the impossibility of avoiding one's fate, Jocasta tells Oedipus that "Chance rules our lives, and the future is all unknown. Best live as best we may, from day to day."[51] No amount of magical divination can reveal all. The future remains unknowable. But this is no reason not to make plans or promises, and certainly no reason to be afraid. In the *Illiad*, Hector expresses contempt for the reading of omens, and he tells his companions, "fight for your country—that is the best, the only omen!"[52] In other words, the best way to know the future is not to wait for a sign, but *to act*.

And this leads me to the next major theme in Heroic virtue: the "Last Chance".

§ 89. The Last Chance

This invites the question: what if the thing you are trying to do is obviously a lost cause? What if there are so many problems, complications, and opposing forces that success seems remote, if not entirely impossible? There are plenty of examples of this. Activists for various political or social causes often find governmental bureaucracy or public apathy to be a nearly insurmountable obstacle. They become frustrated as over time their victories end up unnoticed, insignificant, and forgotten. All of us, moreover, find ourselves from time to time facing Death itself, the situation against which it seems no kind of success or victory is possible. For part of the metaphysical 'function' of fate, if I may speak of fate this way, is to provide each person with her death, that is, to fix the time and place of each person's death. The presence of death is always close to the heroes of epic poems.

In the *Illiad*, there is an interesting exchange between Achilles and a Trojan fighter named Lycaon, whom Achilles had just defeated. First Lycaon begs for mercy, saying that he is no relation to Patroclus' killer, and so Achilles has no reason to vent his rage against him. But after the death of Patroclus, Achilles had no sympathy in his heart for any Trojan. He tells Lycaon:

Come, friend, you too must die. Why moan about it so?
Even Patroclus died, a far, far better man than you.
And look, you see how handsome and powerful I am?
The son of a great man, the mother who gave me life
A deathless goddess. But even for me, I tell you,
Death and the strong force of fate are waiting.
There will come a dawn or sunset or high noon
When a man will take my life in battle too—
Flinging a spear perhaps
Or whipping a deadly arrow off his bow.[53]

There is grim irony in Achilles' use of the word 'friend' here, as it is addressed to an enemy whom he is about to kill. We have seen how in Greek society the name of friend is reserved for the closest and most beloved of one's companions. The friend is the one who you trust with your life, and who you are prepared to die to protect. But the point of this speech is to affirm that no one, not even the great and glorious like Achilles, can escape death. Achilles and Lycaon are equals in that they must share the same violent fate. Lycaon acknowledges this by letting his weapon fall from his hands, and spreading his arms wide, to willingly receive the killing-blow. Achilles knows that the death he deals to Lycaon will come to him some day as well. And there is something a little chilling in the way Achilles acknowledges this fact—for true to his own prediction, it is an arrow through the heel that eventually kills him.

We are all destined to die. It cannot be avoided. To the heroic soul, however, this too is no reason to shirk from action. The third response to Fate, in this little account of the qualities of the heroic soul, is *the Seizing of the Last Chance*. This type of response is particularly apt in circumstances when, whatever you do, death is likely to befall you. The philosopher Lévinas wrote, "Prior to death there is always a last chance; this is what the hero seizes, not death. The hero is the one who always glimpses a last chance, the one who obstinately finds last chances."[54] The story of the death of Cu Chullain is a wonderful, albeit heart-wrenching, illustration of this attitude toward death. A prophesy had foretold that three of his spears would kill three kings. His enemies got three spears from him by trickery (although with great loss of life in the process!), and they shot them back at him. One killed his charioteer, Laeg, son of Riangabra; one struck one of his chariot horses, the Grey of Macha; and the last one struck Cu Chullain himself. The story makes it clear that the prophesy was fulfilled: the three spears killed the king of charioteers, the king of horses, and the king of heroes. Knowing that he was dying, Cu Chullain went away to wash himself in a nearby lake, and then called to his enemies to find him.

There was a pillar-stone west of the lake, and his eye lit on it, and he went to the pillar-stone, and he tied himself to it with his breast-belt, the way he would not meet his death lying down, but would meet it standing up. Then his enemies came round about him, but they were in dread of going close to him, for they were not sure but he might be still alive... Then the Grey of Macha came back to defend Cuchullain as long as there was life in him, and the hero-light was shining above him... Then a bird came and settled on his shoulder.[55]

Tradition holds that the bird on his shoulder was the goddess Morrigan, in the form of a raven. The picture of the great fighter, dying but still standing, with the bird standing above him, is to my mind the most profound image of an honourable death from all heroic mythology. It sets the precedent for us even today, showing us how to act when hope is lost.

I have always held Cu Chullain in awe, ever since I was first taught the story as a boy, for his obstinate will to stay on his feet, even when about to die. The Lithuanian-French philosopher Emmanuel Lévinas defined "Tragedy" as "the victory of fate over freedom". Yet the hero who seizes the last chance is able to accept fate without passive resignation or submission. As Lévinas says, "for through the death assumed at the moment of the alleged victory of fate, the individual escapes fate."[56] Not that his end becomes other than what fate has decreed: fate is still a force of the universe, still bigger than any individual, and still inescapable. But the fate of the hero who seizes the last chance becomes a product of his free will. It becomes something he chooses, rather than a product of circumstance and accident. Cu Chullain accepted that he was dying, and did whatever he could to make sure his death happened as he wanted it to happen. To be taken by fate while never relinquishing one's initiative and one's values, and especially one's dignity—that is what it means to seize the last chance.

We find another illustration in the death of Beowulf. Near the end of the story, an escaped slave robs the treasure-hoard of a dragon, and the monster sets about marauding the countryside in retribution. It falls to Beowulf to find it and kill it. By this time Beowulf is an old man, having ruled his people for fifty years. He enters battle knowing fully well that whether he succeeds or fails, he will die. Therefore just before he engages the dragon in combat, he tells his companions:

> Not one foot will I retreat
> From the barrow-keeper, but here by the wall
> It must go between us as fate decides,
> The Lord, for each man. My heart is bold,
> I forego boasting against this war-flyer.
> Wait on the barrow safe in your mail,
> Men in your armor, to see which of us
> Shall better survive the wounds dealt out
> In the rush of battle. It is not your business,
> Nor fitting for any, except me alone,
> To test out his strength against this monster,
> Do a hero's deed. I must succeed,
> Win gold by courage, or battle seize me,
> Final life-hurt take your lord away![57]

Here is Beowulf telling his companions that he plans to fight the dragon, but as to whether he will win, 'fate, the master of us all, must decide'. Then he tells his men not to intervene to help him. One could read this, uncharitably, as his selfish wish to keep all the glory of victory to himself. But victory is not guaranteed here. It is not certain that there will be any glory to win. Again, Fate decides it. By asking his friends to wait and watch, and not join in, he is doing them the good turn of saving them from his fate. Beowulf knows he is almost certainly about to die, but yet he carries on. The prospect of death is not a reason to hold oneself back.

> It was no easy journey when Ecgtheow's son,
> Renowned and brave, had to leave the field,
> Make his dwelling in another place,
> As each man must give up loaned time.[58]

This statement is one of the most important in the story. Beowulf accepts his mortality, even welcomes it, for 'everyone has to die'. There is no sense of failure or despair in this welcoming. Rather, the heroic last stand is a fulfillment of fate and destiny in a manner that befits a heroic life. This is the hero showing by his example what it looks like to do the right thing when the highest possible stakes are in play.

§ 90. Heroic Women

Two thousand years or more have gone by since the age of the Celts, the Norse and Scandinavians, the Greeks, and other ancient heroic people. Ideas have changed, and so have some of the facts of social reality. We are in a good position, then, to ask some critical questions of the form of ethics ancient people bequeathed to us. Here's one to start with. In most heroic myths, the primary characters are men. I think it may be undeniable that heroic virtue is strongly rooted in ancient conceptions of masculinity, and especially in aggressive and self-promoting forms of masculinity. Therefore, can heroic virtue offer anything to women?

In Homer's *Odyssey*, it would appear at first glance that there is at least one virtue for women: 'constancy', that is, commitment and loyalty to her husband. Odysseus' wife Penelope remained loyal to her absent husband despite twenty years of separation (during which Odysseus himself spent years with several other women), as well as harassment from other men wishing to wed her, and various threats to her children. The Roman historian Tacitus wrote that German women are noteworthy for their chastity: "Clandestine love-letters are unknown to men and women alike. Adultery is extremely rare, considering the size of the population." He also adds, as a jibe to the aristocratic women of Rome, that "no one in Germany finds vice amusing, or calls it 'up-to-date' to seduce and be seduced."[59] From other sources in parallel cultures one gets the impression that the virtues of women in the Heroic age are the virtues required for the maintenance of a household and a family. She rules the roost absolutely; but her sovereignty of the household also locks her into that household, and offers her little or nothing outside of it. (Incidentally, the same arrangement that locks women in the nursery also locks men *out* of it.) This does not appear to us today as a fair bargain.

The case of Helen of Troy offers an interesting counter-example. The story says that she was given to Paris by the goddess Aphrodite, and abducted from her home in Sparta. But did she really go unwillingly? The size of the fortress where she lived, the steep slope of the hilltop on which it sits, the number of bodyguards and warriors surrounding her (a feast after a peace conference was in progress at the time), and other factors lead me to believe that she eloped of her own free will. Not only that, but she got help from inside. The impression is *not* that she was treated like a kind of football by the men in her life, each trying to catch her and keep her. It is more like that of a woman who got tired of being treated like a football, and made her own choice to elope with Paris and go to Troy, to start her own life anew.

Similar examples can be found in Irish storytelling. Cathbad the Druid prophesised that Deirdre would be the most beautiful women of all time, but on account of her beauty terrible battles would be fought and many men would die. To prevent that from happening, King Conchobor arranged for her to be raised in secret, and married to him as soon as she came of age. But when she met a young hunter named Naoise, she immediately eloped with him and his brothers to Scotland. Similarly, the Irish heroine Grainne, betrothed to marry a man she did not love, eloped with Dairmud. When Dairmud was reluctant to go, she threatened him with satire; knowing that like most men of the Heroic age he would do nearly anything to avoid public humiliation. May it be added, though, that these three women did these things not so much for honour or glory, but primarily for *Love*. Certainly their love was borne of a feeling, a magical impulse, a moment of spiritual recognition which could not be denied without sacrificing a chance for true happiness. But their love was also a deliberate, rational choice. They *decided* who they wanted to be with. They were prepared to endure exile, homelessness, hunger, combat, and other hardships, in order to live the life they wanted to live. In this way, their lives portray the very same Heroic virtues that in other respects seem to be the province of men. And like the virtue of honour, Heroic literature sometimes portrays Love as more important than life itself. At the end of Deirdre's story, when her lover Naoise had been betrayed and killed by Conchobor, she chose suicide instead of an enforced betrothal to a man she hated and feared.[60]

Queen Maeve of Cruachan, another Irish heroine, fought a major war to assert her equality in her marriage. The story starts with an occasion called "The Pillow-Talk", when she is in bed with her husband Ailill. As they lay down together, he says to her "It struck me... how much better off you are today than the day I married you". Maeve counters this by describing how much wealth she had before her marriage, and the size of the army she commanded, and so on. She also described the reasons she agreed to marry Ailill: he was not miserly nor jealous nor timid. These were important qualities in a husband, since Maeve has none of Penelope's famous constancy: instead she boasts, "I never had a man without another in his shadow". She finishes by telling him: "if anyone causes you shame or upset or trouble, the right to compensation is mine... for you're a kept man." (*The Táin* pg. 52-4)

Ailill, of course, balks at this; and so he orders a complete accounting of all the property he and Maeve own. The argument is important because whoever had the greater wealth would be the controller of all the marriage assets. They soon discovered that they both held exactly the same amount of wealth in every respect, save one. Ailill owned Finnbennach, the White Horned bull. Maeve asked a messenger if there was an equal to that animal anywhere in Ireland, and was told that a farmer in Ulster owned the great Brown Bull of Cuailnge, an animal so large that fifty children could dance on his back. Maeve offered its owner a herd of fifty yearling heifers in return for the loan of the bull for one year, and added that if the farmer came with the bull he would receive gifts of land, a fancy chariot, and "my own friendly thighs on top of that". (*The Táin* pg. 55) The farmer, Dáire mac Fiachna, at first agrees to the terms; but soon learns that if he hadn't agreed, Maeve would have sent an army to take it by force. He therefore refuses to lend his prized bull. When Maeve hears of this, she does indeed raise an enormous army from three provinces of Ireland (Munster, Leinster, and her own Connaught) to attack the fourth (Ulster), where the bull was kept. As it turns out, Maeve's army did eventually capture the Brown Bull, but she did not get to keep it. As soon as the two great animals came together they attacked each other. They had in them the spirits of two ancient farmers who had hated and fought each other through many lifetimes and transformations. The Brown Bull of Cuailnge kills Finnbennach, the White Bull, and carries the corpse on his horns all the way back to Ulster.

Similar observations about heroic women can be found in historical accounts. Tacitus wrote that "Britons make no distinction of sex in the appointment of their commanders."[61] And of the women of Germanic tribes, he says "the woman must not think she is excluded from aspirations to manly virtues or exempt from the hazards of warfare."[62] Several historical British Celtic queens like Cartimandua of the Briganti, and Boadicca of the Iceni, were the rulers of tribes and the commanders of armies. Boadicca seems to have been motivated by nationalism and by revenge (her daughters had been molested by Roman soldiers). And Cartimandua fought and won three civil wars that the Roman outposts in her territory had provoked.

For the record, there need not be anything un-heroic about so-called 'feminine' qualities like compassion, care-giving, and nurturing. Someone who consistently gives her time and work and love to another person might still be leading an *active* life. It is this emphasis on activity that makes it heroic. It need not be un-heroic just because it is attached to the lives of others: rather, it is un-heroic if it is based on obedience, self-denial, or passive resignation. But if it meets the needs of the time and place with something decisive and life-affirming, and results in the creation of a sense of identity which one may properly be proud of, then it deserves to be called excellent indeed.

Finally, it is worth adding that the men of Heroic literature are not necessarily the barbaric, bloodthirsty, brainless bullies they are sometimes believed to be. In many Nordic sagas it is often the case that the men are reluctant to do anything too confrontational, even when they could benefit themselves thereby. Sometimes they have to be egged on by their wives or sisters. Gunnar's spiteful wife Hallgerd, from the Icelandic story of *Njail's Saga*, is one of the worst of them. Whenever Njail and Gunnar would come to an agreement, she would provoke the tension anew, for instance by getting one of her servants to murder one of Njail's servants. Strong-willed women in Heroic societies were not simply taking on a male social role or a male identity. They were taking on a Heroic identity, which was fully available to them, and not the exclusive field of the men. They were 'fair and fierce' as Yeats wrote: strong, brave, intelligent, persevering, and certainly Heroic—and still women.

§ 91. Ordinary People

The sources I have consulted may seem to portray the virtues of a narrow section of heroic society: the warriors and warlords. And some of the wisdom-texts we've looked at, like the *Testament of Morann* and the *Instructions of Cormac*, were originally composed to offer ethical advice to kings and leaders. It is, of course, appropriate to judge an ethical idea by its paragons, just as we judge a religion by the conduct of its saints. But Heroic virtue may strike many as excessively 'macho'. Does it offer anything to ordinary people?

In fact Heroic mythology offers a great deal. Everyone, whether a warrior or not, and even today, must face the unpredictability of the future. It may follow that friendship, hospitality, generosity, courage, trust, and all the other heroic qualities are still useful and valuable for everyone. Similarly, there is nothing in the idea of Excellence that excludes people who are not warriors. Honour can emerge from being highly skilled in a trade of profession, and from a job well done. Other heroic qualities can be developed in the course of practicing agriculture, blacksmithing, carpentry, and musicianship. They can emerge from parenthood and family life, friendship, and love. All the different ordinary things people did in the Heroic age, and still do today, are still occasions for heroic excellence.

Storytelling, the source of heroic virtue, was also meant for everyone, and not just the warriors. Njail Thorgeirsson, the central hero of *Njail's Saga,* is not a sword-fighter but a farmer, and he is sometimes consulted by his friends as a prophet. He is also a part-time lawyer, and much of the action of the story takes place in courts of justice at the Althing (Iceland's annual parliament), and not on battlefields. The *Hávamál*, the wisdom-text from *The Poetic Edda*, is not an advice-text to the kings and nobles like the *Testament of Morann*. It is an ordinary person's guide to etiquette in the feasting hall. It speaks of how one should behave in friendship and in love, in trade and business affairs, in raising families, and a variety of other situations. It even has warnings about the dangers of gossip and of talking too much, especially when one really has nothing to say! Here is a passage from the *Havamal* on the respect owed to people with disabilities:

> May the halt ride a horse, and the handless be herdsman,
> The deaf man may doughtily fight,
> A blind man is better than a burned one, ay:
> Of what gain is a good man dead?[63]

It would seem that the author of the *Hávamál* regarded everyone as having some use, and that only a dead man is totally useless. One could infer that therefore everyone is worthy of respect, one way or another. Heroic virtue, we may conclude, is available to all.

There have been several practical experiments in re-creating ordinary Heroic Age life, and they have tended to produce many of the qualities of character described in the literature. In the year 2001, the BBC produced an educational 'reality TV' series called *Surviving the Iron Age*, and published an accompanying book. Volunteers were taken to an original Celtic hill-fort in Wales to live as Iron-age people for seven weeks. They were given various tasks, such as to elect a chieftain, to produce their own food, and to create various Iron-age materials like honey beer, tallow candles, wicker baskets, clay pottery, charcoal, and an iron bloom. They even had to build their own Wicker Man! On the last day, one of the participants made this observation about what life must have been like for ancient Heroic-age people.

> When we lit the wicker man, it was so warm and the evening was pure fun. I began to realise what the Celts must have felt like. Theirs was a life of extremes. They would have worked hard and worried about eating enough, then they would really enjoy themselves and eat whole steers and have lots of fun. It felt really decadent. It was sheer abandonment.[64]

And what kind of people were produced by this situation? Barry Cunliff, one of Britain's best archaeologists, observed:

> The sort of thing I am learning is people's different concept of time. Yesterday I was watching people moving about the place. They were moving slowly and fairly purposefully but not in a busy way. All of their sense of time was different... I was talking to the blacksmith in the house that was used as his forge. There was a girl there working the bellows and it was the most beautiful, quite relaxing time. This must have affected the minds of the people the way they responded to nature, the way they responded to each other, the way they responded to their own creative abilities.[65]

What struck me the most, as I watched the series and read the book, was the reaction most of the participants had on 'returning' to the twenty-first century. Their attitudes towards materialism, work, friendship, civil society, even personal hygiene, and much more, was radically changed.

> Ron was taken aback by how rude and aggressive people were on the street and Brenda wanted to go back to the fort, where she found life simple, peaceful, and hassle-free. Jody too remarked on people's behaviour. 'Everybody always seems to be in a bad mood. I went to Tesco's and everybody was jostling each other and giving each other bad looks. It was so different in the community...[66]

It seems to me that the volunteers of the BBC project, in re-creating Iron Age life for only seven weeks, also re-discovered many of the values and moral priorities described in Heroic age myths and sagas. In particular, "all the volunteers remarked on how important friendship had become."[67] Not only did they miss their families and friends at home, but after the project was over they very much missed each other. It appears, then, that many of the virtues of the Heroic age emerged not just from politics and warfare, but from their survival demands, the world they lived in, and the way they related to each other.

But here's a critical question. Some of the qualities for which a person may be honoured in Heroic society are not what we might call properly 'ethical'. In a heroic society, one can be praised for being tough and strong, being naturally talented in some practical craft or skill, being a dangerous fighter, being handsome or good-looking. One can even receive honour for being 'lucky'. It was believed that Fate has a hand in shaping the kind of person you are, not just the circumstances in which you find yourself. In this respect Virtue is an aristocratic idea: the virtues portrayed in heroic literature seem to belong to superior people, not to everyone. The contemporary philosopher John Casey wrote that part of the distinctiveness of Pagan virtue is in the way it attributes ethical significance to 'accidental' or 'non-moral' qualities like these.[68] To our modern ears this strikes a dissonant chord. The familiar side of virtue does not like to praise or blame anyone for things they do not choose or control. How can things that are a product of fortune, not a product of people's choices, be morally praiseworthy?

The answer is that what one *does* with the gifts of fortune is what earns a hero the most praise or scorn. Even today, we respect and admire pop celebrities of all kinds, from hockey players to fashion models, for their non-moral 'excellences' like beauty or athletic skill. (Or perhaps it would be better to say we secretly envy them.) But we also offer more respect, and better quality respect, to celebrities who put those gifts to good use. We are born with various potentials and powers: some 'properly' moral, like an instinct to respect people, and some 'not', like the ability to win an Olympic marathon. But I assert that the way we practice and develop them is what makes us finally virtuous, and deserving of the highest kinds of praise. Perhaps that is part of the reason why many celebrities support charities or promote humanitarian causes. Paul Robeson, a well known baritone singer of the middle 20th century, through his choices of what to sing and where to perform, used his celebrity to draw public attention to racism and to promote civil rights for American Black people. Bob Geldoff, lead singer of The Boomtown Rats, organised the Live Aid international rock concert, to raise money for famine relief in Africa. Twenty years later he organised another international concert, Live "8", to encourage world leaders to do more for third world poverty. Bono, lead singer of Irish rock group U2, has been championing the cause of poverty relief for decades. In the course of his activism he speaks directly to some of the most powerful political leaders in the world. Angelina Jolie campaigns against child poverty; and she has personally adopted several children from third world countries. These people are using their celebrity to promote important moral causes. In this way, the honour they possess is rooted primarily in what they do.

Some readers might not be satisfied with this answer. But I cannot ignore the conclusion that various non-moral excellences, like beauty, strength, and 'luck', usually do contribute positively to the flourishing of whoever has them. They therefore usually count as Virtues, as the Heroic age defined them. Aristotle himself also claimed that the Virtuous person must possess certain non-moral qualities to succeed: for instance he must be tall and handsome.[69] Similarly, in Irish tradition, a chieftain must have no physical blemishes or disfigurements of any kind. King Nuada, for example, was deposed from the leadership of the Tuatha de Dannan when he lost his right arm in battle. Within the logic of Virtue there is always a tension between two ideas that do not normally sit well together. On the one side, there is the requirement for universal unconditional benevolence and compassion, which we have learned from Christianity. On the 'other side', there is the pursuit of excellence in all sorts of human affairs, and the elevation of what it is to be human. I must put off my solution to this tension until later. For the moment, let me say that this tension is no reason to dismiss Heroic Virtue altogether. Even with this tension unresolved, the Virtues still teach the deep truth that lasting happiness comes primarily from who you are and what you do, not from what you possess. It is the intelligent use of the gifts of fortune, not the mere possession of them, which in the end will make you flourish.

In the Heroic age, non-moral qualities might not be excellences of *character*, but they are excellences nonetheless. In terms of the social response, while ancient people would praise (or envy) those who were benefited by fortune, they would also judge most harshly those who squandered what fortune gave them. Similarly, we today have very little pity when wealthy, powerful, or famous people find that their high and mighty place does not make them happy. Indeed we sometimes take smug delight in the watching their downfall. It is not until the time of Plato and Aristotle that the notion of the practice and development of Virtue for the sake of happiness becomes fully explicit. But even in the earliest reaches of the Heroic age, Honour is ultimately something you *earn* by your *actions*. It does not automatically belong to those who are born into wealthy upper-class families. It belongs to those who work for it.

§ 92. Atonement

I have described Heroic virtue as tied to the social order. What did Heroic society make of people who violated that order? What was done to its criminals, and how did the community restore its sense of well-being?

Petty crimes and misdemeanors might be punished with something mildly embarrassing, like a satirical retelling of the act in songs and stories. In the case of murders, the killer could usually pay a fine to the victim's family, and the amount would depend on the social rank of both the killer and the victim. This fine was called the *wer-gild* in Anglo-Saxon, meaning 'man-payment'. Among the Irish this fee was known as the *eiric*, or 'honour-price'. But sometimes no amount of money could quell the desire for vengeance, and honour-killings would go on. Repeat offenders would receive heavier fines, and more serious forms of public humiliation. Eventually their whole reputation would be tarnished and their honour left worthless. They would find it hard to live and work with others as fewer and fewer people would trust any promises they might make, or would even be unwilling to associate with them.

Finally the most serious crimes would be met with exile, that is, dismissal from the human community (and not execution, as one might expect). Tacitus wrote that among the Germans, "to throw away one's shield [i.e. to commit an act of cowardice] is the supreme disgrace, and the man who has thus dishonoured himself is debarred from attendance at sacrifice or assembly." This punishment was deemed worse than death: "Many such survivors from the battlefield have ended their shame by hanging themselves."[70] An outlaw was someone who had no lord, and so could not benefit from the lord's protection. Others could harm him, steal from him, or even kill him, without any legal penalty. Being an outlaw also meant the near-total loss of honour and self-esteem, the loss of all his friends, and even the loss of his standing as a human being, in the eyes of others. In Heroic society, being an outlaw is almost on par with being a wild animal, or a monster, and not a fully human person. This is what made it feel like a fate worse than death.

But what of those who seek to re-enter human society after having been exiled? What must they do to earn the right to return, or to be invited back into the community? The Greek story of Hercules gives an interesting example of *atonement*: the criminal who seeks re-admission to society must undergo some kind of quest. The Greek hero Hercules, in a fit of uncontrolled rage, threw his children into a fire. He was therefore assigned a dozen different quests, known to storytellers as the Twelve Labours of Hercules. Note that he had to undergo these dangerous tasks *away from the community*. First he was sent into exile, and then he was told not to return until he had done something to prove his honour again. Similarly, in the Irish story of Brian and the sons of Uisneach, Lugh Lamh-Fada imposes a quest upon Brian and his brothers in punishment for the slaying of Cian, who was Lugh's foster-father. Like Hercules and his Labours, they were ordered to go abroad to procure various treasures. The story shows the Blood Feud at work: Brian and his brothers killed Cian in retaliation for Cian's slaying of their sister. The story makes it fairly clear that Lugh's punishment was heavy-handed, far out of proportion to the crime they committed. When Brian and his brothers return from the quest victoriously, but with their life's blood seeping away through terrible wounds sustained in their last battle, Lugh's stern and unforgiving response is likewise judged harshly. One of the treasures that Brian and his brothers had to retrieve was a magical pig-skin with the power to heal all wounds. One word from Lugh and the treasure would be brought to them. But Lugh does not give that word, and so they die. The story is counted as one of the three great Sorrows of Irish storytelling.

This form of punishment, the pattern of exile → quest → re-admission, expresses two main moral ideas to which I want to draw attention. First, since a person's whole sense of identity and purpose came from his membership in a community, to commit a crime was to damage or even to sever one's relations to others in society, and thus to harm himself. In this way, criminals invite their own punishment. Second, the great energy possessed by the warriors is more like a sudden flood in springtime than like a gentle river that flows all year round. It has great potential for both good and evil—that is, for both protecting a community and doing benefit to others, and for destroying a community and doing harm. One must dig channels and watercourses for it lest it burst the banks and destroy the surrounding landscape. That is to say, one must temper it with honour and other noble qualities lest it cause harm to oneself and others.

§ 93. Apotheosis

Ancient people believed that every human being possess an immortal soul that can survive death. Sometimes it remains in this world, in the form of a ghost or a disembodied spirit. Sometimes it travels to an Otherworldly resting-home for the dead. Sometimes it reincarnates as an animal or another person. They believed in various gods who could intervene in human affairs, and who required offerings and sacrifices in return for the things they gave to us. Some also believed in the existence of an impersonal magical energy that radiated from various places, people, and things. Heroic literature is full of accounts of these beliefs. The Roman commentator Pomponius Mela wrote this about the beliefs of the Celtic Druids:

> One of their dogmas has come to common knowledge, namely, that souls are eternal and that there is another life in the infernal regions, and this has been permitted manifestly because it makes the multitude readier for war. And it is for this reason too that they burn or bury, with their dead, things appropriate to them in life; and that in times past they even used to defer the completion of business and the payment of debts until their arrival in another world.[71]

Imagine telling your banker that you would like to defer the payment of your credit card to the next life!

A similar belief was held among the Vikings. As Snorri Sturlson describes in *The Prose Edda*:

Most important, he [the All-Father] created man and gave to him a living spirit that will never die, even if the body rots to dust or burns to ashes. All men who are righteous shall live and be with him in that place called Gimle or Vingolf. But evil men go to Hel and from there into Niflhel, which is below the ninth world.[72]

Snorri was writing well into the Christian period, and so these remarks here may be a Christian interposition on pre-Christian mythology. But whether or not this fragment represents a Christian interposition or a genuine piece of Pagan lore, I think this notion of immortality is not worth serious attention. It tells us almost nothing about how we are to live in the here and now. We could believe, as Christians do, and as Snorri Sturlson did, that the course of our lives in this world determines which Otherworld we will go to after we die. If we made our life decisions on this basis, we would find ourselves living in various ways for the sake of that next life, and not for the sake of this one. And we would therefore miss much of what makes life enjoyable and worthwhile.

People in Heroic societies also believed in another kind of immortality: it is called *apotheosis*. This is the reward for people who are courageous and honourable, and who seize the last chance when facing death. But it is different from the immortality of the soul in that deserving heroes can benefit from it while they are still alive. When Beowulf finally posted Grendel's severed arm in the hall of Heorot, King Hrothgar gave him the greatest praise that anyone in a heroic society could ever earn: "But now, by yourself, you have done such a deed that your [fame] is assured, [and] will live forever."[73] And Queen Wealhtheow gave him a gift of a special coat of armour, a precious heirloom, and praised him saying:

You have brought it about that far and near
None but admire you, and always will,
A sea-broad fame, walled only by wind.[74]

This is the highest kind of reward anyone can ever hope to receive in Heroic society. Heroes therefore often begin their careers with an announcement of their intention to earn it. The story of Cu Chullain's boyhood deeds exemplifies this. Cu Chullain went to King Conchobar mac Nessa and demanded to take up arms, saying that Cathbad the Druid had told him to do so. Later, when Cathbad denies it, this is what Cu Chullain says in his defense:

> "I told no lie, King," said Cu Chullain, "for it was he indeed put it in my mind when he was teaching the others, for when one of them asked him if there was any special virtue in this day, he said that whoever would for the first time take arms today, his name would be greater than any other in Ireland, and he did not say any harm would come on him, but that his life would be short." "And what I said is true," said Cathbad, "there will be fame on you and a great name, but your lifetime will not be long." "It is little I would care," said Cu Chullain, "if my life were to last one day and one night only, so long as my name and the story of what I had done would live after me."[75]

As we now know, this omen turned out to be true. By tradition, Cu Chullain died at the age of twenty-seven. Similarly, in the *Illiad*, when Achilles rebuffs the embassy from Agamemnon, he reveals that his mother allowed him to choose between the short life of glory and the long life of comfort.

> Mother tells me,
> The immortal goddess Thetis with her glistening feet,
> That two fates bear me on to the day of death.
> If I hold out here and I lay siege to Troy
> My journey home is gone, but my glory never dies.
> If I voyage back to the fatherland I love,
> My pride, my glory dies,
> True, but the life that's left me will be long.
> The stroke of death will not come on me quickly.[76]

Again, as we all now know, Achilles chose the short life of glory. Similar to Cu Chullain's reasoning, the short life of glory was preferable to Achilles because it also entails immortality. And true to his own prediction, it was not long after Achilles killed Hector, an act which both avenged Patroclus and also secured his place as the greatest of all Hellenic fighters, that Achilles himself is killed.

Apotheosis is the immortality of a life-story that continues to be told long after the person dies. It is achieved by the doing of something so glorious that the story of one's life becomes part of the legends and mythologies of a community. And these legends, so it was believed, would last forever. As it is said in the Hávamál:

> Cattle die, and kinsmen die,
> Thyself eke soon wilt die,
> But fair fame will fade never,
> I ween, for him who wins it.[77]

A good name, says the Havamal, never dies. There may be some substance to this idea. For example, Thor Heyerdahl, the famous Norwegian adventuring scientist, believed that narrative apotheosis transformed an ancient Russian chieftain from the area around the north shore of the Black Sea into the Nordic father-deity Odin.[78] Before he died in April of 2002, he was working on archaeological explorations of the area in pursuit of this theory. The *Prose Edda*, one of the great literary sources of Norse mythology, seems to confirm this theory. It says that Odin originally came from the city of Troy (the same Troy of *The Illiad*) and that he led a mass migration of his people up to northern Europe.

> Odin had the gift of prophesy, as his wife also did, and through this learning he became aware that his name would become renowned in the northern part of the world and honoured more than other kings. For this reason he was eager to set off from Turkey, and he took with him on his journey a large following of people, young and old, men and women. So, too, they took with them many precious things. Wherever

they went on their travels, tales of their splendor were told, making them seem more like gods than men.[79]

The narrative continues from there, describing how Odin and his people settled Saxony and Westphalia (both in modern-day Germany), as well as Denmark, Sweden and Norway, and how the royal families of those countries are descended from him and his sons. [c.f. pp. 7-8] Indeed the original meaning of 'divine right' was the justification of a noble or royal family's right to rule based on that family's genealogical descendant from a god—who was a mortal hero who became a god through this process of apotheosis.

Some people may be disappointed by this form of immortality. They may prefer the Judeo-Christian belief that 'true' immortality is the psychic survival of the soul, after death, in an other-world paradise; not the survival of a trifling thing like a story. But the immortality of Apotheosis has a number of advantages which I think are worth considering.

First, it is not dependant on an immaterial, immortal soul, nor on an other-worldly after-life, the existence of which may be impossible to prove scientifically. It is therefore an open prospect for humanists, skeptics, atheists, and religious believers alike. In this respect I think it has the ability to bring people together. Furthermore, since it need not rest upon a belief in an immaterial soul, Apotheosis forces people to focus their attention on their actual lives. And many of the rewards which it offers for being virtuous are available in the here-and-now. We need not wait until after death to receive them. It is therefore a very practical, very accessible principle.

The second advantage to Apotheosis concerns the rewards themselves which it offers people who live virtuously, and who develop various praiseworthy talents. It rewards qualities which benefit others, such as generosity, hospitality, and friendship. It also encourages qualities which are rewarding on their own, such as courage, integrity, and intelligence. The most obvious reward is the praise of our peers: we all have deep psychological needs for acceptance and for respect. But a person can also determine independently whether she is living a virtuous, heroic life, by deciding whether she finds her life satisfying, enjoyable, and complete. As a 'mere incentive' for virtue, Apotheosis may seem disingenuous. But there is nothing particularly irrational about offering incentives to live a good life. Even Plato and Aristotle took time to show why it benefits a person to be virtuous, and why it harms a person to be wicked. They described how the development of one's natural talents, and the activity of directing those talents towards the aim of a worthwhile life, is the very essence of happiness itself. I think this notion of happiness deserves to be revived in our own time, once again. If anything is disingenuous in ethics, it is the promise that the rewards for living a good life are delivered after death!

Third, Apotheosis gives the heroes good reasons to carry on doing heroic things, even when there is little hope of success, and even if the hero's own death is a likely consequence. Apotheosis could therefore be taken as another 'mere incentive' for virtue, not a reason why virtue is intrinsically desirable. But as an incentive, the immortality offered by Apotheosis may seem hollow: it becomes available only after death. (And whatever one may believe about the survival of the soul after death, Apotheosis offers a benefit one can never personally enjoy while alive.) But a Virtuous person, in the heroic sense, is motivated primarily by her sense of self-worth. The desire to create a total life-story that would be worthy of remembrance is one way that sense of self-worth may be expressed. To the virtuous person, the prospect of one's own death is not a reason to shirk from being virtuous. This is part of the point of the Seizure of the Last Chance.

Fourth, and finally, Apotheosis encourages people to think of their lives in a holistic, comprehensive way; that is, as a story. Many contemporary philosophers claim that storytelling is a powerful way of both recognizing and configuring personal identity. It is in the story of your life that you will recognise yourself; your biography is the largest part of your identity. Insofar as personal identity is bound to storytelling, it will follow that to tell someone's life story is to call up that person's presence. To continue to tell someone's life story is to give that presence a continued life. Indeed this is a large part of what we mean when we say that someone's 'spirit' lives on. If one's story lasts forever, then that may be just as good as one's presence and identity living forever.

There are two obvious objections to the idea of Apotheosis as a goal for the worthwhile life. One is that human memory is fallible and fickle, and that no amount of fame can possibly last all eternity. Some people's life stories may be told for a few centuries, others for only a few months. Many people never have their stories told at all. It might follow that Apotheosis is a false immortality. I believe this objection is weak. A Heroic person is not so dependant on others that he cannot tell for himself whether his life is worthwhile. The point of Apotheosis is that a good life can be represented as a good story: a heroic life is a life with a story that deserves to be told after the person has died. Whether other people do, in fact, tell that story, is up to them. And they may commit a great injustice if they neglect to tell the stories of deserving people. But you can be responsible for living in such a way that others *ought* to uphold your life as a model of excellence which future generations can learn from, and perhaps emulate.

Another objection is that cruel and evil people sometimes have the stories of their lives told after their deaths too. Does Apotheosis therefore also reward lives of outstanding wickedness? The reply to this objection is similarly obvious. No sane, self-respecting person would *want* to be remembered as a criminal. It seems to me more like a *punishment*, than a reward, to be made famous for causing great suffering to others. However, it is true that the same forces are at work in the lives of the heroic and the terrible. It can sometimes be said of both kinds of people that they possess great spirit. But I shall deal with this issue elsewhere.

As a final word, may I say that the idea of Apotheosis is still with us. We still think it is important to remember outstanding people of the past. This is why we have war memorials, headstones on graves, monuments, and public ceremonies to honour fallen soldiers. During the Renaissance in Italy, princes and wealthy people would seek a kind of surrogate immortality by commissioning paintings or sculptures of mythological gods and heroes with their own likeness somewhere in the work. Today, rich people do the same thing by creating charitable foundations in their name, or by

bestowing philanthropic gifts upon hospitals, universities, and other insti-
tutions with the condition that some part of the institution be named after
them. For reasons that remain unknown, U.S. Secretary of State
Condoleeza Rice has an oil tanker named after her. But just like in the Iron
Age, we today still bestow immortality on the people we love and admire.
Britain's Princess Diana, for instance, is already well on her way towards
becoming something like a saint. We continue to be fascinated by the story
of her fairy-tale wedding, and the mysterious circumstances of her death.
Something similar can be said of "the gods of rock and roll": John Lennon,
Jimi Hendrix, Elvis Presley, Buddy Holly, Kurt Cobain, Janice Joplin, and
Jim Morrison. Apotheosis, in the heroic world-view, is the measure of a
successful life, and indeed the means to achieve victory over the fates.

THIRD MOVEMENT:
THE CIVILIZED

§ 94. High Classical Society

At the end of the heroic age, the idea of the life of adventure capped off with a glorious last stand began to lose its appeal. Many warriors were just as prepared to kill for the sake of honour, as they were to die for it. Never-ending blood-feuds were wearing people down. The *Saga of the Volsungs*, a Nordic epic story, is all about the destruction and suffering that the blood feud can create. In *Njail's Saga*, Njail undertook many attempts to dispel people's grudges and create peace, from arranging oaths of friendship to manipulating Iceland's constitution. They all fail when one last hold-out lets his wounded pride get the better of him. In Homer's epic tale of the *Odyssey,* the sequel to the *Illiad*, the Greek heroes finally come to the underworld of Hades and are allowed to choose their next life. Odysseus chooses the life of an ordinary man. It was the last one available, as all of his friends had taken their turn before him. But he says he would have chosen the ordinary life anyway, as he has had enough of adventure.

We leave behind the heroic world and come to the classical world. Cities displace fortresses and farming settlements as the main centres of population. Standing armies replace militias and singular heroic champions. The Greek orator Pericles declared that not just individuals, but whole cities, like his own Athens, can be heroic in the Homeric sense. Clann chieftains and heads of tribes become landlords. Some of them have even become hereditary monarchs, and are no longer elected, although they must still have the support of the aristocracy. But some classical societies are also republican or humanist in nature. Either way, the position of women deteriorates significantly: these are definitely male dominated societies. And things get a lot worse for the poor, as the upper classes become more entrenched and institutionalized. Even the community meeting place becomes institutionalized: the *agora* of Athens, the *forum* of Rome. The written word overtakes the spoken word as the primary means of expressing the society's most important ideas and values. Responsibility for magic, religion, and the supernatural is mostly handed over to specialists like priests and sorcerers. There may be a movement towards monotheism. And perhaps as a result of all these changes, the notion that human beings are part of the world, and but one type of earthly creature among others, loses ground. It is replaced by the notion that human beings are the masters of the world, with the right to rule over it. As said by Marcus Aurelius, an important Stoic philosopher and Emperor of Rome to boot: "The rest of creation is constituted to serve rational beings, just as in everything else the lower exists for the higher".[80] In the ancient world, a 'civilized' society did not mean a society were people are 'civil' to each other: it meant a society united by a hierarchical order.

Still, Fortune's shadow had not been banished. As an example, have a look at the story of "The Sword of Damocles". It concerns Dionysius I, dictator of Syracuse from 405 until 367 BCE, and one of the most tyrannical and paranoid rulers of his time. One of his courtiers, a spineless sycophant named Damocles, exclaimed how wonderful the life of the monarch must be. Dionysius immediately arranged for Damocles to have a taste of it. Here is the story as it appears in one of the works of Cicero, the *Discussions at Tusculum*.

Dionysius had [Damocles] installed on a golden couch covered with a superb woven coverlet embroidered with beautiful designs, and beside the couch was placed an array of sideboards loaded with chased gold and silver plate. He ordered that boys, chosen for their exceptional beauty, should stand by and wait on Damocles at table, and they were instructed to keep their eyes fastened attentively upon his every sign. There were perfumes and garlands and incense, and the tables were heaped up with a most elaborate feast. Damocles thought himself a truly fortunate person. But in the midst of all this splendour, directly above the neck of the happy man, Dionysius arranged that a gleaming sword should be suspended from the ceiling, to which it was attached by a horse hair. And so Damocles had no eye for those lovely waiters, or for all the artistic plate. Indeed, he did not even feel like reaching out his hand toward the food. Presently the garlands, of their own accord, just slipped down from his brow.[81]

The story of a man invited to enjoy a wonderful banquet, on the condition that a sword be suspended above him by a hair, is one of the most famous symbols of the unpredictability and fragility of life. Cicero's larger philosophical point, which is often missed, is that "happiness is out of the question if you are perpetually menaced by some terror."[82] Fortune is that terror: it is the terror of the future, the unknown, of loss, and of catastrophic change. Fortune is too transient, too unreliable, to give anyone lasting happiness. The blessings it brings simply cannot be trusted to stay. Even the very rich and powerful are subject to it: indeed they may be more vulnerable, since they have much more to lose. Cicero, himself a very wealthy man, elaborated at length about how wealth cannot create sustainable happiness for anyone. And in the end, that thread holding the sword eventually snaps: fortune always resolves itself in death.

The same point is made some four centuries later by Boethius, in a well-known work entitled *The Consolation of Philosophy*. This is how he described the goddess 'Fortuna', and the reason she cannot be trusted.

Change is her very nature. In the very act of changing she has preserved her own particular kind of constancy towards you. She was exactly the same when she was flattering you and luring you on with enticements of a false kind of happiness. You have discovered the changing faces of the random goddess... Do you really hold dear that kind of happiness which is destined to pass away? Do you really value the presence of Fortune when you cannot trust her to stay and when her departure will plunge you in sorrow?... Commit your boat to the winds and you must sail whichever way they blow, not just where you want.[83]

The story of the lives of these two authors are dramatic illustrations of this very point. Cicero was a politically powerful orator, and advisor to several emperors: he wrote the *Discussions* while he had been banished into exile by his political opponent, Julius Caesar. Boethius had it worse: he was a

Consul and a political advisor to King Theodoric the Ostrogoth, who ruled the Western Empire from Rome in the 4th century CE. Boethius had wealth, luxury, political power, and nearly everything he could ever want. Then one bright sunny day, he was indicted in a plot to overthrow the senate. Although he pleaded his innocence, he was exiled to a jail in Ravenna, and sentenced to death. From his prison cell he composed *The Consolation of Philosophy,* a book in which he imagined that the goddess of wisdom, Philosophy herself, appeared in his cell and started a conversation. After chastising him for having excessive self-pity, the goddess told him his despair is caused by the trust he placed in Fortune.

It may seem as if these writers of the Classical age were merely repeating what their Heroic forbears said. But this is not the case, for two reasons. First of all, Classical society held that the most important problems in life emerged not from nature, nor from metaphysical or supernatural powers, but from *relations with other people*. Cicero said, "The worst calamities in the world are likewise those which man inflicts upon man."[84] He considers the challenges posed by natural disasters, animal attacks, and so on, but concludes that "much more frequent are catastrophes such as the annihilation of human beings by one another, formed up in armies."[85] In the first century BCE, Lucretius named the pursuit of wealth as one of the primary sources of misery and suffering in life:

Men craved
Power and fame, that their fortunes might stand
On firm foundations, so they might enjoy
The rich man's blessed life. What vanity!
To struggle toward the top, toward honour's height
They made the way a foul and deadly road,
And when they reached the summit, down they came
Like thunderbolts, for Envy strikes men down
Like thunderbolts, into most loathsome Hell...[86]

For this reason, Lucretius speculated that the first laws that human beings created for themselves were non-aggression treaties: "Do not hurt me, please, and I'll not hurt you, were the terms they stammered. Men asked protection for their little ones as well as their wives…"[87]

As a final example: at the time of the founding of Athens as a city-state, Plutarch wrote that there were 'Seven Sages' almost universally regarded as the wisest men in Greece. He said that the philosopher Thales was "the only sage of the period who pursued his speculations beyond the limits of strictly practical problems; all the rest gained their reputation for wisdom from their prowess as statesmen."[88] In other words, most of the people renowned for knowledge and wisdom at the time were not mystics or prophets, nor poets, nor philosophers, but politicians! Try to imagine someone saying the same thing in our world today.

Our biggest problems, as these writers conceived them, are not metaphysical or supernatural: they are *social* and *political* problems. Other people have different beliefs and ideas. They might speak a different language. They might be saints and sages, but they also might be thieves and murderers. They may want to do different things. All these differences produce conflict. The kind of questions being asked in this situation were questions like, How are people to get along with each other—at the very least, without killing each other? What is justice? What does an ideal human society look like? Is it better to be virtuous or to be wicked? What kind of people should our lawmakers be? Who shall rule?

Classical writers also prescribe a very different kind of proper response to fortune. The poets of the Heroic epics and sagas described characters who happily jump on the Wheel of Fortune as if it was a carnival ride. Fate offered a shot at immortality to those who rode the wheel with honour, courage, and so on. The philosophers of the classical world say one should not climb on the wheel in the first place: one will only be thrown off. Instead, they suggested that the way to protect yourself from fate, or more precisely, to preserve happiness despite what fate may do, is to train up your faculty of *reason*.

§ 95. Reason

Consider this passage from Plutarch's *The Rise and Fall of Athens*, which was written just as Greek society was changing from a collection of warrior-tribes to a league of city-states. Expressing a view that seems to have been prevalent at least among the upper classes, Plutarch says that only Reason can prepare you to handle the ups and downs of Fortune.

> Those who have failed to learn how to fortify themselves with reason against the blows of fortune lay up endless troubles and fears for themselves, and it is not affection but weakness which brings this about. Such people cannot even enjoy what they long for when they get it, but allow themselves to be obsessed with continual anguish and anxieties and apprehensions, because they are forever anticipating some future loss. The wisest course is not to guard against the loss of our wealth by taking refuge in poverty, nor of our friends by rejecting friendship, nor of our children by having none, but rather to forearm ourselves with Reason against every kind of misfortune.[89]

The power of Reason, with the prominence given to it by the Greeks, is a shield against fate. This is not to say that the people of previous societies were any less capable of critical thinking. But with Classical societies, Reason takes centre-stage as a supreme principle of human life for the first time. To practice Reason means to look inward to your own mind to find answers to the problems that beset your life. You can no longer look to oracles and prophets, to the precedents of tradition, to popular opinion, nor to so-called common knowledge. You must do your own thinking. Popular culture today thinks of Reason as something dispassionate, cold-hearted, and impersonal. But in the ancient world's understanding, this view is simply wrong. Reason emerged from a relationship with spiritual values that transcended the self, and sometimes transcended the world as well.

Heraclitus, the ancient Greek philosopher, confirms this in several of his fragments, such as these ones:

- What understanding or intelligence have they? They put their trust in popular bards and take the mob for their teacher...
- I searched myself.

- It belongs to all people to know themselves and to think rightly. [90]

Heraclitus is saying that instead of searching for truth in 'popular bards', or 'the mob', he searched for wisdom within himself. To Know Yourself—the famous inscription at the temple of the Oracle of Delphi—is to him something like an ethical necessity for everyone. Other philosophers of the Classical period confirm this. Cicero's account of the Sword of Damocles, for instance, was not meant to be pessimistic. He wrote it to encourage and uplift people, and show them how philosophy offers the way to permanent and lasting happiness. As he says, you must not look to external circumstances or possessions, but to what you possess in yourself:

> When misfortunes appear on the horizon, we exaggerate them from sheer fright, and when they are right upon us we exaggerate them once more, because of the pain they are causing us. These feelings impel us to put the blame on circumstances when what we ought to be blaming is a deficiency in our own character.[91]

If you search within your own character for happiness, what will you find? The philosophers believed you would find that the transience of fate and fortune is only the surface appearance of things. Beneath this mere surface the world is unified, ordered, and especially *intelligible*. We mere humans *do* have the ability to understand it. Heraclitus gave us Fire as the metaphor of the transience of things. Yet his most important contribution to philosophy is his granting of a name for this fire: the *Logos*. He also gives us a philosophically concise expression of its nature:

- This *logos* always holds but humans always prove unable to understand it, both before hearing it and when they have first heard it. For though all things come to be [or happen] in accordance with this logos, humans are more like the inexperienced when they experience such words and deeds as I set out…
- Although this *logos* is common [i.e. universal], most people live as if they had a private understanding.

- Listening not to me but to the *logos* it is wise to agree that all things are one.[92]

The word *Logos* has a dozen or more possible equivalents in the English language: reason, order, principle, saying, speech, or "the word". It is this *logos* which is enshrined as the very word of God in the first paragraph of Saint John's gospel: "In the beginning was the Word". This famous line was originally written in Greek and not Aramaic. And it was written in the Greek city of Ephesos, in Asia Minor (now Turkey), which was also Heraclitus' home town![93]

The message of Heraclitus, philosophical rather than mythological in spirit, is that the world is organised not by an inevitable yet mysterious fate, but by a fully rational and non-mysterious order: the *logos*. One can therefore learn, by observation and deep thought, that there are reasons for why things happen the way they do. In this way, the power of Reason offered not just a new defense against Fortune, but also a chance to overthrow her sovereignty. For *Logos*, the rational order of the world, which the contemplative person could find within himself, was not subject to fate. This is what is implied by claims that the *Logos* is 'common to all', and that through *Logos* 'all things are one'. Therefore, so it was claimed, it could be trusted to bring lasting happiness.

Despite this contrast, a comparison can be made between the classical and the heroic understanding of virtue, in the ways the two traditions responded to death. As an example, when Socrates was put on trial for blasphemy and for corrupting the youth of Athens, and faced with the possibility of execution, he told the jury:

To fear death, gentlemen, is no other than to think oneself wise when one is not, to think one knows what one does not know. No one knows whether death may not be the greatest of all blessings for a man, yet men fear it as if they knew that it is the greatest of evils.[94]

In other words, Socrates asserts it to be a deep truth that we mortals know nothing of what happens to us after we die, and so it is irrational to fear death. Reason is presented as a defense against fate, or more precisely in this case, as a defense against fear of the unknown. But note that this is also similar to the Heroic idea that you must do the noble and heroic thing even if you may die in the process. As Socrates also told the jury:

> You are wrong, sir, if you think that a man who is any good at all should take into account the risk of life or death; he should look to this only in his actions, whether what he does is right or wrong, whether he is acting like a good or a bad man. [95]

Socrates put his life on the line in a court of justice, not a battlefield, but otherwise the principle is the same. Yet this is nothing like the Apotheosis offered by Heroic virtue. Indeed several classical writers asserted that Apotheosis is ultimately superficial and worthless. Marcus Aurelius, for example, wrote:

> ...will a little fame distract you? Look at the speed of universal oblivion, the gulf of immeasurable time both before and after, the vacuity of applause, the indiscriminate fickleness of your apparent supporters, the tiny room in which all this is confined. The whole earth is a mere point in space; what a minute cranny within this is your own habitation, and how many and what sort will sing your praises here! (*Meditations*, IV.3, pg. 24.)

Where the *Hávamál* claims that a good name will last forever, Marcus Aurelius wrote the exact opposite: lasting fame is 'oblivion'. Yet as he saw it, this was not a cause for despair. It is, first of all, the reason why virtue is to be practiced for its own sake, and not for the sake of being praised for it by others. Indeed, this transformation of the meaning of honour, from a public to a semi-private quality, is one of the large differences between heroic and classical virtue.[96] Secondly, it was also a major theme of Marcus Aurelius' philosophy that one must:

> ...think always of the universe as one living creature, comprising one

substance, and one soul; how all is absorbed into this one consciousness; how a single impulse governs all its actions; how all things collaborate in all that happens; the very web and mesh of it all. (*Meditations*, IV.40, pg. 31.)

This 'single impulse' that governs all things is the *Logos*. Reason gave the people of classical society a chance to align their souls with this Logos, and so be united with something eternal, permanent, even divine. And that, so they believed, was the basis for a true and lasting happiness. In a nutshell, the idea is that if you could grasp the divine with Reason, then you would be totally undisturbed by anything fate put in front of you. No matter what happened, your peace of mind would be unassailable and complete. Indeed they had a name for someone who could do this: the Great Soul. But I shall have more to say about that after examining some other branches of the Classical view of virtue.

§ 96. "By Nature A Social Animal"

Next, the philosophers of the Classical period asked themselves, How do we apply Reason, this half-intellectual, half-divine technique for finding knowledge, to the problems of social life? Plato turned to the stars and the cosmos for his answer. He said that the wisdom-loving person can easily find what justice is because "there is a model of it in heaven, for anyone who wants to look at it and to make himself its citizen on the strength of what he sees." (*Republic* 592b) The very meaning of the word 'civilisation', in the ancient world, was a human society modeled after the order of the cosmos. Plato concluded that the rulers of society should therefore be philosophers, because only they have the ability to perceive the rational order of the world. Aristotle, by contrast, sought the answer in human relations. In *The Nicomachean Ethics* he wrote "It is by taking part in transactions with our fellow-men that some of us become just and others unjust." (*NE*, 1103b12). Raphael's famous painting, "The School of Athens", elegantly portrays this difference of opinion. Plato, an older gentleman, stands in the centre of the picture with one hand pointing upward to the sky. Aristotle, a younger man, and Plato's former student, stands in the centre next to him and gestures to the room below. Plato holds a copy of *The Timaeus*, his work on cosmology and the structure of the universe; Aristotle, by contrast, holds a copy of his *Ethics*, which discusses human relationships.

Aristotle is generally regarded as the first writer in the European tradition to speak of Virtue directly and systematically. In his *Nicomachean Ethics* (named for his son Nicomachus who compiled it from lecture notes), virtue begins with an obvious starting place. Every human being wishes to be happy. What we all really want, overall, is to have a fulfilling and worthwhile life. Happiness is always chosen for its own sake and never for the sake of something else (*NE* 1089b5). It is also "a thing which merely standing by itself alone renders life desirable and lacking in nothing". (*NE,*1097b13). It requires no extra props or plug-ins; for it is its own reward, an end in itself. And everyone, through his actions either directly or indirectly, aims towards what he thinks will bring him happiness. For Aristotle, the desire for happiness is an unquestionable fact of human psychology. The definition of Virtue, with this starting place, is 'a quality of character which is necessary for success in the pursuit of happiness'.

But what is happiness? Even Aristotle conceded that there can be a lot of disagreement about what it is. The word for Happiness in the Greek language is 'eudaimonia'. The word has an interesting precedent in one of the fragments of Heraclitus: *ethos anthropoi daimon* ("Man's character is his fate").[97] 'Daimon' is the Greek word for 'Fate' and 'Fortune'. This fragment seems to be saying that the quality of someone's fate or fortune is determined not by external powers but by her character, and by the kind of person she is. Happiness, or 'eudaimonia', is a good, beautiful, or favourable fortune or destiny. For Heraclitus, *eudaimonia* is a good or favourable fortune which someone creates for herself through her habitual actions and the way she lives her life. For Aristotle, it also comes from the things you do, especially activities which are inherently pleasurable and self-rewarding, and are launched from the highest and most noble aspects of ourselves. The idea of *eudaimonia* is thus associated to the word 'kalon', which is usually translated as 'the noble', but can also mean what is 'fitting', 'praiseworthy' or even 'beautiful'.[98] Therefore, an alternative translation of *eudaimonia*, preferred by many philosophers today, is 'flourishing'. It captures the original Greek meaning a lot better, and it is somewhat less ambiguous than 'happiness'. It involves the expression of one's powers and potentials to the limit of their possibility, and the pleasure and joy that such expression gives. To flourish is, quite unambiguously, to be all that you have in you to be, to express your powers as fully as possible, and to create for yourself a wonderful world thereby.

If your conception of right and wrong is based on laws and commandments, your notion of happiness will be very different. In fact it will usually be the case that happiness and the law will have nothing to do with each other. The Ten Commandments and the Golden Rule are totally silent on the subject of happiness. Immanuel Kant wrote that upholding duty will not make you happy, but rather will make you 'worthy of happiness'.[99] But with happiness understood as Aristotle understood it, as what life feels like for someone fully flourishing as a human being, then the good and beautiful life can easily come together with the moral life. The emphasis on personal flourishing and the quality of one's own life may sound egotistical. But this is tempered by Aristotle's belief that human flourishing is always intertwined with one's friends and with the community. We find this in the proud assertion that "man is by nature a social being". (*NE*, 1097b10) The phrase could also be translated as 'a political being'. In *The Politics*, Aristotle similarly claims that a human being is "a political animal" (*Politics*, 1253a1). The idea is that it is natural for people to live in organised communities, and that a capacity for sociability is among the potentials and endowments of nature with which a person is born. By participating in society, and 'taking part in transactions with our fellow-men', we properly discover and develop our potentials, find a place to express them, and become fully Virtuous.

The Greek word that Aristotle uses here is "polis", meaning a politically organised community. We get English words like 'politics' and 'police' from this Greek root. I should specify that Aristotle's *polis* is not at all like our idea of a nation-state. For Aristotle, the *polis* combines two ideas which modern political theorists tend to separate carefully: the state on one hand, and civil society on the other. 'Civil society' includes groups like families, friendships, trading partners, and special purpose associations like theatre troupes, service clubs, and sports teams. The state, by contrast, is a formal institution responsible for the provision of various public functions within a specific territory, such as protection from criminals and from military attack. When Aristotle claims, then, that people flourish best only in the right kind of *polis*, it is this holistic, inclusive sense of the whole of society, including but not limited to a specific set of political relationships, which he has in mind. The contemporary philosopher Alasdair MacIntyre explained that the indispensable thing which the *polis* provides is *dikaiosune* (the Greek word for Justice). To be separated from the *polis* is to be without *dikaiosune*.[100] Without the *polis*, then, one's various natural talents and abilities would go undeveloped, or would be developed to serve unjust ends, and "what could have been a human being becomes instead a wild animal."[101]

It would be worth asking at this point, how does someone develop into a Virtuous person? In Aristotle's account, there are three stages. At the first stage, we are born with various endowments of nature, called 'faculties', such as the ability to move, grow, think, and speak. Among them Aristotle singled out the social and intellectual faculties as being higher and nobler than others, because they appeared to be specific to humanity. Reason, in his system, is the highest faculty we have, the "spark of the divine within us". At the second stage, we are thrust into social situations which require us to respond appropriately. We become virtuous (or un-virtuous) through the ways in which we interact with other people. The process of 'moral education', which is the process of developing the virtues, is for Aristotle a social or a public affair, and not a private matter. We are, after all, 'social animals'. The third and final stage obtains in the way in which we regularly and repeatedly respond to and interact with other people. That is the practice, so to speak, that will produce virtue or vice, and which will ultimately produce the happy life. If we respond to a situation by acting upon that faculty within us which is highest and most noble, or in Aristotle's words 'closest to the divine', and with just the right application of it, neither too much nor too little, then we act rightly. To continue to respond the same way is habit forming. If you make a habit of responding to other people in this way, you will have installed within your character a virtue.

These various considerations: the power of reason, the emphasis on social and political problems, the process of moral education, the aim for happiness, and so on, are at the root of the classical meaning of Virtue. Of course, other cultures and civilizations have different lists of virtues, and different ways to decide what should be on the list. Sometimes the same culture will have different conceptions of virtue at different times in its history. Nonetheless, the Classical tradition outlines with great clarity the elements of Virtue which all conceptions seem to have in common. I have already described many of them, but it may be useful to gather them together into a complete list:

- A virtue is a quality of a person's character and identity. It is a disposition, or a habit, to act in a certain way, and it is closely connected with each person's sense of who they are. As Aristotle said, a Virtue is "a settled disposition of habit."
- Virtues are learned, developed, and practiced over time, for instance in the process of growing up from childhood to adulthood. This is generally called 'moral education'.
- Virtues are also taught by the way certain outstanding people are held up as role models and as paragons, whose exemplary lives are admired and emulated. Indeed the stories of such people's lives are often used to explain and justify the importance of various virtues.
- A virtue must be deliberately and rationally chosen. But the emotional and passionate dimension of each person's being has a place in the process as well. A virtue is a habit of one's whole self, not just one's intellect.
- Virtues are almost always embedded within communities and human relationships. Even though the Virtues focus one's attention on one's own self, there is usually no such thing as a stand-alone, totally independent and self-reliant Virtuous person.

- Virtues are not utilitarian in nature. Their main purpose is not to produce some kind of material outcome or consequence. Their purpose is to produce a certain kind of person.
- Similarly, Virtues are not rules, nor are they laws. Their purpose is not to produce a desire to follow rules and laws. But Virtues often exist in a complicated relationship to rules and laws.
- Some traditions claim that the virtues are necessary for the attainment of certain ethical goals, and that vices generally impede or prevent their attainment. Such goals may be practical, or abstract, or both, such as 'leadership', or 'the sustaining of a community', or as in the classical tradition, 'happiness'.
- Most traditions assert that living virtuously is self-rewarding, and that possession of a virtue benefits he or she who possess it.
- Similarly, it is generally held that a vice harms he or she who possess it. Someone who lives un-virtuously is said to be punishing himself.

These ten elements constitute the basic logic, or perhaps I should say vocabulary, of the classical understanding of Virtue. Yet every culture or philosophy or tradition that promotes the idea of Virtue will hold to at least some, of not most, of these ideas. They may appear with varying degrees of emphasis. They may not all be present at the same time. They may even be part of an argument with a completely different kind of conclusion. But when any of these ideas appear as part of some discussion about how people should live, they are signs that the logic of Virtue is at work in the speaker's mind.

The classical world which gave us this conception of virtue also gave us a list of four special qualities which have come to be known as the 'canonical' Classical Virtues: Courage, Prudence, Temperance, and Justice. Let us have a close look at each of them now.

§ 97. Courage (Again!)
This quality should already be familiar: it is also one of the Heroic virtues. To the heroes of mythology, Courage involves the overcoming of fear and the single-minded pursuit of some goal no matter what physical pain or

other hardship may be involved. It is invoked for the sake of honour, and reaches the pinnacle of its praiseworthiness when used to face death. The classical tradition adds that courage is virtuous only when it is displayed in the service of a noble cause. That noble cause is something the courageous person must deliberately choose. According to Aristotle, the highest of noble causes is national pride. In his words:

> For even though it be the case that the good is the same for the individual and for the state, nevertheless, the good of the state is manifestly a greater and more perfect good, both to attain and to preserve. To secure the good of one person only is better than nothing; but to secure the good of a nation or a state is a nobler and more divine achievement. (*NE*, 1094b1)

This nationalist courage is the courage of someone who aims to bring honour and benefit to his community and his country, not simply to himself alone. Aristotle also claims that this kind of courage is displayed most perfectly on the battlefield, that is, by the person who puts his life on the line to protect his people. Courage, in this interpretation, is primarily a political virtue.

Our notion of courage tends to be more personal. We are inclined to think that the perseverance of someone suffering a traumatic injury or enduring a painful disease is a form of great bravery. We call it courageous when someone 'puts up a strong face' while experiencing loss, disappointment, or grief. Even so, the public dimension of courage is not lost to us. Every year on the 11th of November, most countries in the British Commonwealth march for Remembrance Day, in which the courage of those who fought the first and second world wars is commemorated. Similarly we praise the courage of those who do daring things in the name of some public good. Terry Fox ran his Marathon of Hope half-way across Canada, while debilitated with cancer and an artificial leg, to raise money and public awareness for cancer patients. (He died before the Marathon was completed). To put one's name and reputation on the line for a public cause, especially a controversial one, takes courage. Fire fighters display profound courage when they battle out-of-control fires in cities and towns, or in remote forests. Rescue workers show it when they head into stormy weather on mountainsides or high oceans to bring stranded people to safety. Environmental activists display courage when performing acts of civil disobedience in the service of environmental protection. Those whose lives or economic interests are disrupted by civil disobedience tend to describe such action as reckless, futile, foolhardy, or even nonsensical—anything other than courageous. But clearly, to stand between a whale and a whaler's harpoon, as Greenpeace activists used to do, takes guts. It is to face the prospect of bodily harm in order to 'save' a part of the environment from excessive plundering. Union workers who go on strike to improve their working conditions often show enormous courage, especially when doing so entails a substantial loss of income, long days or cold nights, the taunts and jeers of passer-bys, or humiliation in the media. It takes great courage to attend an anti-globalisation rally or an anti-war protest, especially when such events are dispersed by riot policemen armed with tear gas, concussion grenades, and wide powers of arrest and detention.

It is clear that there are many noble causes which can be a venue for courage. There can even be conflicting ideas of what counts as a noble cause. Like any other virtue, courage is configured by choice—the cause which one pursues with courage must be chosen carefully and intelligently. Indeed it is the wise choice which separates true courage from foolhardy bravado. The wise choice requires an understanding of two things. The first is the danger involved. In the old conundrum "Who is more courageous—the one who feels fear yet acts, or the one who feels no fear at all?" the answer is the one who feels the fear, and yet acts. Someone who doesn't feel fear when about to undertake something dangerous may be someone who doesn't fully understand what he is about to do, nor the risks involved to himself or others, nor the likelihood of success. If this fearlessness impairs the ability to judge whether the cause is truly worthy, then it is not courage. It is, instead, mere recklessness.

This leads to the other thing that is necessary for making a wise choice about when to be courageous: a proper understanding of what a noble

99

cause is. I define a cause as truly noble when it aims to change the world, in some great or small way, into a condition better suited for human flourishing. A courageous person aims to benefit others, and benefit the society she lives in, and perhaps future generations too. And courage ultimately benefits its possessor, and not just because the courageous person has less fear. It is an affirmation of the world's potential for goodness and beauty, and an active will to participate in the world. To be prepared to accept danger, suffering, hardship, and even death in the attempt to change the world is to be most fully courageous, and most sincerely loving. These qualities are, it seems to me, self-rewarding; a worthwhile and flourishing life cannot do without them. As Aristotle said, "the virtuous man's conduct is often guided by the interests of his friends and of his country, and he will if necessary lay down his life in their behalf." In so doing the courageous person "chooses great nobility for himself." (*NE* 1169a19) What benefit does the person gain from doing such a thing? He gets to be the one to perform the courageous act itself, which in the Classical understanding of virtue, is its own reward.

§ 98. Prudence

According to Aristotle, a person becomes Virtuous by developing the various parts of his nature so as to be able to respond well to other people, and to all the various situations in which you may find yourself. How shall you tell *which* parts of your nature to train up so? And how far should they be developed? *Any* endowment of nature can be developed and expressed to the level of greatness, even a capacity for cruelty and violence. How shall we tell which of our virtues is the right one to use in any situation? Traditionally, the job of sorting this out fell to an ability which in Greek was called '*phronesis*': and in English is usually translated as Practical Wisdom, or Prudence.

Aristotle's definition of Prudence appears in his discussion of the "doctrine of the mean". It is the job of prudence to determine what virtue is called for, how much of it is too much, and how much is not enough. This 'right amount' is called by Aristotle 'the Mean'. Vice is defined as the wrong amount of that disposition: it is too much, or it is not enough, of what is required. We find this in one of Aristotle's definitions of Virtue itself:

> Virtue then is a settled disposition of the mind determining the choice of actions and emotions, consisting essentially in the observance of the mean relative to us, this being determined by principle, that is, as the prudent man would determine it. And it is a mean state between two vices, one of excess and one of defect. (*NE*, 1107a1)

For every virtue, then, there are *two* vices, not one: there is a vice of "too much", and a vice of "not enough".

The notion of 'the prudent man' and 'right reason' is introduced here because it is often not enough to say that the virtuous person is one who aims at the mark between deficiency and excess. "This bare statement however, although true, is not at all enlightening", says Aristotle, because it is true of "all departments of human endeavor that have been reduced to a science." Therefore "a person knowing this truth will be no wiser than before." An act must also be "in conformity with the right principle" to be completely virtuous. (*NE*, 1138b24) Prudence, or 'right reason', therefore holds an important place in his system as the virtue associated with choice, with truth-attainment, and with mature decision-making. Here are Aristotle's words on prudence in the context of determining ethical choices:

> Now it is held to be the mark of a prudent man to be able to deliberate well about what is good and advantageous for himself, not in some one department, for instance what is good for his health or strength, but what is advantageous as a means to the good life in general. (*NE*, 1140a24)

Prudence, it may be inferred here, is the ability to discern what is and what is not conducive to the good life. This isn't a question of balancing short term and long term interests. It is also not precisely right to say it balances one's own interests with those of other people. Prudence discerns what is good for humanity in general, both now and in the future, both near and far, and not just for yourself or any particular other person, except that individuals are representatives of the species. Aristotle is quite emphatic about this in his discussion of prudence: he observes in several places how prudence is "commonly understood to mean especially that kind of wisdom which is concerned with oneself, the individual", but that this understanding is wrong: for "a man cannot pursue his own welfare without domestic economy and even politics" (*NE*, 1142a6), and so when he chooses something in pursuit of his own happiness, he does so in reference to what is good for all people, and not just for himself. In other words, one should chose not only for oneself, but for all humanity. When Aristotle writes that a Virtuous action not only strikes the mean, but is also in conformity with right reason, it is this faculty of prudence which enables one to evaluate whether this is so.

§ 99. Temperance

Over the door to the Oracle of Delphi was cut a second proverb: "Everything in moderation and nothing in excess." This is the motto of the god Apollo, to whom the Oracle was dedicated. The message is like our own modern saying, "too much of a good thing is bad for you." The passions can make life a lot of fun. But they can also be destructive if they are given free and unfettered reign. The third of the four classical virtues, called Temperance, is concerned with the regulation of the passions.

Of all the four classical virtues, Temperance represents the greatest break from the preceding Heroic culture. Heroic age warriors were passionate, noisy, violent people. But even in their time, something like Temperance was being advocated in their wisdom-teachings. The *Hávamál*, for instance, contains warnings against drinking too much:

> For good is not, though good it is thought,
> mead for the sons of men;
> the deeper he drinks, the dimmer grows
> the mind of many a man.[102]

Against gluttony, it similarly warns:

> The greedy guest gainsays his head,
> and eats until he is ill.
> His belly often maketh a butt of a man,
> On [the] bench 'midst the sage where he sits.[103]

Although I have previously described Heroic virtue as a moral system that approves of boastfulness and bombast, there was also an understanding that too much pride can be un-virtuous. Consider as an example the Greek story of the heroine Arachne. She was the finest weaver of her time, and famous all over the world for her skill and artistry. One day she let her reputation go to her head, and bragged that she was a better weaver than the goddess Minerva herself. The goddess, in disguise, therefore challenged Arachne to a weaving competition. Arachne lost (no surprise there). *Hubris* is what becomes of pride when it exceeds proper bounds: for instance when someone claims more honours than he or she really deserves. The story is a little ambiguous about what becomes of the excessively prideful person. One version says that Minerva punished Arachne by transforming her into a spider. Another suggests that Arachne fell into a deep depression and tried to hang herself, and Minerva changed her into a spider to save her life. In this second way hubris is seen as self-punishing, not a sin against the gods. It is self-punishing because it sets oneself up for devastating failures. Hubris is also the quality possessed by those who set impossible tasks for themselves, with a false belief that they will succeed. Proper pride is 'tempered'. It does not boast of what it cannot do, nor does it make any promises it cannot fulfill. It does not compete with the gods, or any other forces or powers against which victory is categorically impossible.

It is not until the classical period, however, that Temperance appears as a virtue of comprehensive self-control, including within itself all considerations of hubris and excess. Temperance is the virtue of someone who keeps their passions and emotions within proper bounds. Aristotle associated it with the bodily pleasures of smell, taste, and especially touch.

But it would be wrong to say that Temperance is the quality of someone who puts a lid on the sensual side of her being. Temperance is not the same as abstinence, and certainly not the same as chastity. The Temperate person is allowed to enjoy sensual pleasure—even encouraged to do so. However, as Aristotle says, "...it is right to be a lover of self, though self-love of an ordinary sort is wrong." (*NE*, 1169b4) Ordinary self-love is that of the indulgent, greedy person. "The bad man ought not to be a lover of self, since he will follow his base passions, and so injure both himself and his neighbours." (*NE*, 1168b10). The idea behind temperance, here, is that one should pursue pleasures intelligently, without becoming 'addicted', so to speak, and so one will not end up causing harm to oneself and others.

What has been said here about too much sensuality, can also be said for too little. Classical Greek society had a religious festival called the Dithyramb, in honour of the god of nature and ecstasy, Dionysus. The rituals they performed in honour of the god of the Dithyramb involved music and poetry, heavy drinking, dancing, and lots and lots of sex. Similar to other European pagan cultures, the ancient Greeks found spiritual fulfillment in the enjoyment of the wonders and bounties of the embodied world. They also believed that the passions and the animal drives are not evil (although they can sometimes be dangerous), but an integral part of the soul. So those who try to suppress them end up harming themselves. The dramatist Euripides wrote a play called *The Baccae*, about a town that outlawed the worship of Dionysus. In the play, Dionysus himself comes to the town, disguised as one of his own prophets. He instills a madness in all the women so that they head off to the Dithyramb, against the orders of King Pentheus. Pentheus of course becomes angry, and, suspecting that Dionysus is responsible, has him arrested. Pentheus then learns that his own sister, Ino, and his mother, Agave, are among the women who went to the dithyramb. Dionysus convinces Pentheus to disguise himself as a woman so he can follow them. "If they see you as a man, they'll kill you" Dionysus explains. Pentheus resists, but eventually agrees, and goes to the mountain in disguise to search for his mother and sister. When he arrives, Agave has become so insane with ecstasy that she believes he is a lion, and in a frenzy she kills him with her bare hands.

Dionysus then drops all the illusions, and lets everyone see the consequences of their denial of his worship. When you suppress the passions, they will find another way out, and not necessarily a safe way out. The chorus concludes:

A free and open mind
Is safe against the excesses
Lurking in the secret juices of your plants [i.e. wine-grapes].
But those who try to strangle you
In the roots of their own nature,
Who oppress and are oppressed
Through you, achieve their own destruction.[104]

The message of Temperance is that intelligent enjoyment of pleasure is ultimately better, and even *more pleasurable*, than unrestrained hedonism. It is not simply a matter of sacrificing the short-term for the long term. It has more to do with the quality of the here-and-now moments in which food, drink, sex, and other bodily pleasures are enjoyed. And it has to do with the kind of person you are. Euripides, speaking through the character of Dionysus, said, "As in all things, moderation depends on our nature. Remember this! No amount of Bacchic revels can corrupt an honest woman."[105] The temperate person has that honesty, that 'free and open mind', and can enjoy the pleasures of the body and of the world without becoming a slave to them. The person without the free and open mind 'achieves his own destruction', that is, he punishes himself.

If any of the heroes of the ancient world lived to see our modern world, I think they would find it extraordinarily luxurious and decadent. We have energy sources they couldn't have dreamed of, like coal, electricity, petroleum, and nuclear power. We have a huge range of consumer goods available to us, precision-engineered with the help of machines and computers, and mass-produced on an industrial scale. Even our food is produced this way, with combine harvesters and factory farms. Some of our food is even genetically modified, to improve productivity, and resistance to insects and diseases. We have a system of international distribution called the Global Market with which we buy and sell huge quantities of goods, to and from almost anywhere in the world. Our material standard of living is far better than what it was centuries ago. But before accepting all this wealth without question, we would do well to learn from the experiences of Heroic societies that encountered Europe's first attempt to create a global market: the Roman Empire. Tacitus wrote of how General Agricola pacified the Celts of Britain not with military force but with trade goods, new building techniques, and various "enervating luxuries". His description of this process has all the smugness of a con-man who has just been thanked by the victim of his latest swindle:

> The population was gradually led into the demoralizing temptations of arcades, baths, and sumptuous banquets. The unsuspecting Britons spoke of such novelties as 'civilisation', when in fact they were only a feature of their enslavement.[106]

Our addiction to the cheap imported consumer goods of the Global Market may end up enslaving us the same way. A little Temperance, then, might be good for us too.

§ 100. Justice.

In the simplest terms, the virtue of Justice is the ability to discern what people owe to each other. It concerns the assignment of benefits and public honours, or punishments, and so on, in accord with some principle of what people deserve. Of all the four classical virtues, it is the one most involved in relations to other people. Indeed it is impossible to practice justice without some amount of giving and taking with others. Perhaps for this reason, Aristotle praised justice as 'the whole of virtue' and even 'virtue itself'. The just person gives to everyone she meets what she believes is properly owed to them. We often owe to each other material things: a fair day's pay for a fair day's work, for example. But we also owe each other immaterial goods like gratitude, respect, and praise. The just person gives the voices and interests of others their appropriate space, and will yield to others when there are good reasons for doing so. She recognizes her own faults and mistakes, and offers appropriate apologies for them. Yet an understanding of justice brings with it an understanding of what each person owes to *herself* as well. She will not submit herself to be humiliated or demeaned. And she will not hesitate to complain or even get angry when wrongly deprived of what others owe her.

Connected as it is with our social relations, Justice is a virtue of communities as well as of individuals. In *The Republic* Plato argued that justice is a harmony of the internal elements of the soul, as corresponded with a harmony of the different classes of society. Aristotle said "the term 'just' is applied to anything that produces and preserves that happiness, or the component parts of the happiness, of the political community." (*NE* 1129b18) To both of them, the virtues all depend on the *polis*, the politically organised community, for their proper development and expression. As seen, it is a basic presupposition for Aristotle that people can attain a worthwhile life *if and only if* they live in the right kind of community. This is an ancient wisdom: it even appeared in the heroic world. Njail Thorgeirsson, the hero of Njail's Saga, said "With laws our land be built up but with lawlessness laid waste."[107] It is with the virtue of justice that we recognise what laws will build up a society, and bring out the best in its people.

The important thing to note here, it must be added, is that the Virtuous person doesn't become Virtuous in order to be a better rule-follower. Rather, he follows some rules in order to be more Virtuous. Laws are authoritative only to the degree that following them tends to bring out the best in a person's character. Whenever problems arise from the following of rules, for instance if the rules conflict with each other, or if the rules ask us to do ridiculous things, then one can always refer back to the principle of reason, the aim for happiness, and the model of the good life, to arbitrate the matter, like a higher court.

Normally when we think of Justice, we think of crime and punishment. Perhaps this is because the sense of *in*-justice tends to be stronger than the sense of justice itself. People often find it hard to describe what kind of a social order they want, but find it easy to describe what they do *not* want. (Hence, perhaps, why seven of the Ten Commandments are phrased in the form of 'thou shall not'.) Indeed people often don't know what justice *is* until someone has done something *unjust*. As observed by Paul Ricoeur,

> It is in the mode of complaint that we penetrate the field of the just and the unjust... people have a clearer vision of what is missing in human relations than of the right way to organize them. This is why, even for philosophers, it is injustice that first sets thought in motion.[108]

Justice, as a virtue, is the quality which enables us to recognise injustice, and motivates us to do something about it. Although this may seem like justice dwells too much in the negative, it is a faculty we could not live without.

§ 101. The Great Soul

Someone who follows these four virtues, guided by Reason, and with *eudaimonia* as her aim, would become what Aristotle called a 'Great Soul'. All of the major writers of the Classical period who discussed virtue painted their own distinct portrait of the Great Soul. But their different pictures were fairly consistent with each other, especially in the way they portrayed the role of Reason in the virtuous life. In the classical tradition, Reason is a spiritual thing. Plato, for instance, claimed that Reason gives us an ability to create a personal, intellectual relationship with the universal *Logos*. Someone who develops his capacity for reason also creates a relationship with the divine, and in so doing, becomes divine himself. As Plato says in *The Republic:* "The philosopher, by consorting with what is ordered and divine, and despite all the slanders around that say otherwise, himself becomes as divine and ordered as a human being can." (*Republic* 500d.) Aristotle appears to have taught a similar idea: for him, Reason and the intellectual contemplation of the world is "the activity of God", and so someone who undertakes the same activity finds lasting happiness.[109] Marcus Aurelius offered a similar message:

> He lives with the gods who consistently shows them his soul content with its lot, and by performing the wishes of that divinity, that fragment

of himself which Zeus has given each person to guard and guide him. In each of us this divinity is our mind and reason. (*Meditations* V.27)

Reason offered the people of the classical world a chance to participate in the divine, and in so doing, become divine. By practicing the virtuous life in accord with Reason, we can achieve not only happiness in this world, but also something like personal ascension to godhood.

This is a different notion of immortality from the Heroic Apotheosis sought by Beowulf, Achilles, and Cu Chullain, and other heroes of the mythological world. Instead of Apotheosis, classical virtue offers a more philosophical immortality in which one cultivates qualities of character that are also divine qualities, and so one shares in their divinity. It is the immortality of aligning one's life into harmony with the very same ultimate powers and forces which, in other respects, render human life apparently small and insignificant. In this way one may participate in the being of higher things, and for a time share in their immortality. That is how the Classical tradition conceived the spiritual dimension of Reason. Someone who grasps this is on track toward becoming a "Great Soul".

To have a Great Soul is to find that life is intrinsically desirable, and to find that the world is a delightful and beautiful place to be. As Aristotle says, it is "the *consciousness of oneself as good* that makes existence desirable, and such consciousness is pleasant in itself" (*NE*, 1170b5). The value of life, then, is something the Virtuous person finds within herself *as* a Virtuous person, or *having become* a Virtuous person. This principle is at the very heart of the original understanding of virtue, both classical and heroic. To have a Great Soul is also to see the world as the field and stage of one's life, the platform from which all one's dreams and journeys are launched, the raw material from which happiness is fashioned. To flourish and to live well is to celebrate the world, to love being a part of it, and to rejoice in being alive. As Aristotle said:

Nor ought we to obey those who enjoin that a man should have man's thoughts, and a mortal the thoughts of mortality, but we ought so far as possible to achieve immortality, and do all that man may to live in accordance with the highest thing in him; for though this be small in bulk, in power and in value it far surpasses all the rest. (*NE* 10.vii.8, 1177b26, pg. 275)

From a philosopher generally thought to be a hard-nosed realist, here he says we can experience the same happiness, the same joyful alive-ness, that the gods' experience. Immortality itself, he says, is not beyond our reach: all we have to do is 'live in accord with the highest thing in ourselves'. This tradition continued in philosophy long after Aristotle. For instance, some eight hundred years after Aristotle, Boethius claimed that the human mind is made in the image of God.[110] It is therefore through the exercise of reason that we can come to know God's thoughts. As he says, "through the possession of divinity" one may become truly happy, and therefore "Each happy individual is therefore divine. While only God is so by nature, as many as you like may become so by participation."[111]

This picture of the Great Soul is not without its flaws. For one thing, it is a very *masculine* vision. These writers usually didn't have much to say about women at all, and some quite unequivocally stated that a woman cannot become a Great Soul. With a few rare exceptions (Cleopatra of Egypt, perhaps?) the time when women could achieve greatness, and be acknowledged and honoured for it, was gone. This vision is also *aristocratic*: the Great Soul is beyond the reach of working class people too. In Aristotle's description of the ideal community, farmers and labourers are not allowed to enter the *agora*, the public square, unless they are summoned there. This is apparently because their livelihoods connect them too much with material productivity.[112] And in Aristotle's other writing he suggests that some people are naturally born slaves, unable to think for themselves, and only good for manual labour. Finally, in some ways this vision of virtue is also remarkable for its *self-absorption*. Especially in the Stoic school of philosophy, which Marcus Aurelius and Cicero spoke for, the function of Reason was to help one humbly and passively accept whatever the world throws at you. Its appeal was the call to look within yourself for one's own happiness, and not tie one's sense of worth to things beyond your control. But this same principle also called for a radical disengagement from the world. Marcus Aurelius suggested that one should "view earthly things as if looking down on them from some point high above" (*Meditations* VII.47), or in other words, as if not involved in the world. Similarly, Cicero said "A man who has the ability to commune with himself does not feel the slightest need for anyone else's conversation".[113] This statement is contrary to Aristotle's claim that 'man is by nature a social animal'. But more to the point, it represents a philosophy of naval-gazing resignation, disconnected from human relationships. If you withdraw into yourself as Cicero recommends, you might be spared some of the suffering of the world. But you may also miss out on much of what makes life go well: friendship and love, for instance. I think it is a great irony that the intellectuals of the Roman Empire, a society known for its imperialist mission to impose its military and political order on the world, were subscribing to a philosophy of passive withdrawal. Such a philosophy, in practice, cannot bring lasting fulfillment in the face of fortune and worldly suffering. All it can do is teach you how to grin and bear it.

Nonetheless, we still believe in the Great Soul. We still believe in heroic virtues like pride, strength, honour, and courage. But much of the time we believe them in secret, deep down, discretely, perhaps guiltily. To the ancient heroes, and to the classical philosophers, 'spirit' was connected to excellence. It had to do with strength of body and mind, and of personality. The Great Soul could give to herself a good and beautiful destiny by acting from that part of her nature which is closest to the divine. And isn't that what we still admire about great people? We respect those who do good and who benefit others, who give to charity and who help strangers in need. But we also admire those who push the boundaries of human nature: those who are a bit stronger, faster, more witty, more daring, more reckless, more full of passion, more capable of love, than the regular run of humanity. We admire the strength and agility of professional athletes, the beauty and charm of pop celebrities. We secretly admire them even if they are rough and dangerous, even if they are hard on their friends and families and even if they are outright criminals. This is why tabloid newspapers are so successful. We often disapprove of their actions in public but we still want to know all about each new outrage they commit, even if only to enjoy passing judgement on them. We are fascinated by such people, both the good and the terrible, because they have such spirit.

FOURTH MOVEMENT:

VIRTUE THROUGH THE AGES

§ 102. Renaissance Humanism

Throughout the time we now call the Middle Ages, almost all European cultural life was dominated by Christianity. Most music and art was Christian devotional art, and almost all intellectual enquiry was Christian theology. And aside from warfare, technological progress was driven by the desire to build bigger and better cathedrals. Indeed the Gothic pointed arch and flying buttress was invented so that the cathedrals could have higher ceilings! Then, around the late 1400's, there was a major resurgence of high classical pagan culture, the first of its kind in Europe for more than a thousand years. And, ironically, the desire to build bigger and better Christian monuments may have been directly responsible for it. How did it happen?

All over Italy, the remnants of the old pagan Roman Empire were still visible, and some of them were truly monumental. There was the Pantheon, with its geometrically perfect spherical dome of enormous size, and with its hole in the centre: given the available technology, it is a truly stupendous engineering achievement. There were many huge decorated obelisks, like Trajan's Column, and the Column of Marcus Aurelius, both more than 30 meters (97 feet) high. There were aqueducts which kept a steady grade for miles, and which took advantage of gravity pressure to make water flow uphill. Wealthy Italians of the middle ages wanted to build big monuments of their own, especially cathedrals and palaces. But the knowledge of how to do so had been lost. So they began looking at old Roman manuscripts that had been preserved in monasteries in Ireland and in the Islamic world, searching for technical manuals. They found what they were looking for, and much more besides: histories, biographies, philosophical discourses, political pamphlets, literature and drama, old maps, business records, military plans, even satirical novels. In short, they found the accumulated knowledge of an entire civilisation. With these discoveries, not only could they change the way they built things, but they could also change the way people think.

It is important to understand that the central Christian teaching of the time, by which people understood themselves and their place in the universe, was the Doctrine of Original Sin. This teaching described humanity as essentially *fallen*, thrown out of the Garden of Eden and deprived of God's presence. We were all being punished for the disobedience of Adam and Eve, the Biblical progenitors of the human race. This doctrine, crafted by the 4th century philosopher Saint Augustine, using the story of Adam and Eve and the letters of Saint Paul as his precedent, is still the hidden cornerstone of Christian spirituality today. Without it, other central Christian concepts like salvation and redemption are meaningless. Christianity taught people to see themselves as wretched and lowly, 'natural born sinners'. The Catholic Mass, even to this day, requires parishioners to repeat self-disparaging refrains like "I confess to Almighty God...that I have sinned through my own fault", and "Lord, I am not worthy to receive you." The path to redemption was to be humble, penitent, dutiful, and especially obedient to authority, so that some day God would give you a better life in heaven after you die.

Enter a young nobleman named Count Giovanni Pico della Mirandola. By the age of twenty-four he had spent seven years studying at various Italian and French universities, where he mastered several languages, helped re-introduce Plato and Aristotle and other Classical writers, and even became a proficient magician and occultist. He had a plan to create a grand synthesis between Classical, Hebrew, and Christian teachings, and to include mystical systems like the Cabbala. Unfortunately he was never to realise it, as he died of a fever before the age of thirty. Nevertheless his name lives on as one of the foremost initiators of the Renaissance. At the end of his apprenticeship he proposed a *disputatio*, a public debating session, with the Fathers of the Church. Newly graduated scholars would earn their wings with a *disputatio* on various principles of theology, philosophy, or politics. The modern day practice of the 'oral defense' of a Masters or Doctoral thesis is descended from this custom. Normally, the speaker would cover about two dozen questions, but Pico offered to debate no less than nine hundred. He was refused by Pope Innocent VIII, who declared him too young and too ambitious to proceed, and also declared some of his questions heretical. The prelude to his *disputatio*, which was also re-submitted as his 'apology' after the event was cancelled, has come to be known as *The Oration on the Dignity of Man*.

The Oration is one of the most important works of the Italian Renaissance; indeed it serves as its manifesto. Its novelty and greatness, as well as its heresy, is in its confidence in human power and greatness. In this vision, humanity is not fallen from the grace of God, nor expelled from the Garden. Rather, humanity is upheld in a place of high honour, "but a little lower than the angels" (*Oration* pg. 4). This doctrine does appear in the Bible too (at *Psalms* 8:6, for instance), but up to and including Pico's time, it was always overshadowed by the Doctrine of Original Sin. Pico rejects that doctrine: as he describes it, God's true message to us goes like this:

> The nature of all other creatures is defined and restricted within laws which We have laid down; you, by contrast, impeded by no such restrictions, may, by your own free will, to whose custody We have assigned you, trace for yourself the linaments of your own nature. We have made you a creature neither of heaven nor of earth, neither mortal nor immortal, in order that you may, as the free and proud shaper of your own being, fashion yourself in the form you may prefer. It will be in your power to descend to the lower, brutish forms of life; you will be able, through your own decision, to rise again to the superior orders whose life is divine. (*Oration* pg. 7-8)

In the potential to be whatever we chose to be, and to pursue our own destiny according to our own will, we have the Renaissance idea of the dignity of man. Note that Pico does *not* claim that human nature is divine, as some of his classical predecessors did. In fact he claims we have no fixed nature at all. But we have a potential to determine by our own actions and choices what our nature shall be. The human spirit is an open field of possibility, with great potential for both good and evil. Pico says this power was given by God, so that there would be a creature in the world that could "comprehend the meaning of so vast an achievement [i.e. the creation of the world], which might be moved with love at its beauty and smitten with awe at its grandeur." (*Oration* pg. 5) The ability to 'trace for yourself your own nature' belongs to no other creature, not even to the angels. As he says,

> The highest spiritual beings were, from the very moment of creation, or soon thereafter, fixed in the mode of being which would be theirs through measureless eternities. But upon man, at the moment of his creation, God bestowed seeds pregnant with all possibilities, the germs of every form of life. Whichever of these a man shall cultivate, the same will mature and bear fruit in him. (*Oration* pg. 8)

With the standing of humankind elevated close to the high place it held in the time of the Greek city-states and the empire of Rome, the way was also opened again for a restoration of high classical virtue. Charity, Intelligence and Justice are mentioned by Pico immediately: they are assigned as the qualities of two types of angels, the Seraphim and the Cherubs, and also the Throne (that is, God himself). The development of these virtues, as he says, can place humankind on par with these beings: indeed they enable human beings to fashion themselves in the image of God. In his words:

> If, consequently, in the pursuit of the active life we govern inferior things by just criteria, we shall be established in the firm position of the Thrones. If, freeing ourselves from active care, we devote our time to contemplation, meditating upon the Creator in His work, and the work in its Creator, we shall be resplendent with the light of the Cherubim. If we burn with love for the Creator only, His consuming fire will quickly transform us into the flaming likeness of the Seraphim. (*Oration* pg. 13-14)

Although the language and terms here are those of mystical Christianity, there is a humanist theme being expressed—a 'theological humanism', if there is such a thing. This position is possible for Pico in part because he does not take the Bible as his sole authority. With equal enthusiasm he invokes Plato and other Greek philosophers, as well as Muslim writers like Avicenna and Averros, the Chaldean priesthood of Zoroaster, and a variety of Hebrew prophets. A teaching of the ancient Greek god Hermes Trismegistus is mentioned on the very first page: "What a great miracle is Man". The three inscriptions over the gate to Delphi are reaffirmed as if their messages are a birthright for us all. To follow those precepts, he says, is "so very necessary for everyone about to enter the most holy and august temple, not of the false, but of the true Apollo who illumines every soul as it enters this world." (*Oration* pg. 28) With enthusiasm he describes the teaching of Pythagoras, which is worth special mention as it re-affirms the Classical emphasis on Reason as the divine part of humanity. It was a Pythagorean teaching, revived by Pico, "to nourish the divine part of our soul with the knowledge of divine things." (*Oration* pg. 29-30) The Pythagorean teachings were attributed to a sacred origin: it was claimed to have been modeled on the teachings of the Greek hero Orpheus, who learned them while traveling the underworld. This gave those teachings a status equal to that of the Old Testament prophets. As with Plato and Aristotle, and the other classical writers, Pico finds that Reason is the basis of human dignity and worth, as well as the means of our access to all things divine.

Pico was the father of Renaissance humanism, but a committed Christian too. Some of what he had to say confirmed, rather than subverted, Christian ideas, such as the emphasis on the immaterial and spiritual over the embodied material world. Citing Heraclitus' statement to the effect that nature is always in motion, so much so as to be constantly "at war", he therefore declares that nature cannot be a guide to spiritual truth. "Nature... is generated by war and for this reason is called by Homer, 'strife'. Natural philosophy, therefore, cannot assure us a true and unshakable peace." (*Oration* pg. 21). Autonomous reason, because it is 'pure' and 'eternal', would be the vehicle to purge the soul of conflict and imperfection. But still only Theology grants divine knowledge.[114] This turning inward to the mind and the spirit, and upward to God in heaven, and in both cases away from the embodied world, was fully in accord with Christian teaching at the time. Not that it is without precedent in Classical thought: in some ways it was endorsed by Plato more than a thousand years earlier. But just like Plato, and unlike the Christian theologians of Pico's own time, Pico calls for the inward-upward turn to be directed by a human power, Reason. This is thus a rejection of passive reliance on faith, Church authority, and divine revelation. That small, subtle distinction is as wide as the ocean: it makes all the difference between passive virtue, and active virtue.

To reiterate an important point: Pico's *Oration* does not directly assert that 'Man was made in the image of God'. Rather he asserts that humankind has the ability to model itself after God by cultivating qualities of character also possessed by God, and by the angels. It is not God who made us in His image, but Man who makes himself in God's image—if only he wills it. In this way, the *Oration* inaugurated something like a tradition for Renaissance humanists, in which it was right and just to take pride in being human.

Enter a second Renaissance man: Dante Alighieri. *The Divine Comedy* is probably the most important epic poem of the Renaissance. It is full of tributes to the classical world of Greece and Rome. Its story begins when Dante (who casts himself in the role of lead hero) stumbles down a hill and into a forest. There he meets the shade of the Roman poet Virgil, who takes him on a tour of the underworld. Although the cosmology and moral teaching of the story is indubitably Christian, there are many direct references to the imagination of the ancient Greeks and Romans. We see the three-headed dog Cerberus who guards the entrances to Hell, and the boatman Charon who ferries the recently deceased across the river. We even see the goddess Fortune herself, and Dante is at pains to present her in a way that doesn't conflict overmuch with the Christian world-view of the time. Dante asks Virgil if Fortune controls all worldly goods. He is told that God controls all things, but that God appointed overseers for various purposes. Fortune was assigned the task of distributing and often re-distributing "the splendors of the world". Her character is described like this:

Your knowledge is powerless against her; She provide, judges, and pursues her reign the way the other gods pursue their own. The vicissitudes she causes never cease; necessity compels her to be swift, so numerous are those who merit change. This is she whom even those crucify who should be praising her, instead of Wrongly blaming her with evil voices. But she is blessed and hears none of this; happy among the other first creatures, She turns her wheel and revels in her blessedness." (1:7. pg. 32.)

The fact that Dante is guided by Virgil, author of ancient Rome's most important epic, the *Aeneid*, is also a tribute to the ideas and images of the ancient world. In Virgil's poem, the hero Anaeus is taken on an underworld journey, guided by a priestess named Sibyl. So it is fitting that the author of that poem should be Dante's guide for his own underworld journey. Dante's positive attitude to the ancient world also appears in his treatment of the 'virtuous pagans', that is, good people who died before the birth of Christ. "None ever sinned, yet their virtue was not enough, because they were never baptized." (1:4, pg. 17) Therefore none of them were eligible for Heaven. But none deserved Hell either. So they are sent to Limbo, where the landscape is surprisingly pleasant: "…a noble castle / That seven times was circled by high walls / And guarded by a lovely stream around". Within the castle was "a fresh and verdant field… a place that was so open, luminous / and high, that everybody could be seen." (1:4, pg. 18-9). Dante speaks with Horace, Homer, Ovid, and Lucan, along with Virgil his guide. His feeling for them is sympathetic, even respectful. Indeed it is fairly clear that Dante thinks of himself as one of them, carrying forth their tradition.[115]

The masters of the Renaissance were responding to fate and fortune, and the problems of social life, as people of the ancient world before them had done. But they were also responding to *something within themselves* which knowledge from the ancient world had re-awakened. The word Renaissance itself, after all, means 're-birth'. What they re-discovered, I think, was a way to take pride in being human. Pico's purpose was to help people throw off the burden of Original Sin, and elevate themselves to enlightenment, *without* the authority of the Church, without the inter-cession of saints and angels, and even without the saving grace of Christ. Salvation may be achieved and the soul rendered divine *by one's own effort*. And that, my friends, is blasphemy. But it is also the foundation of *The Other Side of Virtue*.

§ 103. Renaissance Art.

Perhaps the most obvious place where the Renaissance gave new life to ancient ideas is in its art. For the Renaissance made ancient Greek and Roman mythology a legitimate subject-matter for the artist. Some of the most well known, iconic images of the Renaissance are scenes from ancient history and mythology, or variations on ancient themes: Botticelli's "The Birth of Venus", Raphael's "The School of Athens", Da Vinci's "Leda and the Swan", Michealangelo's "Baccus", and Peter Paul Rubens' "The Judgement of Paris", for example. And there are hundreds of others. Mantegna's "Parnassus" features Cupid, Hermes, Vulcan, and other divinities, all attending a marriage between Venus and Mars. One gets the impression that Mantegna wanted to fit as many gods and goddesses into the frame as possible, as if to maximize the blessings bestowed on the happy couple.

Someone familiar with all these pieces is likely to notice that most of them depict the gods and heroes in the nude. This was a major theme of Renaissance art which seems to have been very new at the time. From the end of the ancient world to the beginning of the Renaissance, Europe had nothing else like it. Donatello's bronze statue of "David" was the first free-standing nude sculpture of the Renaissance. The historian Jocelyn Godwin says that "there is no lineage of artistic development leading up to it, and no sign of its having been copied or emulated before the 1470's."[116] Pictures of *goddesses* are also very important here. Europe had not venerated a female deity for centuries. Although the Blessed Virgin Mary provided Christianity with a *de facto* Goddess, she had much less power and prestige than the all-male prophets of the Old Testament, and the all-male apostles of the New. But in the Renaissance, goddesses were re-appearing everywhere: in statues in town squares and the facades of public buildings, and hundreds and hundreds of paintings. It's also impossible not to notice that many of these images are also flagrantly *erotic*. The posture of Donatello's "David" is not just a little bit seductive. Giorgione's "Sleeping Venus" and Titian's "Venus of Urbino" depict the Goddess of Love reclining on a bed, completely exposed. In Giorgione's picture she is asleep, and the viewer is a bit like a voyeur. Titian depicts the goddess awake and looking at the viewer with an inviting smile. A curtain divides the picture in half, forming a line that points straight to—well, what the picture is probably all about.

It is worth repeating, one more time, that these artists and authors did not see themselves staging an overthrow of Christianity. But one may ask, how did they reconcile the paganism of the ancient world, as they portrayed it in their art, with the Christianity of their own world? One explanation is that the gods and heroes were allegorical representations of good Christian virtues. Certainly, Renaissance art was strongly influenced by the philosophy of Plato and the whole Classical tradition, in which art must serve an intellectual purpose. It must direct the mind to 'higher things', the eternal and timeless realities of the disembodied, spiritual world. This may explain some of the imagery in marriage paintings like Mantegna's "Parnassus". The love of the newly wedded couple for each other stands for the love between God and the human soul, in which all is pure, and nothing concealed. But this explanation isn't good enough for other, more obviously pagan images like Titian's "The Worship of Venus", in which a large crowd of Cupid-like infants practically topple over each other to get close to a statue of the Goddess. The best explanation I have found so far comes from historian Jocelyn Godwin, who wrote:

> I do not suppose that anyone in the fifteenth or sixteenth centuries was a pagan, in the sense of rejecting Christianity and adopting a pre-Christian religion... What I do suggest is that some people during this period "dreamed" of being pagans. In their waking life they accepted the absurdities acknowledged as the essence and *credenda* of Christianity, all the while nurturing a longing for the world of antiquity and a secret affinity for the divinities of that world.[117]

In other words, the artists who portrayed the heroes and gods of the pre-Christian world had a kind of private nostalgia for that classical pagan world. As they saw it, that world never bore the burden of Original Sin, for The Fall never happened. Therefore the heroes and gods of that world still lived in Paradise. Certainly, this explains Titian's "The Andrians", or Bellini's "Feast of the Gods", both of which depict crowds of people adoring the gods while gorging themselves with food, drink, and sex. They are portrayed indulging in carnal desire, but without any guilt or shame. As in the ancient world, the animal passions like the libido, the intellectual powers of the thinking mind like reason, and the material bounties of the world like food and drink, were being presented in Renaissance art as sources of spiritual fulfillment in their own right. The re-discovery of this source of spiritual power helped the people of the Renaissance overcome Original Sin—or at least temporarily forget about it. And that, it seems, is another thing the people of the Renaissance re-discovered in themselves.

It should be said, however, that this was only a small part of the force behind the Renaissance. The larger force was the desire of the rich to out-do each other with ostentatious displays of wealth and power. If Renaissance art represented nostalgia for a lost paradise, it was also a way of glorifying the patrons who bought the paintings. And if it was an affirmation of the sacredness of the embodied world and all its good bounties, it was also a male sexual fantasy. Indeed the patrons who commissioned the works often gave specific instructions to the artists for how the models would be posed, what the background scenery would be like, and so on. To attribute spiritual significance to the embodied world was a very bold, very pagan, very subversive kind of move, for the time. But it probably didn't do much to improve the position of women. A goddess in Renaissance art was either a muse, who offered intellectual inspiration, or a nymph, who offered sexual pleasure; in either case, she was an object of male attention. She could not be both mind and body at the same time, nor could she be her own person.

The story of how the goddesses restored their integrity will have to be told in another book (and I am preparing just such a book). For the moment, let us turn to another important writer who made the Renaissance what it was. But his vision was far different from that of Pico, or Dante, or any of the artists.

§ 104. Machiavelli

Italy was nothing like a unified nation in the 15th century. There were more than a dozen independent political powers on the peninsula. The largest and most influential were Florence, Venice, Naples, Milan, and the Papal States. Lorenzo de Medici became the ruler of Florence in 1469, and by means of brilliant diplomacy created a brief period of peace. But in 1494, two years after Lorenzo de Medici died, King Charles VIII of France invaded and claimed the throne of Naples. His successor Louis XII partitioned Naples with the Spanish king Ferdinand of Aragon. Eventually Spaniards held Milan, Naples, Sicily, and Florence, and had garrisons practically everywhere else. Dante himself in The Divine Comedy, entreated his listeners to "Look everywhere, from coast to coast and seashore, O wretched land, then look within your breast and see if any part of it knows peace!" And then he entreats God himself to intervene, for "the cities of Italy are full of tyrants." (II.6, pg. 182). In the midst of this fracas was born a writer whose name has become synonymous with the uncompromising pursuit of power by any means: Niccolo Machiavelli.

To begin, here is one of the most salient passages from *The Prince*, his infamous treatise on how to gain and hold political power.

Many have dreamed up republics and principalities which have never in truth been known to exist. The gulf between how one should live and how one does live is so wide that a man who neglects what is actually done for what should be done learns the way to self-destruction rather than self-preservation. The fact is that a man who wants to act virtuously in every way necessarily comes to grief among so many who are not virtuous. Therefore if a prince wants to maintain his rule he must learn how not to be virtuous… (*The Prince*, XV, pg. 90)

Two things must be noted here. First of all, this passage is meant to snub the followers of Plato, and that meant practically every other intellectual at the time. The 'dreamed up republic' is Plato's *Republic*, the philosophical masterwork in which Plato defines Justice as the structure of an ideal society. Secondly, this passage advocates a 'realistic' view of human affairs, in which Virtue doesn't pay. So one must learn 'how not to be Virtuous'. But I submit that despite remarks like this, and despite his reputation for being a supporter of tyranny (which in many ways is quite deserved), Machiavelli is no less a supporter of the idea of virtue. His interest is not just the means of gaining and holding power, but also the character of the ruler. The spirit of Virtue still guides him, at least in this small way. It is just that *his* picture of the great soul, i.e. "The Prince", is very different from Plato and Aristotle's picture; and vastly different from our own. Indeed he turns the idea of Virtue on its head. For instance, he claims that the wise Prince:

...must not flinch from being blamed for vices which are necessary for safeguarding the state. This is because, taking everything into account, he will find that some of the things that appear to be virtues will, if he practices them, ruin him, and some of the things that appear to be vices will bring him security and prosperity. (*The Prince,* XV, pg. 92)

The virtues he says the Prince must un-learn are the passive, humble virtues of Christianity. Then, the Prince must learn new virtues like ambition, and ruthlessness. Contrary to the whole classical tradition which holds that the ruler should concern himself with justice, Machiavelli claims the Prince should concern himself only with warfare. "A prince, therefore, must have no other object or thought, nor acquire skill in anything, except war, its organisation, and its discipline. The art of war is all that is expected of a ruler." (*The Prince*, XIV, pg. 87) All politics, in his view, is war. Machiavelli then asks, what qualities must one possess, and what qualities must one avoid, in order to win?

In contrast with both the classical and Christian traditions, Machiavelli claims that the prince should *not* practice the virtue of generosity, but rather should be conservative, even to the point of appearing miserly. An overly generous prince may end up impoverishing himself, and will be forced to tax his subjects excessively in order to sustain his position. "Miserliness is one of those vices which sustain his rule." (*The Prince*, XVI. Pg. 94) The prince should also not be excessively compassionate, but rather on occasion he should be cruel, especially when it comes to punishing criminals. Those who are too compassionate "allow disorders which lead to murder and rapine. These nearly always harm the whole community, whereas executions ordered by a prince only affect individuals." (*The Prince*, XVII, pg. 95) A prince need not even be honest nor keep his promises, when it does not suit him. Yet a prince must portray the *illusion* of being generous, compassionate, honest, and even peace-loving. Actual possession of such qualities may leave him vulnerable, but projecting the appearance of possessing them may benefit him. (*The Prince*, XVIII, pp. 99-101). A prince must be both man and beast: that is, he must fight his wars with laws, like a man, and with force, like a beast. He must be a lion to keep the wolves at bay, but he must also be a fox to avoid getting caught in traps. "Those who simply act like lions are stupid." (XVIII, 99-100) Finally, a prince may benefit from being loved by the people, but would prefer to be feared. The passage where this point is raised has become famous for its extraordinarily disparaging attitude toward the general character of humanity:

> ...it is far better to be feared than loved if you cannot be both. One can make this generalization about men: they are ungrateful, fickle, liars, and deceivers, they shun danger and are greedy for profit... The bond of love is one which men, wretched creatures that they are, break when it is to their advantage to do so; but fear is strengthened by a dread of punishment which is always effective. (*The Prince*, XVII, pg. 96-7)

Each of these requirements directly contradicts the classical tradition he inherited. And each of them are dead ends. He should have remembered his Cicero, who wrote that "to make people frightened is the way not to maintain one's position but to lose it... [and] no amount of power, however enormous, can stand up against widespread unpopularity."[118] Yet one of Machiavelli's own sternest warnings is that while a prince may be feared, he must never let himself be hated, for a hated prince is soon overthrown.[119] In August of 2004, U.S. President George W. Bush told his people that the War on Terror may never be won.[120] Just as Machiavelli recommended, Bush has maintained his power by keeping his people in a constant state of fear (that is, fear of foreign religious fanatics and terrorists, not of himself). But it takes energy to be constantly afraid, even of terrorists, and people eventually grow exhausted. In August of 2006 U.S. Senator Joe Lieberman, an experienced and popular politician who supported the War on Terror, was defeated in a Democratic party leadership race by what appeared to be grass-roots support for Ned Lamont, a rookie candidate who advocated ending the war.[121] Then in a general election in November of 2006, the Democrats took over the Congress and the Senate, with a strong anti-war platform. One possible explanation: the people are growing tired of living in fear.

Furthermore, a Prince who is feared may find himself isolated from regular human relationships, or even excluded from them. Joseph Stalin was described by his associates as full of paranoia. Nikita Krushchev described Stalin as "sickly suspicious". Another associate of his, Milovan Djilas, said "he [Stalin] had become the slave of the despotism, the bureaucracy, the narrowness, and the servility he imposed on his country. It is indeed true that no one can destroy another's freedom without losing his own."[122] Again, as Cicero wrote, "Men eager to terrorize others will inevitably become frightened of the very people they are intimidating."[123]

One quality Machiavelli shares with the classical tradition is *prudence*. As he seems to define it, prudence is the ability to discern what is 'necessary', to know what truly are one's best interests. Here are two of the many appearances of this quality in his text.

So a prince has of necessity to be so prudent that he knows how to escape the evil reputation attached to those vices which could lose him his state, and how to avoid those vices which are not so dangerous, if he possibly can; but, if he cannot, he need not worry so much about the latter. (*The Prince*, XV, pg. 92)

A prince must be slow to take action, and must watch that he does not come to be afraid of his own shadow; his behaviour must be tempered by humanity and prudence so that over-confidence does not make him rash or excessive distrust make him unbearable. (XVII, pg. 96)

This prudence is supposed to separate the successful Prince from the bullish tyrant.

Machiavelli is most like a Renaissance man in his treatment of Fortune. Like his forebears, he was very interested in how one may be fend Fortune off, and preserve one's standing in the world. As he observed, "many have held and hold the opinion that events are controlled by fortune and by God in such a way that the prudence of men cannot modify them, indeed, that men have no influence whatsoever." But against this popular opinion, Machiavelli himself believed that "fortune is the arbiter of half the things we do, leaving the other half or so to be controlled by ourselves." (XXV, pg. 130). Prudence, again, comes to the rescue: it responds to fortune by helping us to read the signs of the times. If he were alive today, he might describe prudence as the ability to "know when to hold, know when to fold, know when to walk away, know when to run!" But most of all, the prudent Prince knows when to recognise a good opportunity when it appears, and knows how to make the most of it.

As fortune is changeable whereas men are obstinate in their ways, men prosper so long as fortune and policy are in accord, and when there is a clash they fail. I hold strongly to this: that it is better to be impetuous than circumspect; because fortune is a woman and if she is to be submissive it is necessary to beat and coerce her. Experience shows that she is more often subdued by men who do this than by those who act coldly. (XXV, pg. 133).

The personification of Fortune as a woman is a time-honoured literary device: Pico della Mirandola and Boethius use it too. For heroic Scandinavians, Fortune was represented by three goddesses named Wyrd, Urverly, and Skuld. In Greece these goddesses were named Clotho,

Lachaesis, and Atropos. In Ireland she was called Morrigán, 'The Great Queen', and her relationship to the chieftain of a tribe was the basis for law and order in old Celtic society. What is new in Machiavelli is the representation of the successful Prince as her oppressor. The Machiavellian Prince is cunning, brutal, arrogant, and occasionally cruel. He regards Fate as an adversary to be defeated. If he courts and charms her, it is only because later on he wants to conquer her. When he is kind or benevolent to others, it is only because it will help advance his purposes, not because people somehow deserve kindness. But for all that, the Machiavellian Prince is no less a 'great' man. He seizes good opportunities when they arise, and creates profound changes in the world. Most of all he makes full use of his potentials, and with them he takes full responsibility for his own destiny. More than any other writer of his time and place, Machiavelli gives us the best Renaissance picture of what it is to be 'great'. I mean 'greatness' here in the broadest sense. It includes excellence and corruption, nobility and wickedness, all in equal measure. This non-moral, even *immoral*, aspect of greatness, is still part of Virtue's rarely acknowledged 'other side'.

What Machiavelli does not seem to account for is that when you set yourself up in conflict with fortune, you eventually lose. As the writers in the Heroic and the Classical periods knew, Fortune is something elemental: you can prepare for it, and do things to mitigate the worst of its effects, but you can never conquer it. A war with fate simply cannot be won. And those who come closest to success also come closest to losing their humanity. Other thinkers, some associated with literary genius, and some just as strongly associated with danger, will glimpse the full meaning of human greatness more completely.

§ 105. Shakespeare

The first of these people whom I'd like to introduce is a near-contemporary of Machiaveilli's: the English playwright William Shakespeare. One example out of his 33 plays will do: *Macbeth*. In its narrative of witchcraft and murder, several important Heroic principles re-appear, especially including The Sovereignty of Fortune, and the Seizure of the Last Chance. Macbeth, who at the beginning is a minor Scottish clann chieftain, is told by three witches that he will become king of all Scotland, and they describe the stages by which it will happen. When the first part of the prophesy comes true almost immediately, Macbeth's conniving wife invokes a magical force to help accelerate the rest of it. All the things the witches foretold do indeed come to pass, but at the cost of the death of Macbeth's best friend, Banquo, the creation of a dangerous enemy, Macduff, the loss of his wife's sanity, and indeed the loss of his own human goodness. Fate, especially tragic fate, is as much an unimpeachable force in Macbeth as it is for the Anglo-Saxons who recited the tale of Beowulf around their fires at night, a thousand years before Shakespeare. When Macbeth learns that his wife has committed suicide, he speaks a lament which expresses the texture of life under this lense most poetically:

> To-morrow, and to-morrow, and to-morrow,
> Creeps in this petty pace from day to day
> To the last syllable of recorded time;
> And all our yesterdays have lighted fools
> The way to dusty death. Out, out brief candle!
> Life's but a walking shadow, a poor player
> That struts and frets his hour upon the stage
> And then is heard no more. It is a tale
> Told by an idiot, full of sound and fury,
> Signifying nothing.[124]

This is one of the most famous expressions of weary despair in the English language. Anyone can identify with it: we all have moments of deep sadness in our lives like this. Death has a way of making everything seem absurd and empty. There is wonderful irony in the use of the stage player metaphor, since this speech is from a work of theatre, intended to be spoken by a player strutting and fretting upon a stage. With this meta-theatricality the audience is momentarily taken out of the world of the story and made to confront the real world of their actual lives. And what a grim world it seems to be! Yet despite this grimness one feels oddly empowered. There is strange strength to be gained from admitting that life is a walking shadow. Clarity of purpose can be found in acknowledging that the tale of life is empty sound and fury. A superior poet like Shakespeare can show this. Death also has a way of forcing us to sort out what really matters from what does not. The Seizure of the Last Chance is one of the ways we do this. Near the end of the play, a messenger tells Macbeth that the forest of Burnham Wood appears to be moving. Soldiers intent upon besieging his castle at Dunsinane have hidden their identity and number by carrying tree branches in full foliage above their heads. This is the first of two signs of Macbeth's impending death, prophesized to him by the three witches. He feels fear, but he does not flee, nor does he hide. His response is to rouse his remaining supporters for a final decisive battle:

Arm, arm and out!
If this which he avouches does appear,
There is no flying hence nor tarrying here.
I gin to be a-weary of the sun,
And wish the estate o' the world were now undone.
Ring the alarum-bell! Blow, wind! Come, wrack!
At least we'll die with harness on our back.[125]

Or to put it another way, 'This is a no-win situation, but at least we'll die trying.' It is a wonderful model of someone unwilling to give up, right to the end.

Not a moment after Macbeth has given voice to his perseverance this way, he meets his enemy Macduff. Here is a man who was "not of woman born", because from his mother's womb he was "untimely ripped". This news reveals the second of the two signs of Macbeth's death. There is no way out for him. But his last mortal words are again of perseverance. Instead of fleeing, hiding, or surrendering, he says:

Though Burnam Wood come to Dunsinane,
And thou oppos'd, being of no woman born,
Yet I will try the last. Before my body

I throw my warlike shield. Lay on, Macduff,
And damn'd be him that first cries 'Hold, enough!'[126]

Something about the words 'Yet I will try the last' always makes my heart flutter. Here is a man absolutely at the end of his rope. He knows that Death is about to befall him. Nonetheless he seizes a last chance. I like to think that in his last moment, with this final act of bravery, his lost humanity is restored to him, the free will he never thought he had rises up in him, and he is enabled to die as a hero.

§ 106. Romanticism

Sometime in the 17th century, Reason came to dominate European high culture. Reason, and Reason alone, so the philosophers believed, could tell us what human nature is, what our true end and purpose is, and why moral laws have the authority they supposedly have. Science and scientific method would explain the world for us. Religious superstition and faith would be eliminated: for religion had given Europe nothing but war. There had been nine different Crusades against the Islamic world in the previous three centuries, and dozens of armed conflicts, big and small, between Catholics and Protestants, within Europe itself. In this period Isaac Newton showed us how the world could be described with mathematics. Composers like Mozart and painters like Jacques-Louis David and Thomas Gainsborough showed us how beauty could be an intellectual experience, defined in terms of symmetry, harmony, and perfection. Religion took on a more scientific character too: God was not a Saviour, but an Architect. He created the world, set in motion the laws of nature, and then left humankind to our own devices. Immanuel Kant showed how Reason alone could serve as the sole measure of human worth. "Rational nature exists as an end in itself" was his proclamation in the *Groundwork to the Metaphysics of Morals*.[127] Indeed Kant believed that history itself had the sole aim of producing a rationally ordered human society. "The history of mankind," he wrote, "can be seen, in the large, as the realisation of nature's secret plan to bring forth a perfectly constituted state as the only condition in which the capacities of mankind can be fully developed, and also bring forth that external relation among states which is perfectly adequate to this end."[128] Politicians and leaders were taking notice of this project. There was a new interest in the old notion of the 'benevolent tyrant', an absolute ruler who governs a perfectly ordered society with serenely rational laws. The period has come to be called The Age of Reason, or The Enlightenment.

But the grand plan of the Age of Reason was not without its problems. Various people, especially artists and intellectuals, began to worry about what it might have excluded. As Euripides had noted more than a millennia before, people cannot live without an avenue for the expression of their passions. The opening of just such an avenue is what Romanticism, as a movement, made possible. Romanticism begins as a political movement of protest and rebellion: an assertion of the rights of individuals and of the working class against hereditary aristocrats and landlords. The storming of the Bastille in 1789, and the rescue of the political prisoners held there, is its effective beginning. But as an artistic and intellectual movement, it was a response to the loss of trust in the 'certainties' of universal Reason and divine providence.

The word 'Romantic' had been in regular use since the Italian Renaissance. It referred to artistic styles that resembled old tales of heroic quests, courtly love, chivalry, and adventure written in one of the languages that developed from Latin. But at that time the word had a negative connotation: it implied arts in which free imaginative improvisation got in the way of the intellectual clarity that Renaissance and Age of Reason art was supposed to embody. But to Romantic artists themselves, Romanticism stood for passions that were spontaneous, not hedged in by rules of form, and therefore more authentic. They were not interested in imitating supposed models of perfection, received from antiquity and tradition, as the artists of the Renaissance aimed to do. They wanted a free and unfettered exploration of their own individual creative powers. They no longer felt bound by the *Logos* of human reason, nor by the *Word* of Divine Providence. Instead, they saw humanity as a being of infinite creative possibility, facing an infinite universe. There was a renewed interest in Shakespeare, and Homer, and in the Heroic epics of the

Norse. Isaac Newton's sublimely rational, ordered universe seemed to be breaking down, and the goddess Fortuna was re-asserting herself. Instead of order, peace, and reason, Romanticism elevates passion, beauty, and especially struggle, to the level of the divine. As an example of this, here is how the German poet Goethe, using the character *Faust* as his spokesperson, criticised the Enlightenment values:

> Well, that's Philosophy I've read;
> And Law and Medicine, and I fear
> Theology too, from A to Z
> Hard studies all, that have cost me dear.
> And so I sit, poor silly man,
> No wiser than when I began. [129]

Similarly, English poets like Wordsworth, Coleridge, Byron, Shelley, Blake, and others were producing a style of poetry not intended for the contemplative mind, but for the heart aflame with beauty and revolution. In Germany, Herder argued that language was the primary creative power of humankind. With language people assert their identity and power without the need for supernatural assistance, that is, without the need for God. The Brothers Grimm, strongly influenced by Herder, published folk tales that they collected from children in their neighbourhood. They believed these stories had as much drama, tragedy, horror, and heroism as any of the ancient sagas available at the time, and any Biblical story as well. Similarly they believed the conflicts between good and evil described in them could teach important moral lessons, without the need for a divine lawgiver.

In his novel "The Sorrows of Young Werther", Goethe's main character describes how he came upon a small country boy asleep with an infant cradled in his arms. He sat and sketched the scene for a while, and described his artistic process as follows.

> Only nature is infinitely rich and capable of developing a great artist. There is much to be said for the advantage of rules and regulations,

much the same things as can be said in praise of middle class society—
he who sticks to them will never produce anything that is bad or in
poor taste, just as he who lets himself be molded by law, order, and
prosperity will never become an intolerable neighbor or a striking
scoundrel. On the other hand—and people can say what they like—
rules and regulations ruin our true appreciation of nature and our
powers to express it.[130]

These lines encapsulate the Romantic response to the Age of Reason.
Sometimes knowledge does not bring enlightenment. The intellectual
person, like Faust, can see all too clearly the problems of the world, and is
capable of seriously contemplating the possibility that the world may have
no meaning, no purpose, no inherent worth. In Goethe's poem, Faust has
mastered all the intellectual disciplines of science and philosophy,
especially medicine, but finds they are not enough. So he turns to
something unscientific, irrational, and yet primordial and immense: he
turned to magic. He conjures the demon Mephistopheles, and trades his
soul for knowledge. Similarly the artistic soul, like Werther, finds that
adherence to rules of form stunts the creative powers and prevents their
full flowering.

That summarizes what Romanticism had to say about the Age of
Reason. What did it offer as an alternative? To be clear, Romanticism did
not enumerate a new catalogue of the virtues, as previous re-appearances
of Virtue tried to do. Rather, it painted portraits of people leading "a
Romantic life". Moreover, there is not a singular, universally-agreed
portrait of the Romantic life: there area several, some artistic, some intellectual, some political, and some quite incomprehensible. But in all
respects, Romanticism asserts the idea that the good live involves
modeling oneself after a portrait of an ideal type of person. This is a
reflection of the original notion of virtue. One is not to follow rules or
laws, but rather to possess a kind of personality, one which exemplifies a
certain model of human life and experience. Instead of describing specific
virtues, then, I'll describe the major themes which contribute to the
Romantic character.

One of those themes is the elevation of love and the passions. Goethe's portrait of Young Werther represents this theme best. Werther is a young artist who falls hopelessly in love with a woman named Charlotte. She likes him well enough, but she is betrothed to another man. Werther spends almost all of his idle hours in her presence, doing little favours for her, having long conversations, playing with her young nieces and nephews, and so on. She, for her part, does not reject these advances: in fact she teases and tantalizes him, continually stoking the fire in his heart. Werther's affection for Charlotte slowly builds over time, until it becomes a pathological obsession. This obsession is not criticized by Goethe: rather, it is confirmed as necessary for the Romantic life. As Werther tells Charlotte's fiancée Albert,

Passion. Inebriation. Madness. You respectable ones stand there so calmly, without any sense of participation. Upbraid the drunkard, abhor the madman, pass them by like the priest and thank God like the Pharisees that He did not make you as one of these! I have been drunk more than once, and my passion often borders on madness, and I regret neither. Because, in my own way, I have learned to understand that all exceptional people who created something great, something that seemed impossible, have to be decried as drunkards or madmen. And I find it intolerable, even in our daily life, to hear it said of almost everyone who manages to do something that is free, noble, and unexpected: He is a drunkard, he is a fool. They should be ashamed of themselves, all these sober people! And the wise ones![131]

As a model of happiness, this message seems counter-intuitive. But what Goethe presents to us is a character who *enjoys* his life more fully, *precisely because* it is frustrating. Werther must struggle with life, in order to have a fulfilling life. He feels his passions with more clarity, more depth, more force than Albert, the upright and rational man who apparently feels nothing at all.

Another of Romanticism's major themes is the human response to the world of nature. Paintings like C.D. Friedrich's "Evening" exemplify this:

it depicts two people abiding in a landscape that is peaceful but its colours are strange, almost otherworldly. Its tall trees are monumental; they dwarf the two human figures. Turner's "Fire at Sea" shows a ships crew struggling in vain to stay afloat while the elements surge and crash ferociously around them. In both ways, the world is beautiful: in peace and in violence, it remains sublime, it remains an Immensity. Indeed the Romantic movement is the first to use the word 'nature' to describe the countryside, the land, sea, and sky. Jean Jacques Rousseau, in his *Confessions* (1782), described walking alone across the Swiss Alps. "Never does a plain, however beautiful it may be, seem so in my eyes. I need torrents, rocks, firs, dark woods, mountains, deep roads to climb or descend, abysses beside me to make me afraid."[132] Rousseau is the first major thinker of modernity to conceive of nature as a 'place', the world that is 'out there' beyond the wards of towns and cities. He is also one of the first to attribute to nature an inspirational power. In a similar vein, Werther, Goethe's emotionally frustrated anti-hero, finds his only solace and release by long walks in the countryside at night: "for only nature is infinitely rich and capable of developing a great artist."[133] Before the Romantic Movement, 'Nature' denoted a principle of order or necessity which exists within living beings and the cosmos. And in typical Romantic style, Rousseau describes nature as a source of both inspiration and danger.

A very important feature of Romanticism is the importance it attributes to music. When the *Nibelungenlied*, Germany's ancient heroic epic tale, was re-published, Richard Wagner turned it into four magnificent operas which together are known as The Ring. He hoped that some day music festivals would replace religious rituals, and concert halls would replace churches. So he raised funds to build a special theatre, called the *Festspielhaus*, to serve as the new cathedral of the divine music he wanted to create. In Beethoven's Sixth Symphony, "The Pastorale", you can hear the Romantic love of Nature. In it he composed musical portraits of sunshine, country dances, thunderstorms, and peaceful evenings; all the things that make the Earth an Immensity. The first few bars of his Ninth Symphony sound like a strange morass of unrelated tones, as if the musicians of the orchestra are still tuning their instruments. But then out

of the disorder comes a sudden exclamation of sound, like a fanfare intro-
ducing the entrance of a king. Romanticism is like that: its vision sees the
world of life emerging from chaos and confusion. The second movement
of the Ninth Symphony is the musical equivalent of a riot. And the third,
although set to slower pace, is occasionally interrupted by loud bursts of
uncontainable passion. Perhaps Beethoven composed such unrelenting
music in order to drown out the constant ringing in his ears from which he
suffered, and to make the most use of the time between his severe migrane
headaches. But I think he also understood something about the Romantic
world view. All things are governed by an irrational yet deliberate passion,
a passion which struggles and endures suffering in order to create
something beautiful. Hence the last movement of the 9th symphony
contains the musical arrangement of Schiller's poem, *The Ode to Joy*, a
thrilling celebration of life, companionship, and beauty, which Beethoven
regarded as a statement of spiritual identity.

Finally, Romanticism is characterized by the theme of sacrifice.
Werther's fire-storm of emotion ends in self-destruction. For when
Werther's unrequited longing has reached its absolute climax, and
Charlotte (who by this time has married Albert) asks him not to call on her
anymore, Werther shoots himself. But this is presented not a refutation of
the Romantic life. Rather, it is a consummation of it: *Werther sacrifices
himself for love*. No other conclusion would fit the narrative, no alternative
end would have the same force.[134] It is a Romantic idea, in its artistic
representations as well as its political manifestations, that a cause is
rendered noble by the extent people are willing to struggle and sacrifice
themselves to attain it. As the philosopher-historian Isaiah Berlin wrote,
"Self-immolation for a cause is the thing, not the validity of the cause
itself, for it is the sacrifice undertaken for its sake that sanctifies the cause,
not some intrinsic property of it."[135]

In the Romantic vision, the world is a vast tempestuous ocean, without
a bottom on which to hook an anchor, nor with any islands or shores to
come to land. And each of us are ships floating on this ocean, without map
or compass, without origin or destination—we have only the wind and
waves, pushing us onwards from one unknown sea to another. A vision of

the world as constantly in motion, constantly changing, the world as *sturm und drang*, and therefore never still, never at peace—this is a vision of pessimism, resignation, dejection. But this is also *amor fati*, the love of destiny, no matter how tragic and passionately sad it might be. And this vision is a direct attack on the precisely structured, geometrically elegant and mathematically perfect world given to us by Newton, and the other architects of the Age of Reason.

§ 107. Nietzsche

Let us turn now to another, better known philosopher of the Romantic Movement: Friedrich Nietzsche. Like his Romantic predecessors (especially Schopenhauer), and indeed like the characters of heroic mythology, Nietzsche sees the world as a storm, constantly in motion, ever changing, and' dangerous. In a rant against the English Utilitarians, Nietzsche expresses an agreement with Schopenhauer that the world is a realm of constant suffering. But there is no room for pessimism in Nietzsche's vision. Indeed as Nietzsche sees it, in suffering there is *opportunity*. "The discipline of suffering, of *great* suffering—do you not know that only *this* discipline has created all enhancements of man so far?"[136] Suffering here is not portrayed as the evil which must be countered with justice. Rather it is the very circumstance *in response to which* human character is developed, and made strong. It is the situation that produces a higher type of being—if, that is, one responds to it properly. In words vaguely reminiscent of Pico della Mirandola, Nietzsche says we have it in us to respond well or to respond badly.

> In man *creature* and *creator* are united: in man there is material, fragment, excess, clay, dirt, nonsense, chaos; but in man there is also creator, form-giver, hammer hardness, spectator divinity, and seventh day... [137]

This is the key to understanding the *Ubermensch*, the 'Higher Man', Nietzsche's portrait of the Great Soul. A human being has it within her to be both creature and creator, both divinity and monster, all at once. Life, as he saw it, had no intrinsic, inherent meaning. According to him, the truth of the world is nihilism. Our biggest choice in life, therefore, is whether to be a subject of other people's values, or a creator of one's own; or to put it another way, whether to be a master or a slave. The Ubermensch is a creator and a master. He is the person who, in the absence of a sense of meaning presented to him by God, or Nature, or anything else, *decides for himself* what the meaning of his life *shall* be, and then impose that decision on his world. By this act of willpower, the Ubermensch creates himself.

If the Ubermensch is Nietzsche's portrait of the Great Soul, then what are his virtues? The first among them is the Will. This is the quality that grounds or justifies any others he might possess, just as Reason was the chief virtue for Aristotle, and the writers of the Renaissance. To Nietzsche, it is the quality which enables one to take control of his life, on his own terms. As he sees it, the Will in living things is something like a basic principle of nature. A person, or even a society, which wants to succeed in life, as Nietzsche says:

> ...will have to be an incarnate will to power, it will strive to grow, spread, seize, become predominant—not from any morality or immorality but because it is *living* and because life simply *is* will to power... "Exploitation" does not belong to a corrupt or imperfect and primitive society: it belongs to the *essence* of what lives, as a basic organic function; it is a consequence of the will to power, which is after all the will of life.[138]

Thus Nietzsche describes the Will as a natural force. But unlike his Romantic predecessors, Nietzsche does not take this to be the cause of all misery and suffering. Rather, he finds that the successful discharge of the will is *pleasurable*.[139]

Most importantly, Nietzsche's Will to Power is the special quality of someone who lives by "master morality". Such people possess sufficient Will to create their own meaning for their lives, decide for themselves what the purpose of their lives will be, and impose their Will on the world.

As he says:

> The essential characteristic of a good and healthy aristocracy, however, is that it experiences itself *not* as a function (whether of the monarchy or the commonwealth) but as their *meaning* and highest justification— that it therefore accepts with a good conscience the sacrifice of untold human beings who, *for its sake*, must be reduced and lowered to incomplete human beings, to slaves, to instruments.[140]

The Ubermensch, then, is a figure who *necessarily* dominates and exploits and sacrifices other people. In order to be able to create himself, and impose his new meaning upon his life, he has to be able to impose it on others as well. The "slaves" are those who lack the Will and therefore must passively accept what the masters impose on them. Theirs is the morality of the person who requires external sources of authority to know what is right and wrong. "Morality in Europe today is herd animal morality",[141] he tells us. It is the morality of those who do what they are told and who do not ask questions. Does this seem familiar? Its modern day equivalent sounds like this: "It is our patriotic duty to support the President in a time of war."

Nietzsche's ideas are fashionable again, being more than a hundred years after his death. I have met many people who described to me a desire to apply Nietzsche's ideas to the political affairs of their country. So it is worth reminding the reader that there have already been a few countries that tried to do exactly that. The result was the Second World War. The Nazi party hijacked much of Nietzsche's thought for its own purposes, as did Mussolini's Facists and Stalin's Communist party. Granted, their use of his thought was very selective and self-serving. The Nazis ignored his total rejection of any belief in God, and his insistence that the superiority of the Ubermensch has to do with his qualities of character and nothing to do with nationalism or eugenics. But the plain fact is that the consequence of applying the Will to Power to real-world politics, is the death camps of Treblinka and Auschwitz, and the gulags of Siberia. This is not a matter of putting powerful ideas in the wrong hands. It is part of the very logic of

Nietzsche's doctrine of master and slave morality. There is simply no way to sweep this aspect of Nietzsche's thought under the rug.

Nevertheless, as I said of Machiavelli, Nietzsche is still a supporter of the idea of Virtue. Much of his whole philosophical project is to enumerate the virtues of the Great Soul, like Aristotle before him. Listen to Nietzsche introduce this project.

> Our virtues?—It is probable that we, too, still have our virtues, although in all fairness they will not be the simpleminded and four-square virtues for which we hold our grandfathers in honor—and at arm's length.[142]

The 'four-square virtues' here mentioned are the four classical virtues of courage, temperance, prudence, and justice. The Ubermensch has virtue—but not the virtues of Enlightenment rationality, nor the virtues of Christian piety. By his own description, his virtues are those of the Heroic age. In various passages he praises the 'barbarian' strength of Norse or Homeric warriors. Here is an example of his treatment of honour, the highest of the Heroic virtues:

> The noble human being, too, helps the unfortunate, but not, or almost not, from pity, but prompted more by an urge begotten by excess of power. The noble human being honors himself as one who is powerful, also as one who has power over himself, who knows how to speak and be silent, who delights in being severe and hard with himself and respects all severity and hardness.[143]

So the Nietzschean noble soul can be generous and hospitable. But his generosity is not motivated by sympathy for the suffering of others, nor by respect owed to others. It is motivated by the giver's sense of himself as powerful, as someone able to give, as someone who, in that power to give, has power over another. In the Heroic age, as shown earlier, generosity was connected to honour in that the generous person is likely to earn the praise of his companions. But the Nietzschean Ubermensch does not care about praise. When he chooses to benefit someone, he does it to confirm his pride in himself, and to express his Will to Power.

Although it may surprise you to learn this, *honesty* featured very highly in Nietzsche's catalogue of the virtues. In *Beyond Good and Evil*, he says: "Honesty, supposing that this is our virtue from which we cannot get away, we free spirits—well, let us work on it with all our malice and love and not weary of 'perfecting' ourselves in *our* virtue, the only one left to us."[144] Honesty finishes off many of his arguments for the supremacy of the will, where for instance he says that the Will to Power "is the primordial fact of all history: people ought to be honest with themselves at least that far."[145] In *The Gay Science* he says that honesty lets one look upon the world and understand it properly, in order to be better able to work on it and change it.[146] Honesty is the quality that keeps the Ubermensch aware of his surroundings, and prevents him from falling into new traps of gratifying self-delusion. Honesty forces the Ubermensch to cling to what is true, however unpalatable, difficult to accept, or controversial that may be.

> And if our honesty should nevertheless grow weary one day and sigh and stretch its limbs and find us too hard, and would like to have things better, easier, tender, like an agreeable vice—let us remain *hard* we last Stoics! [147]

Hardness, here mentioned, is probably second only to the Will in Nietzsche's thought. "Truth is hard",[148] and requires great fortitude when false or misleading alternatives are easier, or more gratifying. Here's another description of this 'virtuous' hardness:

> What is good?—Whatever augments the feeling of power, the will to power, power itself, in man. What is evil?—whatever springs from weakness. What is happiness?—the feeling that power *increases*—that resistance is overcome. Not contentment, but more power; not peace at any price, but war; not virtue, but efficiency (virtue in the Renaissance sense, *virtu*, virtue free of moral acid.) The weak and the botched shall perish: first principle of *our* charity. And one should help them to it.

What is more harmful than any vice?—Practical sympathy for the botched and the weak—Christianity.[149]

Nietzschean hardness, as this passage reveals, is also the quality that enables the *Ubermensch* to steel himself against feeling sympathy for others. This he must do lest other people's values ever override his own.

The final quality of the Ubermensch that must be mentioned is Pride. Like Nietzsche's treatment of honour, another quality shared with the heroes of mythology, Pride is turned toward the possessor. It is the love of a noble soul for itself. Two related epigrams in *Beyond Good and Evil* bring this out.

- Whatever is done from love always occurs beyond good and evil.[150]
- Jesus said to his Jews, "The law was for servants—love God as I love him, as his son! What are morals to us sons of God!"[151]

In these two aphorisms, Nietzsche is pointing directly to the absurdity of declaring ethical imperatives with love as their object, imperatives like "Love your neighbor as yourself". Love can only arise from free spontaneity; it cannot be commanded by a law. The passion, the commitment, the sincerity, of an act of love makes the act real not its fulfillment of a rule or a duty. Love is thus beyond any analysis of moral right and wrong. Hence the title of the masterwork in which these aphorisms appear.

But love of *what*? What idea of love is in play here? Certainly not Christian love, the universal neighborly love of everyone, even one's enemies. The love Nietzsche has in mind here is pride in one's standing as a higher type of being, pride in being an Ubermensch: for "the noble soul has reverence for itself".[152] This statement was probably the most concise, poetic, and profound expression of what it means to be *noble* since the Heroic age. The self-love of a noble soul is the very essence the original idea of virtue. Aristotle himself taught very nearly the same thing, in his observation that the virtuous person finds that life is desirable. But as Nietzsche describes it, this self-love separates people and keeps them apart. It does not want to reach out to people and share its life with them, but rather wants to affirm its own superiority. "The noble soul… does not like to look 'up'—but either *ahead*, horizontally and slowly, or down: *it knows itself to be at a height*."[153]

This completes the program, begun in the Renaissance and continued by Romanticism, to overcome Original Sin, and restore dignity and pride to humanity. Someone who follows this program to the Nietzschean conclusion would become a monster. Yet it must be possible to reject this praise of people who become monsters without at the same time giving up our heroic virtues. It must be possible to affirm the self-love of the noble soul without becoming hard-hearted egomaniacs. There must be a way for us, too, to say that what is done for love goes beyond good and evil.

§ 108. Heroic Virtue in The Shire

At last, we have arrived at the twentieth century. Despite the glorious fire-storms of Romanticism, the Enlightenment vision of an ordered, rational world won out in the end. We have astronomy and physics to tell us about the origin and nature of the world, and we have evolutionary biology to describe the origin of humanity and of life. We have parliamentary democracy, independent courts of law, and free capitalist markets to organize our society. These are the hallmarks of our own 'Age of Reason'. But we too have our resurgences of virtue. We have our own mythological stories where portraits of heroes are painted for us, and models of excellence are upheld.

In the 1930's, J.R.R. Tolkien started writing *The Lord of the Rings*, the first fantasy novels of modern times. They were published in 1954 and 55. Around the same time his friend C.S. Lewis began publishing the *Chronicles of Narnia*. Both were well versed in the sagas and epics of the Celts, the Greeks, the Anglo-Saxons, and others. (Hence why in *The Hobbit*, Bilbo steals a cup from a dragon's treasure-hoard: it echoes a similar event in the story of *Beowulf*.) And both authors were was dismayed that England had no indigenous mythology of its own. The tales of King Arthur may seem distinctively English, but Tolkien regarded them as Norman-French, because of the language in which they were first written. Tolkien and his friends therefore decided to create an indigenous English mythology themselves. There were other forces at work, however. The United Kingdom at the time was the largest empire the world had ever known. In terms of the territory it controlled and the number of people who lived under its rule, there has been nothing like it before or since. But the First World War stretched its resources thin, and killed almost an entire generation of its young men. Tolkien was himself a soldier in the trenches of the Great War, and saw its terrors first-hand. Furthermore, industrialization and urban sprawl was rapidly taking over the English landscape. This made Tolkien and Lewis and many of their associates fear that the magic of 'Merry Old England' might be lost forever. They were determined to create a literature that would save as much of it as possible before it all disappeared.

The beginning of *The Fellowship of the Ring* reads like a children's fantasy. But from about the time that Frodo and his three companions leave the Shire, it suddenly becomes a very adult story. The Ring of the Dark Lord has been discovered. His servants and spies are out looking for it, and the Ring itself *wants* to be found. What the Ring ultimately represents is *power*, but not a type of power, nor an amount of power; nor is it an allegory for some type of technology.[154] The Ring represents *power without responsibility*. Its basic function is to make its wearer invisible. It enables one to act without revealing himself, without being accountable to anyone. After all, while invisible, no one could see you and demand an account of your actions. Would such power ultimately corrupt you? Would you be able to resist it? What kind of person *could* resist it? These are some of Tolkien's questions. Indeed Tolkien revealed in a letter to a friend that part of the reason he wrote The Lord of the Rings was "the elucidation of truth and the encouragement of good morals in this real world".[155]

The virtues of Hobbits, then, although they are not great warriors, nor counted among the very wise, may be worth looking at. The first thing Tolkien tells us about Hobbits is that they live in holes in the ground. But hobbit-holes are well appointed, clean and dry, with decorated front gardens and with wood-paneled interior walls. They are so well melded into the landscape that they look like natural hills. A symbiotic, unobtrusive, and loving relationship with the landscape is affirmed here. There is an easy continuity between what is wild and what is cultivated, between areas designated for labour and areas designated for play. Every character, every landscape, every city and town, indeed every rock and tree, has a history, and sometimes a voice as well. The incredibly detailed description of The Shire is a message about the virtues: it is about what environment is best suited for the kind of life Tolkien regarded as happiest. Moreover, The Shire is modeled on the "Home Counties" and "West Country" of England as Tolkien remembered them as a child. Having personally visited these areas, I like to think I understand what he had in mind. It is a landscape of gently rolling low hills, with friendly-looking fields for crops or for grazing animals separated by wide hedgerows, and occasional thickets of tall old trees. The whole of the landscape is a garden.

Hobbits live uncomplicated yet pleasant lives: "they love peace and quiet and good tilled earth: a well-ordered and well-farmed countryside was their favourite haunt." (*Fellowship*, pg. 17) Their unique talent among the people of Middle Earth is the ability to find delight and pleasure in simple things: gardening and farming, smoking 'pipe-weed', singing pub-songs, and especially eating and drinking. They have "long and skilful fingers" with which to make "useful and comely things" (*Fellowship*, pg. 19). Their clothing is simple yet handsome and brightly coloured. Generosity is important to them: the story begins at Bilbo's one hundred and eleventh birthday party where it is the custom for the celebrant to *give* birthday gifts rather than receive them. Furthermore, Frodo's sword and armoured shirt, Sam's rope, Aragorn's ancestral sword, the phial containing the Light of Ëarendil, and other treasures which turn out to be indispensable for the victory, are all gifts from friends. There is so little criminal activity among Hobbits that most of them do not lock their doors at night. And as Sam says, "no hobbit has ever killed another on purpose in the Shire" (*Return*, pg. 347). The virtue of generosity is affirmed here. It is therefore no accident that the Ring of Power, unlike other treasures in the story, is *stolen* by Sméagol, not given to him as a gift. And of the characters who ever carried the Ring, only the most honourable and good-hearted are able to give it away (Bilbo Baggins and Samwise Gamgee, for instance) or able to decline it as a gift (like Gandalf and Galadriel).

A hobbit's instinct for cheerfulness manifests itself no matter what the situation. Even after Merry and Pippin were abducted by Orcs and carried roughly to Isengaard, they were found at the gates by their friends relaxing and enjoying some pipe-weed as if right at home. When King Théoden engages them in conversation, Gandalf interrupts him, saying: "These hobbits will sit on the edge of ruin and discuss the pleasures of the table, or the small doings of their fathers, grandfathers, and great-grandfathers, and remoter cousins to the ninth degree, if you encourage them..."[156] This instinct cannot be repressed, not even by the worst circumstances. When Sam and Frodo are crossing the plain of Gorgoroth, in Mordor, the most blighted and harsh landscape imaginable, Sam looks up to the sky and finds something beautiful:

> There, peeping among the cloud-wrack above a dark tor high up in the mountains, Sam saw a white star twinkle for a while. The beauty of it smote his heart, as he looked up out of the forsaken land, and hope returned to him. For like a shaft, clear and cold, the thought pierced him that in the end the Dark Shadow was only a small and passing thing: there was light and high beauty for ever beyond its reach. (*Return*, pg. 238)

Hobbit optimism, as this moment of beauty shows, is connected to endurance and stalwart perseverance. Even in the most desperate and dangerous times, a hobbit stubbornly *finds* reasons to be hopeful. He'll *invent* a reason to be hopeful, if he has to. In this way we know the Hobbit character, while simple, has an inherent maturity and goodness.

The fundamentally good-natured Hobbit disposition is part of the reason why Bilbo, Frodo, and Sam are able to resist the corrupting influence of Sauron's Ring. Tom Bombadil is totally immune to it: he can flip it in the air as if it is a toy, see through the invisibility it confers on Frodo, and nothing happens when he himself puts it on. The Ring has nothing to offer him: as his wife Goldberry says, Tom is already "Master of wood, water, and hill". (*Fellowship* pg. 172) His 'mastery' is not the domineering over-lordship sought by Sauron, the Dark Lord. Rather, he is master of the world because he *loves* the world, and so the world loves him in return. Tom delights in being alive and receives his life as a great gift, and wants nothing more than what he already has. And like a hobbit he is a generous gift-giver: when we first meet him, he is bringing a bouquet of flowers to his wife. He is Tolkien's portrait of the perfectly happy man.

Other characters are not so pure, and so the Ring is able to seduce them. Boromir, although he is a good man, is totally unable to understand why the Ring should be destroyed. Thus he wants to use it to defend Gondor against Sauron's army. His suggestion is of course rejected, and he says no more of it until he follows Frodo into the forest near Amon Hen. There he asks to use it again, but by then his motives have become more selfish. "It is not yours save by unhappy chance," he tells Frodo. "It might have been mine. It should have been mine. Give it to me!" (*Fellowship*, pg. 519). This attempt to steal the Ring costs him his life, although he redeems himself partially by admitting his mistake to Aragorn, and by trying to protect Merry and Pippin.

When Sméagol first encounters the Ring, he kills his friend Déagol to get it. Then he flees, ostracizing himself as a murderer, away from all social contact. The Ring slowly transforms him into the cave-dwelling creature named for the coughing noise he makes: "Gollum, Gollum!". The nine Nazgul, the servants of Sauron who hunt for the Ring, became the twisted, ghostly creatures that they are precisely because they let their lust for power consume them. They are symbols for how the craving for unlimited power can cause the loss of one's humanity.

It is significant, then, that when Galadriel refuses to let Frodo give the Ring to her, she says "I shall diminish, and go into the West, and remain Galadriel." (*Fellowship* pg. 475) The Terrible Queen she would become if she took the ring, however beautiful and strong, is not her true character. Indeed she is already beautiful and strong, just as she is, and she recognizes how the Ring would turn those qualities into something corrupt. By rejecting the Ring, therefore, she remains *herself*.

§ 109. Heroic Virtue at Hogwart's School

As a final example of a resurgence of heroic and classical Virtue in the twentieth century, let us look at J.K. Rowling, and the *Harry Potter* series of fantasy novels. The virtues which she portrays in the main characters, like Hermione's intelligence and drive, Ron's loyalty and perseverance, Harry's extraordinary courage, would find a ready home in any of the Heroic sagas. There is friendship, for instance between Harry and his mentors Dumbledore and Hagrid, and with Ron, Hermione, and Neville, his friends. There is Justice, for example in the pranks that Fred and George Weasley pull on Dolores Umbridge, the Ministry-appointed Inquisitor who turned Hogwarts into an Orwellian police state. There is integrity, as when Harry sticks to his story of how Cedric Diggory died, even though the Ministry of Magic and the wizard-community newspapers all painted him as a liar, and destroyed his reputation. Dolores Umbridge physically tortured him, and he still kept his word. Indeed in Harry's world the cultivation of Heroic virtue is veritably institutionalized. When new students arrive at Hogwarts School, they are first sorted into their Houses by a magical talking hat. Each of the Houses is known for a group of related virtues. Hufflepuff is the house of persevering and patient workers. Ravenclaw is home to the sharpest and brightest minds. Slytherin, ostensibly the House of those who have 'pure blood', prizes cunning, ambition, and willpower. And Gryffindor holds honour and courage in high esteem. These are not the only instances of Virtue-thinking in the series. Rowling occasionally puts wisdom-teachings into the mouths of her characters. Harry's foster-father Sirius Black spoke of justice when he said, "If you want to know what a man's like, take a good look at how he treats his inferiors, not his equals."[157] Dumbledore spoke of moral development and the priority of character when he criticized House Slytherin's obsession with racial purity: "You place too much importance... on the so-called purity of blood! You fail to recognize that it matters not what someone is born, but what they grow to be!"[158]

Some of the principles of Heroic virtue have an important place in the series. In *The Goblet of Fire*, after the death of Cedric Diggory, Dumbledore tells the students of Hogwarts School to follow Cedric's noble example:

> Lord Voldemort's gift for spreading discord and enmity is very great. We can fight it only by showing an equally strong bond of friendship and trust. Differences of habit and language are nothing at all if our aims are identical and our hearts are open... Remember Cedric. Remember, if the time should come when you have to make a choice between what is right, and what is easy, remember what happened to a boy who was good, and kind, and brave, because he strayed across the path of Lord Voldemort. Remember Cedric Diggory.[159]

This passage is distinct as it cites several Heroic principles. Friendship and trust, as defenses against wickedness, are affirmed. Apotheosis, the re-telling of someone's life-story after the person dies, is Cedric's reward for his goodness, kindness, and bravery. It may seem an empty reward, since he had to die to earn it. But in *The Order of the Phoenix* his memory helped inspire the students to create 'Dumbledore's Army', and stand up to the powers of darkness as Cedric did. His spirit, one could say, therefore lived on.

Similarly, there is a place in Harry's world for the Classical virtues. One of the most important moments in the first Harry Potter book, *The Philosopher's Stone*, is the hero's encounter with a magical artifact called 'The Mirror of Erised'. Listen to Dumbledore describe what it does.

> "The happiest man on earth would be able to use the Mirror of Erised like a normal mirror, that is, he would look into it and see himself exactly as he is. Does that help?"
>
> Harry thought. Then he said slowly, "It shows us what we want... whatever we want..."
>
> "Yes and no," said Dumbledore quietly. "It shows us nothing more or less than the deepest, most desperate desire of our hearts. You, who have never known your family, see them standing around you. Ronald Weasley, who has always been overshadowed by his brothers, sees himself standing alone, the best of all of them. However, this mirror

will give us neither knowledge or truth. Men have wasted away before it, entranced by what they have seen, or been driven mad, not knowing if what it shows is real or even possible."[160]

This is a highly sophisticated message about the virtue of Temperance. 'The happiest man on earth' is the one who finds his life perfect and fulfilling just as it is, and so has no need of anything more. The word 'Erised', after all, is 'desire' spelled backwards. The mirror reminds me of the many warnings against the pursuit of material wealth to be found in classical Greek and Roman philosophers. Similar messages can be found in Eastern writings such as the Vedas, the Upanisads, and the Dhammapada. Indeed the mirror reminds me of Tom Bombadil, from Tolkien's fantasy. Harry is then told that the mirror will be moved, and he is warned not to go looking for it again. "It does not do to dwell on dreams and forget to live," says Dumbledore.[161] This piece of wisdom is somewhat ironic, as it appears in a fantasy novel—precisely an escape from reality into a world of dreams. But perhaps a fantasy is an excellent place to express an idea like that.

In any portrayal of Virtue, even in fantasy literature, there will normally be a 'chief virtue', a quality that stands out above the others. It will show us how to tell the difference between a virtue and a vice. In the Heroic age, the social order served that purpose, and the chief virtue was Honour, the quality for which you earn the respect of your peers. To writers in the classical age, and the Renaissance, the chief virtue was Reason. For Romantic writers, it seems to be the sincerity of one's passion and the beauty of one's creative works. In Harry Potter's world, the virtues embodied by the main characters are, for the most part, those which they need to defeat the evil wizard You-Know-Who, and his servants. But there is more to it than that. In *The Half-Blood Prince* Harry learns of a prophesy that apparently ties his destiny to his greatest enemy. Dumbledore tries to help Harry understand that his *ability to love* sets him apart. At first Harry is dismissive, but he quickly realizes the importance of this quality.

It was, he thought, the difference between being dragged into the arena to face a battle to the death and walking into the arena with your head held high. Some people, perhaps, would say that there was little to choose between the two ways, but Dumbledore knew – and so do I, thought Harry, with a rush of fierce pride, and so did my parents – that there was all the difference in the world.[162]

Later, in *The Deathly Hallows*, Harry finds he must put this realisation into action. Near the end of the story, the Dark Lord attacks Hogwart's Castle with an army. Harry knew that if he presented himself to the Dark Lord, the attack will end and his friends will be safe, but the Dark Lord would kill him. Yet Harry accepted that to defeat the Dark Lord and save his friends, he must sacrifice himself, and die. The last treasure he required to help him defeat the Dark Lord is not given to him until he acknowledges this. He unlocked the Golden Snitch and discovers the third Deathly Hallow hidden within it by whispering to it the words "I am about to die". A moment later, the half-ghostly shades of his parents Lily and James, and his friends Sirius and Lupin, appear before him. Harry understands that he is about to join them. "He was not really fetching them: they were fetching him."[163] They protect him from the Dementors until he is able to face the Dark Lord directly, and he gains from their presence the extra measure of strength and confidence to go on. In this way Harry grasps the Heroic idea of the Last Chance, by which heroes strive to preserve their honour and do the noble thing right to the very end. In Harry's case, the ability to love is the wellspring of his nobility and honour. It is the engine of his courage, and the binding force of his friendships. It enables him to take control of his own destiny, regardless of whatever the prophesy may have said. This ability to love is presented not simply as a force that protects the characters from evil, as when Harry was an infant. It is also an inherently worthwhile quality in its own right. It assures him of *the preservation of his sense of self-worth*: and therefore enables the characters to do heroic things.

Similarly, You-Know-Who's *inability* to love is the root of his evil. In *The Half-Blood Prince*, Harry and Dumbledore explore the Dark Lord's childhood, to try and guess what his next moves might be. We see a very detailed portrait of his progress from a strong willed but troubled child to the tyrant he became. We see how his family neglected him; we see his resistance to being tied to others, even in friendship; and we see his dislike of being 'ordinary' (hence why he changed his name from the rather mundane Tom Riddle to the more impressive Lord Vol—er, you know.) We see how he comes to enjoy exercising power over others, especially inflicting misery and pain on others. We see how he even takes 'trophies' from the other children at his orphanage: a yo-yo, a thimble, and a mouth-organ.[164] The objects had no special significance except for the fact that he caused other children misery by stealing and keeping them. Rowling's message is that wicked people like him are not born. Rather, they are *created* by their circumstances and their choices. There are no natural born killers. To fight them, one must also understand them; and ensure that in the course of fighting them, one does not become like them. And this, too, seems a startlingly mature message for a book that is presented to the world as a children's fable.

The effect this fable has on children is overwhelmingly positive. When children who enjoy the stories re-enact them as part of their games, they also re-enact the courage and integrity of the main characters. They don't just role-play being wizards and witches: the also identify with one of the four Houses, and they role-play the virtues of that house. I have seen my own nieces and nephews doing this many times. (One of my nieces placed a woolen touque on my head and declared that I was Sorted into House Ravenclaw!) Although they are involved in a child-level role-play game, they are also learning what it is to be strong and brave, and learning what reasons and circumstances rightly call for strength and bravery. In short, they are learning how to be Virtuous.

There is much more to see in each of the times we have visited in this grand tour of the origin of Virtue. Similarly, there are so many other places that we could have visited, where the virtues took root. But perhaps it is best to bring this long historical narrative to a close. The story of Virtue, of course, will go on. Our Virtues will surely change in the future, just as they changed over time in the past. But I am certain that the biggest part of the future of Virtue will be in the 'new mythology' of Harry Potter, the Lord of the Rings, the Chronicles of Narnia, Star Wars, and so on. This is the form that heroic mythology takes in our time. I'm convinced that as Virtue moves forward, the artists and storytellers will lead the way.

FIFTH MOVEMENT:

THE CALLING OF THE IMMENSITY

§ 110. The Ancient Problem

At the heart of human life beats an ancient impulse. *We desire to know who and what we are.* We wish to discover ourselves, to examine our powers and our limitations. We want to explore the ways we reach for greatness and the ways we fall to wretchedness. We wish to know what we have the potential to become. I call this a *problem* since the matter of who and what we are is not always very obvious. But it is not like the problems of repairing engines or of programming computers. It is more like the problems involved in mountain climbing, house building or portrait painting. A human being is a creature capable of knowing itself. But this self-knowledge is obtained through an enquiry: that is, we ask questions, conduct experiments, observe the results of various challenges and conflicts, and we draw conclusions. A human being is a creature capable of posing itself as a field of enquiry: indeed, while we can claim to know ourselves, we can also claim that we do not know ourselves. We are a type of creature that can claim to be mysterious to itself. In the very adventure of self-discovery, our own souls appear to escape us. And why is this? How can this be possible? Such is the essence of the ancient problem.

What could be a more natural starting place for the examination of virtue? And yet, what could be more *unnatural?* In my ordinary attitude toward life, I do not question that I know who I am any more than I question that I exist at all. I couldn't carry out any of my practical affairs if I did not presuppose my own identity and existence as a given fact of reality. This remains true even as I change through the course of my life: growing up and growing older, for instance. In our ordinary lives we are engaged in all sorts of ordinary activities—jobs, games, hobbies, careers, and so on—that do not need to be spiritual to be successful. And most of the time, we can make good moral decisions very quickly, in a straight-forward Utilitarian way: "harm none, and do what you will", for instance.

It is normally very easy to see what actions will benefit people, what actions harm them, why it is right to do the former, and wrong to do the latter. And much of the time, that is all we need to know to get through life successfully.

But once in a while, something strange may happen. A circumstance may arise in which it is not clear what the right choice is, and also not clear how the right choice should even be made. These situations cannot be resolved in a utilitarian way: not only because the consequences of one's choices might be unclear, but also because what is at stake is more than just the consequences. A situation may arise in which your sense of self-worth, and direction, your world-view, indeed the very purpose of your life, stands at a threshold. In most people's lives these situations arise rarely: perhaps only once a year, perhaps once in a lifetime. We might not immediately recognise them for what they are. But when they appear, they are often unavoidable. Once in a while, people find themselves in situations where they are almost inevitably bound to ask questions about what they should be doing with their time on earth. They are forced to re-consider who they are, what they believe to be the purpose and meaning of their lives, or even what it is to be human. I believe the origin of the good and beautiful life is in the encounter with that kind of situation. Indeed, the origin of virtue itself, I believe, is in *the dynamic meeting between our ideas of who we are, and the various events and experiences that call those ideas into question.* Such situations tend to become the launch platform for a journey of self discovery. This can be true no matter where the destination may be—and even if there should be no final destination at all, but an ongoing adventure. We begin to question ourselves, and produce answers to guide our lives, when confronted with a presence or a situation that seems, at least at first, to break our regular expectations of the way things are. I shall call this kind of situation *The Immensity*.[165]

Allow me to explain. Ordinary life is characterised by familiarity and safety. When we are living in a familiar world, things appear to us only inconspicuously: they are recognised for what they are and how we may use them, and then we can instantly turn our attention on to something else. In the ordinary world, we take almost everything for granted. We usually look closely and honestly at things only when they break down. When your bicycle is working properly, you forget about the mechanics of gears and ball bearings. When the trains are running on time, you don't care about the workings of the diesel engine. When familiar things do not conform to our expectations, suddenly they become conspicuous: they stand out, they call attention to themselves. The Immensity is like that. But it asserts itself on a larger scale, and with a deeper significance. The Immensity confronts us with the possibility that *the world itself* may be changing, in some great or small way. It therefore invites difficult questions about who we are, what we are doing with the whole of our lives, or what we think our purpose or place is. It may appear to be enormous, awe-inspiring, and powerful, it may also appear to be dangerous, life-threatening, even terrifying. An Immensity fixes our gaze upon itself: it has this power to compel our attention. It may seem to *subordinate us*, and make us feel insignificant, frail, transient, and small. The Immensity is the unexpected, the mysterious, the strange: so it is often a bringer of tension, doubt, and uncertainty. It is an experience or event in response to which it is not immediately clear what to do, or even how to decide what to do. It therefore surprises us, and so pushes us out of the ordinary and familiar world. It forces us to confront things about ourselves that sometimes we may not wish to confront.

Finally, may I say that the motto written above the gateway to divine knowledge, "Know Yourself", is an *ethical* requirement: it tells us to *do* something. That this statement was inscribed above the door to the most important temple in the ancient world implies that to follow it is something like a religious undertaking. So an appropriate response to it may be similarly spiritual in nature. At Delphi, the Immensity which summoned the seeker to self-knowledge was the Pythian Oracle, a deity embodied in a human priestess. With the Oracle as my precedent, I too shall claim that the Immensity is something spiritual. Yet I shall claim the Immensity is a feature of the embodied world. It is not a transcendent presence, to be seen only through intellectual contemplation, or through trance-ecstasy, or with the use of psychic senses, or drugs, or by the soul after the body has died. If it is a divinity, then it is an *immanent* divinity. It will soon need to be asked what we have in us which enables us to respond, and what an excellent response is like. But first it must be asked, just what is the Immensity? What makes the encounter with it an occasion for virtue?

§ 111. Time

Imagine, for a moment, that you are alone in an art gallery, standing in front of your favourite painting. First of all you place yourself just the right distance away from it, to be able to see all of the painting at once, so that just the painting and nearly nothing else fills your field of view. You relax your attention, so that things may catch your eye as if of their own accord. Your eyes trace the main shapes, colours, and figures that interest you. Your attention goes from one to the other, in the sequence that is perhaps suggested by the shapes and figures themselves. Then you might step forward a little to examine a detail or two. You might read the caption on the wall beside the painting to learn a little about the artist, the circumstances in which the painting was created, the technique the artist used, and perhaps something about why the genre or subject matter is important. Then you step back again to take another look at the whole picture. The imagination begins to play on the canvas, and you find yourself wondering what the human figures are saying or what their next move might be. In a landscape painting we imagine ourselves moving in the environment, touching the trees or buildings, feeling the wind on our face. If the painting is abstract, we imagine how the shapes and colours might move if they were somehow animated, like the fragments of coloured glass in a kaleidoscope. With your attention relaxed, more details catch your eye which were in the background. You might step closer again to examine them. Then you might take one last step back to take in the whole image once again, to embed it in your memory, before moving on to the next picture.

The experience of the sacred, the presence of the Immensity, is very much like that. It too has details and relations which we can examine and discover. Part of the attraction of the Immensity is precisely the way in which its details and relations compel our interest. This occurs in part because when we encounter an Immensity, as when we enjoy art, we adopt a new relationship to *time*. The activity of looking at works of art and enjoying them is a *temporal* activity. Everything about the experience of a good work of art, all the looking in, looking back, and so on, are time-extended activities. But the time that passes in this experience is *not ordinary time*, that is, it is not the time of clocks and calendars. Someone else might click a stopwatch and measure how long it took for me to enjoy the painting. But I myself, immersed in the painting, have forgotten all about stopwatches. Ordinary time is suspended, and a kind of internal sense of time takes over, a conception of time which is a function of intentionality, or one's own consciousness. It is a sense of time that exists only in the present moment, the "now" of a first-person narrative. Yet it is tied in with recollections of the past and anticipations of things to come. The spiritual experience is similar. It too cannot be contained in minutes, hours, and seconds. In the presence of the Immensity ordinary time seems suspended, held in check, made to wait. Then sacred time takes over.

Ordinary time is measured using definite units, like hours, days, months, and years. These units enable people to co-ordinate their activities with others, make schedules and promises, and get a variety of things done. For other purposes, we view time as a series of occasions and events. These events are not necessarily measured with clocks and calendars, but still regarded as discreet units that follow one another in a linear sequence. This is the time of turns in a game, of conversations at a party, and so on. We need to have this way of accounting time in order to function. Suppose I need to get a train from Galway to Dublin today. If I suspend my everyday attitude towards time, I would question the meaning of the schedule, and the train would leave the station without me. If the engineer suspended his ordinary attitude towards time, the train would never leave the station. This ordinary attitude towards time also provides a straightforward and useful response to the requirement to "Know Yourself". Personal identity over time, in this ordinary way of thinking, is a sequence of events, such as physiological changes or psychological experiences, all connected to each other in a linear continuity. I point to a photo of myself as I was twenty years ago, and say it is "me", because that image is psychologically and physically connected to who I am now. That continuity of transformation forms one part of the unity of my life from birth to death.

But when an Immensity calls one's life into question, this ordinary way of understanding personal identity no longer seems to fit the case. Your job, your social place, your home town, and so on, become theoretically separate from the problem of *who you are*. While in the presence of the Immensity, things are still happening: you are looking up and looking around, holding your breath with wonder, expressing astonishment or amazement, perhaps giving thanks for being there. Like observing a work of art, the seeker steps closer to examine a detail, and then steps back to see the whole. She becomes curious, asks questions, and makes judgements. Time is still happening, but there is no clock or calendar which can measure it. The time of the clock is suspended and another kind of time takes over, a sacred time, a time that bridges the distance between the seeker who faces the Immensity in the present, and the early morning when the world was born. This time is measured in breaths and heartbeats, and counted in moments and in lifetimes. We might look back on the experience and fit it into the history of our lives, for instance by saying that the revelation appeared at a certain stage of our life, or at a certain time of day or year. But in the moment itself, the ordinary way of accounting for time does not seem like the *right* way.

Ancient monuments, buildings, landscapes and seascapes, and the constellations of stars in the sky, can look as if they have existed unchanged forever. They do not appear to be subject to the transformations of time. We therefore implicitly understand them as utterly unlike ourselves. In antiquity, the power of time to force people to question the significance of their lives was discovered through astronomy. Time was connected to the steady movement of stars, planets, and the sun. The stars were once thought to be immune to time: everything 'above the sphere of the moon' was unchanging and eternal, without blemish or disturbance, moving with perfect mathematical predictability and geometric elegance—hence, totally unlike ourselves. The sun, whose face appears featureless to us (we need special equipment to see its spots and prominences), is an ancient symbol for the unchanging perfection of the order of the cosmos. The moon, with its detailed face and regularly changing cycles, stands half way between the timeless celestial realm and the temporal world of humankind. Unlike the life of the mountain or the sun and stars, human life is always changing, always in motion, always passing into the future. On a simple level, mountains impress us with the presence of time just because they are ancient. But they may also have features that call forth the presence of time in other ways. For instance, we now know that coastlines and mountains do change: wind, rain, and ocean waves erode them. We also now know that stars do move, as they rotate around the centre of the galaxy at different rates (this is called 'stellar proper motion'). But we have to change our temporal frame of reference to grasp this. We have to think beyond the decades of a human lifetime to the centuries or millennia of geological time and cosmic time. Thinking about the world in such *inhuman* time scales can change the significance we attribute to the facts of our lives. We might suddenly feel smaller, perhaps insignificant, or foolish.

Allow me to relate a personal example. When I first saw the hill of Knock Na Rae, in county Sligo, Ireland, I was very excited. I had been told stories of Maeve of Cruachan, who is buried on a cairn on its summit, since I was a child. I first saw it from the road, and it appeared as if floating above the trees and fields and walls, commanding the territory for miles. The climb up the hill is quite steep in some places, although not exhausting. Though the cairn was visible for long distances from the motorway, at the parking lot and for most of the climb it is invisible, over the ridge, and one doesn't encounter it again until near the summit. And indeed this only adds to the anticipation of reaching it. I had a few minutes alone on the top of the cairn, and despite the roaring wind I found it very peaceful and easy to slide into a timeless condition, as if it would be perfectly natural to find the modern buildings and asphalt roads of sprawling Sligo town replaced by the old fishing village with its horse cart streets and wooden boats. When it was time to go, I didn't want to leave. I felt as if for a short while, I no longer belonged to the twenty-first century.

One way people respond to the Immensity of time is by building monuments. The architecture of some ancient buildings like Newgrange, Stonehenge, the Great Pyramid, the many circles of standing stones in

Ireland and Britain, and so on, are designed to bring celestial perfection of the stars down to Earth. They are built in such a way that light rays from the rising or setting sun on certain special days of the year align with its major entrances and corridors. The solar and astronomical alignment draws down the cosmic order to the human level. Having 'humanized' cosmic space, people become able to 'universalise' themselves. That is to say, the solar and stellar alignments in the sacred buildings provide a human reference to the cosmos, enabling people to think of themselves as belonging to the cosmos. They can feel able to participate in the great immensities which otherwise appear to render them fragile, insignificant, and small.

Another way people respond to the Immensity of time is by story-telling. We craft mythologies of the supposed origin of the world, the beginning of history. This responds to the Immensity of time by human-izing time in a way similar to how architecture humanizes space. The philosopher Paul Ricoeur says,

> ...between the act of narrating a story and the temporal character of human experience there exists a correlation that is not merely accidental but that presents a trans-cultural form of necessity. To put it another way: time becomes human to the extent that it is articulated through a narrative mode, and narrative attains its full meaning when it becomes a condition of temporal existence.[166]

Mythology projects on to the cosmos certain human experiences and realities: birth and death, in particular. Creation stories can be understood as a projection of the experience of sowing crops in the springtime, the birth of animals or of children, the waxing of the moon, the blooming of spring flowers, and so on. Similarly, stories of the harvest of crops, the onset of winter, the death of animals and of people, the setting of the sun in the evening, the waning of the moon, and so on, are projected on to the cosmos in stories of the end of time. Mythology re-casts these experiences in to a 'sacred history', a history in which certain events belong to the past and the future, yet they can not be pinned on a calendar. There are many examples of stories like these. The Biblical stories of the Seven Days of Creation, and the Garden of Eden, and the Second Coming, are part of our popular culture. The Norse had a story about how the world was formed from the body of a giant named Ymir, who was defeated in battle by Odin and his brothers Vili and Ve. There are similar stories of great battles in the origin stories of the Greeks (between the Olympians and the Titans) the Celts (the Tuatha de Dannan and the Fomhoire), and some near-east cultures (The Babylonian myth of Tiamat and Marduk). There are also stories of the end of history, when the primordial chaos returns. The Norse believed that the world would end following a cataclysmic battle called *Ragnarok*. In this battle the world will be torn asunder and most of the gods will die. The few survivors, including only two human beings, will have the task of starting all over again. Interestingly, the gods themselves already know this will happen, and are powerless to stop it. Through their prophetic powers they know how they will die, and they know whose hand will kill them. But they also know they will fight on anyway: in part because of the honour they attributed to a death in battle, and in part because it is consistent with the principle of the Last Chance. Stories like these help people understand where they belong in history. Mythology translates the Immensity of time into human terms: once the universe is so narrated, it need no longer be feared.

It may be tempting to think of certain events in the last hundred years such as terrorist attacks, nuclear bombings, mass deportations, genocide massacres, even environmental disasters, and so on, as signs that something like Ragnarok is about to begin. Conservative Christians and New-Age practitioners alike speak of 'end times' in remarkably similar terms: 'apocalypse' or 'the quickening' followed by 'the Kingdom of Heaven' or 'the Age of Aquarius'. But I claim that this interpretation of history is a profound mistake. The Immensity of time might seem to threaten you with a future of loss and despair. But all it really does is present you with a future of unpredictable change. This presentation calls into question your beliefs about who you are, and the world you live in. The Immensity is not a situation in which some predicted or feared future manifests itself. Rather, it is the situation in which the *mysteriousness* of the future manifests itself. In the normal way we look at time, we may predict that certain broad patterns or trends will continue. But the prediction, no matter how accurate, is the anticipation of the future in the present, and not the actual future. The actual future is always beyond our reach. As soon as it arrives, it becomes the present, and is no longer the future. It is like Rhiannon, the goddess from Welsh mythology who rides her horse slowly and yet cannot be overtaken, no matter how fast she is pursued. It follows that the future itself, the future of real-time history, is always mysterious. It will never be possible to know exactly what will happen. Because the future is unknowable in this way, it may hold anything. It is a world of surprises. It is thus something about which we often have anxiety: all of the suffering, heart-break, and tragedy that has ever happened in the past may yet be ahead of us again. But for the same reason the future may also be looked to with positive hope. All the happiness and goodness which we have ever experienced, or could imagine experiencing, may well be ahead of us too, on a return path to the present time. Pandora's insatiable curiousity compelled her to open the box and inadvertently release everything that is painful and evil into the world. But at the last moment, she also released hope.

§ 112. Greatness

Nietzsche wrote that in the absence of the traditional sources of moral authority, such as divine revelation, natural law, and pure reason, a person's morals can only derive from, and must derive from, his own choices and his own will. He asks, "We have killed god—must we ourselves not become gods?"[167] This is a bit of an overstatement. Many people no longer accept the usual sources of moral authority. But they do not therefore take themselves to be gods. Moreover, certain facts remain, for instance the fact that we live in and with certain limitations on our possibilities. Some of these limits are non-moral in nature, like the physical limits of our bodies. Others are quasi-moral such as the fact that we are social animals. The Immensity is a limit situation of this kind. It casts all monumental acts of egotism, like Nietzsche's Will to Power, into radical doubt. Having done so, it forces you to revisit and change your ideas about who you think you are, and what you think you know about the world you live in.

The Immensity is an experience of something which appears to surpass the reach of human power. Because they appear powerful we become aware of our weaknesses. Because they appear eternal we find our own transience. Rudolph Otto wrote in *The Idea of the Holy* that the most singular property of the spiritual experience is that it shakes us, overwhelms us, makes us feel small, and leaves us changed. This is the greatness of the Immensity. The mountain is larger and older than we are, and so it appears *greater* than we are. We say that a mountain "soars", "towers", "ascends" above us. This is not a fact about the mountain. The mountain itself does not actually move anywhere. It is simply there. And yet it is not really wrong to speak of the mountain that way. The reason here is essentially *phenomenological*. For the mountain's shape draws our attention upward, it makes us look up—we literally tilt our heads upwards—and we experience a conscious or unconscious projection of what it would be like up there. Thus it is the imagination that moves, and then projects the motion to the mountain. With that projection comes certain expectations, such as an expectation of what effort it would take to climb the mountain, and what the world might look like from up there. This expectation is part of our experience of looking at it. We also become aware of how dangerous and risky it would be to try—we become aware of the possibility of failure. To experience the IMMENSITY is to anticipate difficulty, frustration, resistance, and challenge. But it is also to anticipate the joy of success, the amazement of further new discoveries, the pride in one's accomplishments, and indeed the ability to rest.

The experience also directs the seeker's attention beyond appearances. It draws attention past itself to what is not yet experienced, and to what may come after it. The experience of what we can see always comes together with anticipations of what is not yet seen. However much of it is apparent and revealed, there is always the sense of more that is not yet apparent, not yet revealed. The top of the mountain is revealed to an onlooker at its foot, but the view from the top is only available to one who climbs it. The Immensity is marked out most of all by the unseen, the unknowable, the ungraspable, the silent and the dark. This is why we sometimes feel as if we are made small and insignificant in its presence. An ancient Stoic philosopher named Epictitus claimed that limit-situations, situations where we feel ourselves at a loss, are the origin of the whole of philosophy. A creeping awareness of being less than we think we are, of being in a world that is greater than we are, of being bounded and finite, or even weak and powerless—of being *something which can suffer*, forces us to confront our situation, the world, and the way of our lives in it. This is how we hope to find some way to understand and to cope. Hence Aristotle's comment that "those engaged in learning are not at play; learning is accompanied by pain".[168]

As odd and as negative as it may sound, we traditionally turn to religion not just to overcome suffering, but also to impart great dignity to our suffering. Christianity, particularly, transforms suffering itself into liberation and enlightenment. Its central image of inspiration is that of a man torturously dying on a cross. Religion teaches not only how to overcome suffering, but also *how to suffer*. This may seem a very morbid, negative view. But it is un-ignorable: any spiritual life worthy of the name will have to confront human suffering. Whether it takes the form of physical or psychological trauma, unrequited desires or frustrated plans, or conflict with other people, suffering is an integral part of human life. *Spiritual suffering* is what life feels like for someone who does not know who she is, who does not know the meaning and purpose of her life, or her place in the world. Confronted by that kind of suffering, one may feel paralysed by indecision, confused by change, terrified of death. It is the task of the spiritual life to confront this suffering. Most images of ancient pre-Christian deities are happy, sexy, strong, in control of themselves and their surroundings, and accompanied by totemic animals, dramatic landscapes, stars and planets, fertile fruit and crops, heroic weapons and trophies, and so on. The equivalent images today are found in advertising campaigns for cosmetics or sports equipment or foreign holidays. We see ourselves in these images as we often wish to be, and it is on such positive images we normally prefer to dwell. But such images do not do justice to the whole of who we are, nor to the totality of our lives. We cannot escape the IMMENSITY and its character of being greater than ourselves. The image of Cú Chullain, lashed to a standing stone as he dies, is a profound and heart-wrenching picture that depicts us just at the moment the Immensity overcomes us. It depicts us as we sometimes actually are: lonely, weary, dejected, at a loss, and failing. One who ignores or glosses over this part of life does not properly understand life. And a spirituality that does not acknowledge suffering has no right to call itself a spirituality.

But observe the goddess Morrigan, in the form of a raven, standing on Cú Chullain's shoulder. She is a harbinger of death, but her posture suggests that she is standing on guard, ensuring that her death will not be interrupted or profaned. She acknowledges and honours the hero who faces the IMMENSITY and does not shirk from it. The greatness of the Immensity, while forcing us to confront the possibility of weakness and failure, opens the way to strength and success to those who do not back down from it. Even as the greatness of the IMMENSITY overcomes us, we may yet take flight.

§ 113. Authority

The *authority* of an IMMENSITY is twofold. First of all, the Immensity is the sort of reality that is in some sense inevitable. An Immensity cannot be ducked or sidestepped, even if it can sometimes be put off. It is an event or experience which is unavoidable for all of us. No matter who we are, where we live, what our age or sex, our occupation, rank or class, or any other 'accidental' feature in life, one will eventually have to face the Immensity. It is a fixed feature of human existence. However different its manifestation may be from time to time and from person to person, it is nonetheless a universal fact of our lives. It therefore defines and configures life, sets the boundaries of possibility, places limits on power. It is, indeed, the sort of universal fact in terms of which life itself has to be understood and interpreted. It is sometimes fashionable to believe that there are no universals in life. Almost everything we normally call a fact is dependent upon contexts of time, place, language, social order, old habits or traditions, and other factors, in the absence of which some alleged universal truth is either false or unintelligible. This is one of the key principles of a school of recent philosophical thought called postmodernism. But an Immensity is not contingent upon anything. It exists as an inextricable feature of life itself, as a primordial given. When I describe three specific Immensities which I believe are the most fundamental, this will be clearer. For now, let it suffice to say that the authority of the Immensity is firstly the way its appearance is a *destiny* for all of us.

The second aspect of its authority is the way it calls upon you to respond in particular ways. It can be a person, an idea, an institution, a work of art, a sensitive ecosystem—nearly anything which must be treated with a certain special respect. There is a distinction here between authority and power. Power is the ability to compel or to force a certain kind of action. You possess power to the extent that you can do whatever you want to do. Something possesses authority, on the other hand, if it demands a certain kind of response to its presence, even if it cannot enforce that demand. Authority is the rightness, the rationality, the justice, the *beauty* of responding to a certain kind of presence in a certain kind of way. You feel as if you know what it is not just because you look at it, but because it seems to look back at you. The mountain, by itself, does not have any power to make anyone climb it. And yet mountaineers say that the mountain "calls" them, "invites" them to climb it, and that they climbed it "because they had to", or "because it was there". They are not simply being metaphorical: this is part of the structure of their experience. The mountain stands out. A masterwork of art, to take another example, is clearly the product of extraordinary skill: the precision of the technique; the attention to detail; the play of colours, textures, and contrasts; and the honesty of its subject matter. That kind of object demands to be respected. Suppose that instead of hanging it on my wall, I use it as a tablecloth. The painting itself cannot punish me. It does not have that kind of power. Yet somehow I know I have done wrong. Things which stand out like that possess authority in that to properly understand and appreciate them, to know them on their own terms, to get the most out of the experience of their presence, it is necessary to treat them in a special way.

By the way, this quality of the IMMENSITY is also normally and regularly attributed to God. Religious people attribute to God an eternal existence, the power to do anything from sending inspirational dreams to creating the universe. We also attribute to 'him' various laws of personal and public morality. But some of God's laws are not really 'laws' at all. They are more like practical instructions for getting to know 'him' better. They take the form of practices like prayers, meditations, pilgrimages, sacrifices, and so on, the benefits of which are not obvious to someone who does not practice them. Some might say that the benefit of obedience is the reward we would receive in the afterlife. But this seems to miss the point. It is to defer or postpone God's authority to the afterlife, about which we know precisely nothing. The benefit of following God's laws, so the practitioners claim, is 'closeness' or 'grace' or 'peace'; in other words, a *transformed and uplifted experience of life*. One who eschews these practices, so the story goes, will miss the beneficial transformation they provide. It is therefore to punish oneself. The Immensity, of course, is not a transcendental divine being, as God is usually described. It is a presence of the mortal, embodied world, in the here and now. It transcends the individual self; and that is sufficient. My only observation here is that between the traditional claims for God, and my own claims for paintings, mountains, and Immensities, the ethical principle is almost the same. To fail to respond to the authority of the Immensity is also to miss a chance to edify and enrich one's experience of life. To 'disobey' its 'command' is to deprive oneself of a beautiful experience, and in that sense, to punish oneself.

The three main three qualities of the Immensity, which are time, greatness, and authority, characterise the spiritual experience. They distinguish the true spiritual experience from the imaginative fancy. The IMMENSITY is the sort of event or experience that changes one's relationship to time; goes beyond one's own skills, abilities, and powers; and demands a certain response. At least one of these elements, usually the third, is always present in the experience of an IMMENSITY. Because of its ability to make a claim upon you, because of its ability to require a response, the Immensity is a source of value and meaning from beyond the individual self. An Immensity, presenting itself to you from outside the horizon of the familiar, *necessarily presents a value that is not of one's own creation*. This kind of value originating from beyond the self is precisely what Charles Taylor claims is missing from the ethics of modern individualism.

Some readers may think that I have been talking about something that fundamentally cannot be talked about. Certainly, the very idea of an 'Immensity', tied to mystery, resists being described. The suggestion that the Immensity goes beyond ordinary human references for time and space may imply it goes beyond words as well. And it is part of the fashionable wisdom of our age to believe that a spiritual mystery is ultimately unspeakable, inexpressible, indescribable. It is even popularly believed that the spiritual mysteries of the world are permanently beyond human intellectual understanding. I claim that this view is false. To say that a spiritual mystery is unspeakable, impossible to express in words, is already to talk about it. To give the IMMENSITY a name, even a vague or noncommittal name like a 'mystery', or a 'state of being', or a 'spiritual experience' is already to express it in words, already to talk about it, already to have given it a name. It is therefore already to know something about it, and already to understand it in at least that small way.

My view is this. An Immensity is not unspeakable—it is *infinitely speakable*. We can and do talk about our spiritual experiences, especially about the countless ways they manifest. It is just that the IMMENSITY cannot be described *completely*. However much we describe or interpret the situation, there will always be something more to say. Thus we can talk about them *forever*. I take my cue from The Poet, who wrote that the IMMENSITY of love is so deep and wide and large a thing that:

There is nobody wise enough
To find out all that is in it,
For he would be thinking of love,
Till the stars had run away,
And the shadows eaten the moon.[169]

This is what makes an Immensity mysterious: not its opacity but its infinite transparency, not its mystery but its infinite accessibility. It is not that we cannot know anything about an Immensity, but that we can never know all that there is to know. When analytic examination seems to fail us, we normally turn to symbolic or artistic representation, such as poetry or mythological storytelling. Then we continue to talk about it. This is part of its greatness. It is also part of its authority, in that to understand it as fully as possible, it is *necessary* to talk about it, explore it, and respond to it. To do otherwise is to never learn what it has to offer, and hence perhaps to miss a chance to enrich and uplift one's life by responding to it.

Further explanation is still required. I shall therefore take you on a tour of three immensities which I think are universal facts, inescapably destined for all of us. They are: the Earth, Other People, and Death.

§ 114. The Earth

First of all, let us look at the Earth. Have you thought recently about the truth of humanity's relation to the world? You haven't? How surprising. And yet how unsurprising as well. For whatever you are doing, you are standing on the Earth. Whatever you are looking at, you are looking at something in the world. Whatever you are using, working on, or affecting, it is a part of the world. As Ricoeur says, "The Earth here is something different, and something more, than a planet: it is the mythical name of our corporeal anchoring in the world."[170] The Earth is the ground, the foundation, the very *prerequisite* for our being. But we have all become used to this fact. We hardly mention it anymore. But once in a while, the Earth can appear as something immense, something capable of making us feel small and at a loss. While I was living in Newfoundland, I met a retired fisherman who told me that he never went to Mass again after having weathered out a sea storm in his fishing boat. This was not because the experience made him question the existence of God, but rather because, in his words, "the waves of that sea taught me more about God than anything the priest ever said in Mass. The huge rollers sure make you small, make you feel mortal. I think it is good for a man to feel that way sometimes." I think this fisherman's chance remark indicated that he understood something important about the Immensity, which is that it alters the perspective you have of yourself.

The Earth can appear as an IMMENSITY even in circumstances that are not actively threatening and dangerous. While living in the west of Ireland I spent a great deal of time walking on the Arran Islands, with their great cliffs that overlook the ocean. I felt troubled by the unreachable horizon: that 'place' that does not exist but nonetheless can be seen in the distance. A horizon is ungraspable. You can sail toward it but you will never reach it. The cliff edge itself, with its dangerous crags, made everything feel heightened, as if every choice was a matter of life and death. It seemed almost as if inviting me to throw myself over the edge, and leave the world behind. Sometimes I felt as if such a leap would be easy, and perhaps even beautiful. But the deadly cliff and the ungraspable horizon also made me feel greatly privileged to be alive, and blessed that such magnificent sights should be revealed to me. I felt close to the ancient Celtic people, my ancestors, who once had so many adventures on the same landscape.

The Earth is the first and foremost of the great Immensities. There are two reasons for this. One is just that the plain fact of existing in the world, having been born into it, being alive in it, is by itself enormously profound. "The world is all that is the case" says Wittgenstein, as the very first premise of his whole philosophy of knowledge.[171] He could have added, "And nothing *less*." For this plain fact alone can be enough to fill one's mind with excitement. Whatever we touch, see, know, or talk about, it is part of the world. Whatever magical or transcendent Other-worlds we might believe exist, it is only through representing them in the mortal world, only through our experiences in the embodied world, that we can imagine them at all. More importantly, the embodied world is where all of our possibilities, opportunities, challenges, and aspirations take place. Whatever else one may believe about after-life worlds, spiritual parallel dimensions, Platonic realms of intellectual purity, nevertheless the embodied world is our present home.

And what a home it is! The second reason that the Earth is the foremost of Immensities is that the Earth is a planet of extraordinary and wonderful variety. On Earth we find sharp mountain crags and flat prairie expanses; hot heavy jungles and cold arctic glaciers; stormy seas and dry deserts; and everything and anything in between. And they are all in motion, all constantly changing in great or small ways. As Heraclitus said in the 6th century BCE, "no one can step into the same river twice". However much you may think you know the world, it will always be slightly different than what you expect. It will always surprise you. And there will always be more to explore. For the most part, we need to travel the world to experience the surprise of its diversity. But it is often the case that one need not travel far to come to a place that is very different from the place you departed. You can plan in advance, by reading maps, weather reports, and traveler's tales, but that is no substitute for being there.

One may believe that we will discover who and what we are in some other, higher spirit-realm. One might even believe that a higher spiritual realm is where we truly belong. In that belief there is a denial of the body, a denial of the Earth, a denial of the here-and-now, and therefore a denial of the greater part of who and what we are. For in a world of pure spirit, such as that imagined by Plato, disembodied and immaterial, we are not whole. Our physical, embodied being-in-the-world is an IMMENSITY with irreducible, un-ignorable authority. It is in the embodied world, it is here on Earth, where life happens. By 'the Earth', then, I mean the planet on which we live, with its lands, seas, and skies. But I also mean the place where we find our home, where we live and dwell, where all of our possibilities find expression, which is both the soil of your home town and also the stars of outer space. The Earth is not an immaterial world, known only to the mind, or to the disembodied spirit described by visionaries. The Earth is the field and stage of life, where the work and the play of life is performed. It is the platform from which any great journey of spiritual transcendence is launched.

With this basic account in mind, there remain two primary ways of thinking about the Earth. First of all, there is the image of the Earth as a benevolent provider. On Earth we find food, building materials, sources of fuel and energy, space to build homes and to run and play, places of outstanding beauty which appeal to our thoughts and emotions. Everything necessary for the fullness of life, from our most basic material needs to our most complex emotional and intellectual needs, is found in the Earth. Thus many ancient people imagined the Earth as a living being, a Goddess, who loves humanity and provides for our needs out of a sense of generosity. In terms of the history of ideas, this may be the first attempt to understand the world in a comprehensive, systematic way. We started to tell stories about Earth goddesses, and these stories served to explain why things are the way they are. As an example of this idea from a Heroic society, here is a passage from the *Prose Edda*, the ancient account of the mythology of the Norse:

> One of the earth's features is that, when the high mountains are dug into, water springs up, and even in deep valleys it is not necessary to dig down any further for water. The same is true in animals and birds, whose blood is equally close to the surface on the head and feet. A second characteristic of the earth is that grass and flowers bloom every year, but in the same year everything withers and drops off. So it is with the animals and the birds. The third characteristic of the earth is that when it is opened or dug into, grass grows over the soil that is closest to the surface. People think of rocks and stones as comparable to the teeth and bones of living creatures. Thus they understand that the earth is alive and has a life of its own. They also know that, in terms of years, the earth is wondrously old and powerful in its own nature. It gives birth to all living things and claims ownership over all that dies. For this reason, they gave it a name and traced their origins to it.[172]

Here is an example from Classical Greece, in the writings of Lucretius, in the first century BCE:

> And truly earth deserves her title *Mother*,
> Since all things are created out of earth.
> I repeat, the earth
> Deserves the name of Mother; by herself
> She made the race of men, and in their season
> The breed of beasts, those mountain stravagers,
> The birds of the air in all their variousness.[173]

We may think that this kind of reverence for the Earth as a living being belongs only to Aboriginal or Indigenous societies. But there are earth goddesses in almost every human culture: Ireland's Morrigan, Scandinavia's Freya, Greece's Demeter and Gaia, India's Durga, just to name familiar examples. As the French theologian-philosopher Paul Ricoeur wrote, "...few images in this regard have marked religious humankind more than that of Mother Earth."[174].

The other outstanding way of thinking about the Earth is that of a foreign place from which we human beings are cut off. Much of the Earth is hostile to us: climates of extreme arctic cold or desert heat, for instance. Storms, floods, volcanic eruptions, earthquakes, and other natural disasters can kill us and destroy our settlements. They are occasions that remind us that the world cannot always be regarded as our home. Natural disasters now account for more refugees than political crises, civil wars, and terrorist attacks. The number of people compelled to cross an international border due to an environmental disaster was at the time of writing estimated to be about 25 million people world-wide. That figure is 3 million more than the estimated number of political refugees at the same time. It was also estimated that there will be as many as 150 million environmental refugees by the year 2050.[175] It is not contrary to our experiences to describe nature as uncaring, unforgiving, impersonal, even cruel. We therefore find it necessary to build shelters, houses, and cities, to protect ourselves from its elements. Strong reasons exist for us to think of ourselves as both connected to the Earth and also set apart from it. Between them, it is easy to become uncertain about our place. We do not automatically know which relation to nature is the proper one. The Earth calls our life into question because we are forced to decide what the Earth means for us and how we are to relate to it. This is why some of the earth goddesses in humanity's pantheon are also stern and cruel. The Hawaiian volcano-goddess Pele comes to mind here, as an earth goddess who destroys as well as gives. India's Kali is another well known example: she is the 'terrible mother' who drinks human blood from goblets made of human skulls.

How can we navigate these two apparently opposite ways of thinking about the earth? Is there any reconciliation between them? I think that in different ways they *both* represent an Immensity. In both its capacity to provide and its capacity to destroy, the earth always suggests possibilities beyond what is visible at any given time. Think of it this way. In the realm of one's ordinary attitude, your world may consist in little more than one's dwelling place, one's workplace, a few places of entertainment such as a cinema, sports arena, or a local pub, a few vacation spots, and the homes of various friends and relations. But however large the size of your home world, there is always something beyond the horizon, always an 'outside' that could be explored. *However large the size of your own home world, the totality of the whole world is always greater still.* There are always more places to see and to visit, more mountains to climb, more rivers to course, and more oceans to cross. The world beyond the self is *absolutely vast*, more so than any single person has eyes to see. To obtain complete safety from the hostile elements of the world, we might think it necessary to become masters of the world: and so we cut back the forests, build roads over the mountains, domesticate the wild animals, plant neat rows of harvest crops. This provides a measure of security, and pushes back the boundaries of the unknown, rendering the world more safe, and less of an IMMENSITY. But the totality of the world is always greater than the range of it which we have brought under our control. We shall never become the undisputed masters of the whole Earth.

Today, the total surface area of our planet has been mapped, down to the last square meter. With our aeroplanes, submarines, land vehicles, and with special sensory devices like radar and sonar, there is no place on Earth we cannot explore. The only remaining physical frontier of the unknown is outer space. But having mapped the Earth and the sky, have we made it into our home? Does scientific understanding render things familiar? If we had complete technological control of the world, would we have subdued its hostile side? The answer is still 'no'. Through scientific understanding of the cosmos, we have come to a greater understanding of how foreign and strange the universe it. Here on Earth, the sciences of meteorology, biology, ecology, and so on, have taught us that the world is more complex than we previously imagined. The more we learn, the more we also find how much more there is to learn. Astrophysics has done more than any other science to reveal how extraordinarily *inhospitable* most of the universe is. Outer space is a vast gulf of utter nothingness randomly dusted with the violent nuclear fires we call stars. We may be impressed to discover that the galaxy has hundreds of millions of stars. Far more impressive still are the light-years of empty space between them. The universe is also older in time than the life-span of any human civilisation, and even the life-span of our planet. The vast overwhelming majority of the universe is a cold vacuum: and therefore hostile to human life in an absolute sense. This too is an Immensity.

Confronted with the size, the vastness, the age, and indeed the grandeur of the world, it may seem very natural to feel small and insignif-icant. The very presence of the world calls one's life into question by forcing us to face the possibility that our lives, individually and socially, are of little or no meaning on any grand scheme of things. The totality of the world will always be large enough to reduce our most magnificent artistic, scientific, cultural and philosophical achievements down to a grain of salt on a beach. We are surrounded by the decaying remnants of previous civilisations: every monumental statement of human presence and greatness is trivialised by space, overcome by time, and eventually left in ruins. The thought that the same will come of our own works and deeds, and indeed of our very lives, can be terrifying. Is it still worth our while to do anything? What could help us overcome this terror? By presenting us with such questions, the Earth becomes an IMMENSITY. We are challenged, questioned, tested, and finally invited to respond.

§ 115. Other People.

Our lives are called into question in a different way by the presence of other people. For everyone is in some small or great way mysterious to each other. The ideas, wishes, fears and dreams of our hearts and minds are hidden, secret things. They cannot be grasped by others, nor even seen by others, except in passing moments when the lamplight of the eye gently flickers. But even then, the curtains are only half-drawn. In *A Tale of Two Cities*, Charles Dickens said:

A wonderful fact to reflect upon, that every human creature is constituted to be that profound secret and mystery to every other. A solemn
consideration, when I enter a great city by night, that every one of
those darkly clustered houses encloses its own secret; that every room
in every one of them encloses its own secret; that every beating heart
in the hundreds of thousands of breasts there, is, in some of its
imaginings, a secret to the heart nearest it! Something of the awfulness,
even of Death itself, is referable to this.[176]

Part of the 'secret' is the fact that each of us lives in a private world.
However much you manage to open your mind and heart to another
person, there will always be some part which remains closed. Whatever
you share, there will always be something more which you cannot share.
For no one else can live you life for you. No one can stand in your place,
nor see the world from your point of view. No one can think your thoughts
for you, no one can feel your feelings for you. Your can reach out by
describing your place and point of view to others. But in doing so, the
others do not experience your point of view like you do yourself. They
experience only your description of it, which they take into their world and
make their own. Loneliness, too, is an Immensity. And just as you cannot
open yourself fully to another, no one can open himself fully to you.

Such is the way to understanding other people as an Immensity. The
mysteriousness of other people is that each person is her own person, the
possessor of her own autonomy and free will. And this autonomy, this
ineffable *selfhood*, cannot be grasped by another person. When another
person meets you, she faces you with her own attitudes, her own values,
her own freedom, her own initiative, and her own power. Her intentionality grasps things in your world—including *you*. Therefore we do not
relate to people the same way we relate to ordinary objects. We tend to
look at objects as examples of types or of kinds, to be used in particular
ways. We also look on them as someone's property, as belonging to
someone. Our possessions, when we use them for any purpose, become
like extensions of our bodies. There's no mystery involved in this. When

driving a nail to build a wall, I do not think of the hammer, unless of course it were to fly out of my hands. The nail becomes the centre of my attention, and the hammer 'disappears', becoming like an extension of my arm. When driving a car, the car feels like an extension of my body. We see this in the way that people involved in a car accident do not say, "He hit my car", but rather they say, "He hit me". Now here is the clever bit. Try as we might, and like it or not, it is impossible to do that to other people.

The philosopher Emmanuel Lévinas described this situation in a difficult but memorable pair of books, *Time and the Other,* and *Totality and Infinity.* His general idea is that the encounter with something foreign, something strange, something capable of surprising you or imposing its presence on you, is the logical origin of ethics itself. This is so because, in his words, "The absolutely foreign alone can instruct us".[177] The face of the other person looking at me is just such an absolutely foreign presence. For another person is an autonomous being, freely acting and speaking of her own accord. By her autonomy, generating for herself her own meaning, the face of the other person reduces or denies my power to impose or ascribe meaning to her, or grasp her as my own possession. The face already possesses its own meaning. As Lévinas says, the other person "is not unknown but unknowable":

…the other [person] is in no way another myself, participating with me in a common existence. The relationship with the other is not an idyllic and harmonious relationship of communion, or a sympathy through which we put ourselves in the other's place; we recognise the other as resembling us, but exterior to us; the relationship with the other is a relationship with a Mystery.[178]

The mystery of other people, the "secret" that Dickens said is enclosed in every human heart, makes it impossible to relate to others the same way we relate to ordinary objects. No one can psychologically assimilate another person as an extension of his being, as he can with a hammer or a car. If he could do so, the other person would no longer be 'other' than him, but would become a part of his own being. This is the other person's mystery, but also, as Lévinas would emphasise, the other person's *authority*. The other person, because he is 'other' than ourselves, is able to make demands upon us. This is usually the demand to share one's world and one's possessions. But at the bottom it is the demand for *acknowledgement* as a free and autonomous person.

Lévinas' philosophy of the face goes further: he defines *time itself* as the relationship with the other person. "I do not define the other by the future," he says, "but the future by the other."[179] We can anticipate and predict the future, but that anticipation is a function of the present, not the actual future. The authentic future, like the autonomy of the other person, cannot be grasped. It is what I have called an IMMENSITY. Lévinas says time appears to us through the face of other people.[180] The idea here is that time itself appears to us in the approach of the other person because the other person's freedom and autonomy, and hence unpredictability, constitutes the presence of an unknowable future: you can never be sure what the other person will do next. When we are alone, we are enclosed in our own home world and there are no surprises there. Surprises come from outside; or else they are not surprises. The other person, coming from outside our home world, brings with her the possibility of the unexpected, and thus brings with her the presence of time and the future.

The greatness of the other person is in the total inability to possess her. The only way to even attempt to possess another person is by negating her autonomy; or in simpler language: by killing her. But to destroy something is to lose it, not possess it. One cannot attempt to possess another person's identity and spirit without destroying it. The genuinely free, autonomous, 'other' person has that element of surprise and unpredictability which always exceeds our expectations, in subtle ways or in overwhelming ways. The only way to exert total power over another person is to kill her. But if one were to succeed in murdering her, the very independence and freedom that one sought to possess instantly disappears.

Lévinas is also drawing on the famous 'Dialectic of the Master and Slave', first described in 1806 by Hegel in his *Phenomenology of Spirit*. The idea is that the master needs to acknowledge the autonomy and personhood of the slave in order to receive from the slave the acknowledgement of mastery that he craves. The effect, philosophically speaking, is that they swap positions. Of course, killing is not impossible: some soldiers and some criminals make an occupation of it. But Lévinas' and Hegel's point is that as an act of domination, killing is ultimately futile. Not even a murderer can possess the freedom of another person.

An important critical objection should be raised here. Lévinas says that the face of the other person "forbids murder" and "commands justice". But what about criminals, slave-owners, serial killers, and other kinds of people who obviously do not see other people as possessing moral authority? The face of a slave to his master is not that of one who commands justice. The master views his slaves as his property to whom he gives the orders, and for him the situation can never go the other way around. Similarly, criminals and serial killers view their victims as not-people, and the appearance of a potential victim arouses in them a will to dominate through torture and murder, rather than respect or sympathy. In the light of such observations, Lévinas' argument may seem unrealistic. One way to respond to this objection is to note that it misses the point of Lévinas' philosophy. Lévinas is saying something about the logical origin of ethics, which are the conditions for its possibility. He is saying something like this: Ethics *begins* in the meeting with another person. One is reminded of the Gospel teaching that whenever two or more people meet, God is there. But what Lévinas has in mind is more of an Old Testament idea. Like the prophets and patriarchs of Judaism, the Other Person is always the master, always the authority figure, always the law-giver, and always the judge.

We shall see more of this objection later. I have attempted to summarise and simplify what is a very complex and obscure system of philosophy. But have no fear: the general ideas here are quite intuitive. If one looks another person in the face, one must immediately see her as another free and independent being who cannot be possessed, not even if she is killed. Other people call our freedom into question by being present as something that cannot be possessed. As Lévinas says, "To welcome the Other is to put in question my freedom."[181] Since the other person cannot be possessed, she is the only being one can want to kill. Yet this killing is futile. The futility of murder constitutes the other person's authority: it constitutes *an invitation to enter into a relationship that is not based on power*. It invites one to engage in dialogue, to become friends, and to share one's possessions. For the other person to remain herself, to remain autonomous, to remain 'other' than myself, I must respect her and speak with her as she is. By speaking with her, I welcome her into 'the house of my being' not as an object which I possess but as one to whom I share my possessions. Thus the presence, the gaze and the voice, of another human being, is a spiritual experience.

§ 116. Death.

Ladies and gentlemen, may I present Death, the final Immensity. Death is timeless: there is never a time where there is no death, and so death itself does not die. Death possesses greatness: he stands over all of us, starting just after the moment we are born. Death is authoritative: whatever we may do to resist him or hide from him, he will find us and he will win. Death comes for us all. Sometimes he bides his time and sometimes he surprises us. He temporarily reprieves many of us, but in the end spares no one. He cannot be bargained with, nor can he be bought off. When he does not come to take you, he comes to tell you that some day you will be taken. There must be no quibbling about this. You are going to die. Let's read that again. You Are Going To Die.

You've probably heard this before. But most people do not grasp its full significance. I sometimes think that the amount of time and attention people put to the possibility of life after death, of reincarnation or of immortality in heaven, is a massive distraction device intended to console us and prevent us from having to face death directly and honestly. The same might be said of medical interventions that prolong the lives of people whose brains and bodies have ceased functioning. Certainly this is true of the pseudo-scientific hope that some day we can cheat death by cloning ourselves and then somehow 'downloading' our minds into our clones. The prospect that we are finite and fragile is simply too uncomfortable, too disturbing, too unpleasant. It puts a damper on every party. The pop singer Kylie Minogue announced in May of 2005 that she has breast cancer. In February 2006 Kate Moss received radiation therapy for the same disease. Fame, wealth, and beauty cannot protect you from the things which make life decline.

There is a delicious scene near the end of the Monty Python film, *The Meaning of Life*, which expresses what I have in mind here. Death, in his billowing black cloak, stands in a barren field holding his scythe. There is a wind-blown bare tree beside him, and a stormy grey sky above him. He approaches the camera not by walking forward but by 'appearing' ever closer in a sequence of camera cuts. It is a beautiful piece of film-making. Then he knocks his scythe on the door of a country cottage where a dinner party is in progress. He announces himself in a scratchy voice: "I am the Grim Reaper!" The hostess invites Mr. Death into the house and promptly chastises him for rudely interrupting the party. They do absolutely everything possible to maintain the veneer of polite superficiality and to avoid facing the fact that they are about to die. It's a very funny scene, but it's also rather frightening. And that's the brilliance of the whole film: it lampoons the ridiculous lengths people will go to in order to *avoid* talking about the meaning of life.

As far as scientists have been able to determine, human beings are the only living things on Earth who can be conscious of their own immanent death. Plenty of animals mourn the deaths of their friends and family. Indeed anything that is alive will do things to protect its existence. But only we, it seems, know in advance that all these efforts are ultimately futile. Only we know that some day we will die. But we may take a little bit of comfort in knowing that we've already had plenty of practice. Some of you may have "survived death". You may have been in a situation in which you might have died: a life-threatening disease or a terrible injury. Some of you may have encountered someone who tried to kill you, if you were once a soldier or the victim of a crime. Some of you may have been present when close friends, family members, or beloved companions have died. I have had several experiences like this, with both family relations and close friends. Some of these people died peacefully after a long and excellent life. Some died after a period of chronic suffering and we were happy that the 'passage' put an end to it. One died suddenly when struck by a car. I also knew someone who took her own life. Experiences such as these reveal life's inherent fragility. To be alive is to be *mortal*, which is to be captured by time. It is to be a transient being, a passing and fleeting being. It is to be vulnerable to change, unable to resist change, always exposed to the possibility of being destroyed.

Another thing that appears to be unique to humanity, not shared with other animals, is the creation of art to represent death. Some of our images of death are meant to console us and reassure us. For instance we collect photographs and memorabilia of deceased relatives and friends. Perhaps it offers a promise that the family line will continue in the children, nieces, and nephews. Perhaps it gives a sense that the deceased friends are still present with us. The anthropologist Marvin Harris described a custom among the Dobuan people of the South Pacific, in which the skull of the recently deceased head of a family was kept in an honoured place in the home, given offerings, prayed to for advice and for protection, and addressed as "Sir Ghost".[182] Like our custom of displaying photos of deceased relatives, these honoured skulls would have given people a feeling that their predecessors were still with them. As another, more macabre example, there is a monastery in the town of Sedlic, near Kunta Hora, in the Czech Republic (it was part of Bohemia when founded in 1142) where the interior is decorated almost entirely with human bones. In 1870 the bones from almost 30,000 people were dug from an ancient graveyard to make room for new burials. A local woodcarver named Frantisek Rint used them to decorate the charnel house. Human bones cover nearly every surface of the walls and ceiling, and were made into chandeliers, candelabras, furniture, and even a family coat of arms. The representation of death in art serves as a potent reminder of the inevitability of death. But it may surprise you how quickly one can come to accept, and even *appreciate*, this reminder. It helps to make the fear of death much less of a burden. And it helps people focus and clarify their minds regarding what they wish to accomplish in life and how they wish to be remembered after death.

Other artistic depictions of death are meant not to alleviate our fear of it, but to make us even more terrified. Think of the art of Francisco Goya, for instance. "Saturn Devouring His Children" is one of the most impressive visual representations of murderous paranoia ever drawn. "The Witch's Sabbath", which features a group of hags carrying a basket of babies and tempting a young man to join them, portray some of our deepest fears not only of dying but also of madness, the loss of reason and autonomy, of evil, and of darkness and the unknown. A second look, however, shows that such works also portray the stupidity and gullibility of those who are afraid of darkness and evil. The witches are cartoonish almost to the point of being comical, and anyone who is seriously afraid of them is himself worthy of ridicule. Again, something resembling a purging of the fear of death is at work here.

Representations of death force people to change their attitudes about life. Anti-war activists, for instance, sometimes use graphic representations of death to motivate us to demand peace. Picasso's most famous painting, *Guernica*, creating in reaction to the bombing of the town of Guernica during the Spanish civil war, is probably the greatest of these. When Colin Powell, the United States Secretary of State, visited the United Nations to make his case for the necessity of military action against Iraq, the tapestry reproduction of Guernica which hangs there had to be covered for him. Diplomats said the painting would send "too much of a mixed message."[183] I wonder if the real reason for covering it was so that nothing would remind Mr. Powell that war is always a disaster, and so that nothing would trigger in him any humanitarian feelings of sympathy for those who would die in the forthcoming war.

An ancient philosopher named Lucretius was the first person in written history to describe Death as an ungraspable Immensity. So long as one is alive, he said, one has not died and so does not experience death. Once one is dead, one no longer exists and so there is no one for death to claim. One travels towards death *but never reaches it*. Lucretius said that we should therefore have no fear of it. His conclusion is a paradox: a logically sound argument that derives an utterly absurd conclusion from otherwise agreeable premises. On the basis of a twist of logic, he asserted death to be a non-event that happens to no one. But this is not quite right. The cessation of existence is a real event that happens to real people. And we are surrounded on all sides by its handiwork. Nonetheless Lucretius' paradox has some wisdom to it. To die is to be removed from time, and to be removed from the possibility of having experiences, even the experience of death itself. It is the only event in the world about which it is possible to say, without contradiction, that it is both an absence and yet a presence. No one experiences her own death. We grasp toward it, but once it is grasped we are deprived of the power of grasping. Death pulls the ground out from under us and throws us into the sea. It leaves no hand hold: no God, no law of universal reason, no law of nature. It answers all our calls for help with silence. It confirms none of our theologies, yet also denies none of them. *Silence itself* is its answer. Hence we can make it mean nearly anything we want it to mean, and we can believe nearly anything we want to believe. This silence is what makes death an Immensity.

But the silence of death is *not* simply that death reveals nothing of what lies beyond it. The silence of death is that we can know nothing about death itself. If the mystery of death was our lack of knowledge about what comes afterwards, and that was the whole of our ignorance, then we would focus on the accounts of people who describe near-death psychic experiences. And the event of death itself would seem quite banal, hardly worth mentioning. But its mystery is deeper still. Death is not a presence that we know nothing about. It is an *absence*, about which there is nothing we can possibly know. For it is also the absence of the person who seeks to know it. This very absence gives it a strange power. It silences not just knowledge, but also the knowledge-seeker. This silence is absolute and final, and so again, strangely powerful.

This should indeed frighten us. Not to be frightened by it is not to understand it.

§ 117. The Threshold

It has been my suggestion so far that the virtuous life begins with an experience of something that is unexpected and surprising, that changes one's relationship to time and to the future, that reminds us of our fragility and limitations, and which presents itself as if making a kind of request or demand. This account might cause some readers to ask, What possible spiritual life could there be if our lives are inevitably hedged in by such things? What choices and possibilities are there if the great monuments of existence are constantly hanging over us? Would it seem to the faint hearted that the only genuine possibilities for life are despair and resignation? There is a proverb from the ancient Greek world called The Wisdom of Silenus, named after the philosopher who coined it, which expresses this point of view. "The best thing for man is to never be born, and the second best thing would be to die quickly." But to be resigned and despairing like this is *not* to commence a spiritual life. However much the Immensity appears at first to overwhelm you, its presence also invites choices and actions. It gives us a chance to rise up to its level. It offers an opportunity for doing something that will change who and what we are, possibly for the rest of our lives. In short, the Immensity calls upon us to *respond*.

The Immensity can appear in simple situations. Here are the words of a friend of mine, as she described seeing a man at a bus stop who "seemed familiar" to her. She eventually approached him and asked him who he was. Her explanation for this choice, as she described it later, included this intriguing remark:

Sometimes the cosmos throws you a curveball, or something comes at you directly out of left field. An opportunity. If you choose to act in one way, your life can remain the same. However, if you choose a different action, something not necessarily typical, something bolder, braver, you can change your life entirely. This is what happened to me this week and it is amazing to me. How one evening, planned as a frivolous outing with friends, solely for our entertainment, turned into a life-altering decision. I am elated and proud to say, I chose the latter option. I acted, partly not knowing why. Something told me to go back, to turn around, to speak, and not walk home without taking the opportunity to make contact. Since that night, I have repeated the phrase "I'm so glad I turned around" several times.[184]

As it turns out, the man she met was someone she knew by reputation. They started dating each other within days. The story of both of their lives took a completely different path than either of them would have taken if she had chosen to go home. Instead, she chose to 'turn around', and that decision unexpectedly created a new direction in her life. The Immensity appears in such circumstances. In this way, it can be thought of as an impetus for *initiation*, which I here take to mean something close to the word's Latin origin, 'initium': a beginning or a commencement of something. It is an impetus for initiatory change because in the course of responding to it, your life may go forth in a different direction than it would otherwise have gone.

As another example, consider the story of a Canadian medical doctor and mountaineer Dr. Stuart Hutchinson. While climbing Everest in 1994, he abandoned his own push to the summit to rescue another climber, who had a potentially fatal pulmonary edema. Two years later, in May of 1996, he was 100 meters from the summit of Everest during a terrible snowstorm. Dr. Hutchinson had already abandoned his own attempt at the summit when the storm came up. So then he went in search of lost climbers who were still on the ascent. Eight climbers died that day. One of the survivors was a man whom Dr. Hutchinson found in the snow and had originally decided not to rescue. As he explained his decision:

When you can't do everything, what do you do?... Do you go to try to bring the highest people down who are most directly at risk? Do you get the people back who are easiest to get down? If you can't go out again, what do you do? The instinct really was to keep more people from dying and stabilize a bad and worsening situation. So much had gone wrong.[185]

The survivor himself, a pathologist from Texas named Dr. Beck Weathers, later confirmed Dr. Hutchinson's decision. "Every mountaineer knows that once you go into a hypothermic coma in the high mountains, you never, ever wake up. Yasuko and I were going to die anyway. It would only endanger more lives to bring us back." [186] But Dr. Hutchinson had complex feelings for his choice on that day, and admitted to being troubled for years afterward.

The Immensity is like this too. It calls for decisions which reveal what our true powers and limitations are. For the things that one can *do* in response to an Immensity are things which put what one normally regards as one's abilities, powers, and possibilities to the test. In the process, we confirm our beliefs about who we are; or else we discover new powers, or perhaps new frailties. We may discover that our limitations and possibilities are greater, or lesser, than we originally believed them to be. In this change, you become a person capable of more life, or perhaps less life, than before. And that too has the effect of taking your life in a different direction. *This is the very discovery of who and what we are.* From that moment forward, you become a different person. An Immensity, approaching the seeker from outside of her familiar world, can enlarge that world or shrink it, as she surpasses or falls short of what abilities she believes herself to have in the course of responding to it. The effect of becoming greater or lesser than who you think you are is thus something that you do to yourself. The Immensity only provides the unexpected impetus to begin. The Immensity is the great initiator standing at the threshold between who you are now and who you could become. And as these discoveries are made in the course of *choices*, they are not only moments of self discovery, but at the same time they are acts self-configuration, and self-creation.

These occasions have many wonderful disguises. A man sees a child about to fall into a well, and feels suddenly compelled to rescue the child even though he is a stranger. A long-time friend comes to visit and announces that he has a terminal disease. A young woman unexpectedly finds that she is pregnant. A car accident leaves a man's leg pinned under the wreckage, forced to sacrifice his leg or else remain trapped. A man with a wedding ring in a box in his pocket knocks on his girlfriend's door. During a storm a lightning flash sets fire to a house, forcing the family within it to rebuild their lives. A report about a serious famine in a foreign country motivates someone to travel to that country and help with the relief effort. A young college student moves out of his parent's house for the first time, to live in his own apartment. All of these events are masks of the Immensity. What you do in this situation becomes part of the story of your life. The Immensity appears in the actions which demand *an irreversible choice*, a choice that cannot be undone. In those choices, your life goes on in a different direction than it would have gone if you had chosen differently. Our choices in the presence of the Immensity are thus the choices which make us who we are; they make us *different* than we would be if we had chosen differently. In this way, once you have chosen a path, the path then chooses you.

Obviously, not all of our choices have this effect on our lives. My future is probably not dependent on my choice to take a train from Galway to Dublin today. Such a choice does not require me to call upon qualities of character which go beyond the needs of everyday life, or which I might believe I do not possess. But the choice to pursue a certain career path, to travel to a place I have never been to before and try to live there, to marry a beloved partner, to speak at a family member's funeral, and so on, are all choices which tend to put important resources of character to the test. We may not realise how often such situations appear. Indeed it may be the case that they are rare. But these are the occasions where we succeed, or fail, as human beings. Think back to your first kiss. Was it what you expected? What happened in your body? How did your feelings change? Did you fall in love? Were you already in love, and what happened to that love? This is the Immensity, working itself through our experiences, changing our lives as we respond to it.

Therefore I do not claim that the immensities represent limit situations, as Epictitus did. Certainly, I would not call them obstacles. Rather, I think they represent *problems*. They are problems because they must be puzzled out, resolved somehow, or answered. They must be faced and met. But however much they may seem to limit our powers and our possibilities, they take none of our choices away from us. Even the encounter with death does not take our choices away from us, however much it may seem that it does at first. In every situation, you *always* possess the ability to choose how you will respond. For the appearance of an Immensity is always at the same time the appearance of a possibility for hope. Even the appearance of death offers a Last Chance at an increase of life. For the appearance of an Immensity is an occasion when one's life stands on the edge of transformation. The Immensity calls your life into question but does not judge you. The seeker passes a judgement on herself by making her choice. The Immensity itself does no more than present the seeker with a problem that calls for a choice to be made. Spirituality consists in answering the call. It consists in the habits we create for living with the great immensities of life, understanding ourselves in relation to them, and perhaps, like the heroes of mythology, being consumed by them.

§ 118. Crossing the Threshold

It is a deep truth that for every manifestation of the sacred there is a corresponding form of action. When in the presence of an Immensity we are engrossed, we stand in awe, but that is not all that we do. We also *respond*. To respond is to become engaged with the experience, to say or to do something with it, for it, about it, or because of it. The response is the essential moment of initiation into a spiritual life. For it is not the experience of the sacred that makes us spiritual, but rather it is our response to it. We are transformed not by standing at the threshold, but by crossing it. The Immensity does not provide you with any answers. It only presents you with questions. The answers must be discovered within yourself, in and through the things you do.

Therefore if the person does not act in response to the Immensity, then he effectively closes himself off from the fullness of the experience. There are parts of the Immensity which are revealed *only* through positive response to it, that is, through works and deeds. Someone who remains humble and passive in its presence will never see this. (It may also be the case that to respond with passive humility is already to choose a response, and in that small way, not to be passive nor humble. But I shall leave that aside for now.) The reason is because the response to the spiritual experience is very much a part of the experience. To affirm that some event or experience *is indeed a spiritual event* is the minimum response called for. It is to declare the experience to be not a part of the ordinary, everyday world. It is also to affirm that all choices made in response to it are life-defining, world-creating choices, in great or small ways. And even this small observation makes a contribution to the experience, without which the experience may be impossible to recognise for what it is. Even to *interpret* the experience is to contribute to it: interpretation gets the mind thinking, and that is, after all, an active response.

The basic principle that needs to be affirmed here, already mentioned, is that there is a general correspondence between appearances of the Immensity and various forms of acting, working, behaving, feeling, and making choices. There is no manifestation of the sacred that is not at the same time an invitation to do something. As Paul Ricoeur put it,

> The sacred does not reveal itself just in signs that are to be contem-plated, but also in significant behaviour. The ritual is one modality of acting (*faire*). It is "to do something with this power or powers". I do not mean by this just (or even essentially) those magical manipulations by which human beings attempt to dispel, appease, render favourable, or capture these powers, but rather every manner of practically signi-fying what is aesthetically signified in space and time. To see the world as sacred is at the same time to *make* it sacred, to consecrate it. Thus to every manifestation there corresponds a manner of being-in-the-world.[187]

There are many, many ways in which manifestations of the sacred give rise to forms of action. As our understanding of the Immensity increases, so does the complexity of our responses. The most obvious and visible ways of responding to the Immensity have to do with artistic and ritualistic expressions of religiosity, especially the drama of ceremony, art, music, and architecture. We might perform some act of personal purification, from removing one's shoes to having a bath, and thus we make ourselves 'properly prepared' or 'worthy' of being in the presence of the sacred. We might also mark off the edges of the area where the Immensity manifests itself; that is we *designate sacred space*. We set up boundary markers on the land or on the calendar designating space and time reserved for celebrations or for rituals. This may be followed by various ways of decorating the space, or various kinds of dramatic performances which are intended to further the impression that this time and space has religious importance. Such decorations may also be intended to enhance and to interpret the experience, in order that it may be shared by a community. Or, they give material representation to what some seekers have seen in their mind's eye. This may eventually be followed by the composition of oral and written teachings concerning the significance of the experience and its possible meanings, and any implications for personal or social morality. The consequences of our response to it may even inspire ideas about humankind's ultimate purpose and destiny.

At the most fundamental level, however, we respond to the Immensity by *making choices*. The personal response is the one that answers the call to know who you are, by doing something that effectively defines and changes you. Once the Immensity appears to someone, a relation between the Immensity and that seeker is established, and through this relation initiatory questions may be asked. The most primal question is the Ancient Problem, "Who are you?", which appears to the seeker through the way the Immensity gives the seeker reason to doubt that she knows herself, and reason to doubt that she is who she believes herself to be. Just by being-in-the-world we are called upon by life itself to know who we are and to give an account of ourselves. Somehow the question "Who are you?" demands an response, and will not be put off or silenced for long. To respond is to accept the invitation, to answer the call. It is also to *change*, to become a new or different person, one way or another. This is because in order to answer the call completely and properly we must summon up our energy, put ourselves to work, or even to the test. In so doing, we discover what powers and capabilities we possess, and what their limits are.

It is often the case that it is impossible to know how we will respond to some situation until we find ourselves in it. For people are capable of surprising themselves with their own actions, by for instance discovering reserves of courage or endurance, or waves of compassion, that they did not know they had. This can happen even in situations that do not seem at first particularly unusual. Thus selfhood, that is, *who we are*, tends to be *revealed* by the response to the Immensity. But it is at the same time *produced* and *created* by our choices, especially the ones that create habits in our character. Actions flow from habits, yet also create habits. Character is both the source of our actions and the product of them. The relation between habit, character, and selfhood on the one hand, to actions, decisions, and choices on the other, is a relation of symbiosis. And this symbiotic process is the means by which we discover who and what we are.

It is time now to investigate this creature that stands at the threshold, this being that wishes to know itself. What do we have within us that enables us to respond to the Immensity? What resources of being can we call upon as we pursue the ancient impulse to know ourselves? To be a human being means, among other things, to be a creature that can take initiative and can make independent decisions. It is also part of what it means to be human that we can be called upon to give an account of ourselves. This is, in part, what the Immensity calls upon us to do. Normally we use the word 'responsibility' to denote some kind of moral requirement, usually having to do with respect for others. But this is not the deep meaning. Responsibility doesn't entail any particular moral requirement or disposition. It entails only the *ability to respond*. It is simply one of the implications of being a creature that can speak and act on its own. Responsibility entails only the possibility of being able to answer, when asked to account for who you are, and what you have done. It thus entails only the *possibility* of being moral, whatever one's idea of morality may be. The questions here are, With what do we respond? What does an *excellent* response look like? What kind of response is worthy of being described as *spiritual*?

§ 119. Spirit

To cross the threshold of the Immensity, you need *spirit*.

Now 'Spirit' is one of those wonderful words that mean so many different things to so many different people. To make matters worse, we live in an age where the prevailing paradigms of social and political life do not need, or are fundamentally opposed to, the belief in spirit—paradigms like science and international capitalism, for instance. I agree with the scientifically minded people of the world that much of what we believe about the soul is quite silly. The traditional idea of spirit which comes to us in the western tradition is that the soul is a kind of psychic 'monad': something indivisible, eternal, singular, unchanging, and indestructible. But isn't there something a little suspicious about that idea? There is nothing in our real-world experience of life which has these qualities. Not even our dreams. Furthermore, other cultures have much more rich and diverse ideas about what spirit is. As anthropologist Marvin Harris observed, "there is nothing in the concept of the soul per se that constrains us to believe each person has only one."[188] Plato, back in the 5th century BCE, claimed we have one soul but that it has three parts. There is an 'appetitive' part which is responsible for animalistic desires, a 'rational' part which makes active intellectual discoveries and decisions, and a 'spirited' part between them which is the seat of willpower, passion, and emotion. Why we modern Westerners should believe in only one soul, while much of the rest of the world believes in three, or four, or even dozens, is rather baffling. It is as if we have been cheated out of the fullness of our being.

We also think the soul is a kind of ghost: it is invisible and immaterial, impossible to see or grasp, but nonetheless real. We are told it is most definitely a *thing*, even if it can't be touched, sensed, or packaged. This too is a great fraud: it is as if we have been given something and then had it stolen away in the same moment. Many people also believe that knowledge of spirit is ultimately intuitive, impossible to express in words. Some people physically resist any attempt to explain or define it. But this too is contemptible. If someone is unable to explain her most deeply held beliefs, we have good cause to doubt that she really understands her beliefs, or even if she really believes anything at all. We should resist the urge to simply say that it is ineffable and that to define it is to kill it. We can, and do, talk about spirit all the time. We write books, sing songs, build monuments, and compose artworks about it. Indeed, the question of spirit itself is something of an Immensity. For whatever answer someone may offer, and however much we talk about it, there is always more to say. It is elusive and ethereal, and yet it is not so far out of reach that we can say or do or know nothing whatsoever.

And finally, as if I have not said enough already, there is the belief that the soul is somehow inside of us. We are told it is within the body even while we are also told no surgeon in the land could find it. But this is another absurdity. Why should the soul be confined within the body? Especially when our minds are not! The mind reaches out to the world through the organs of perception, flies through time and space on the wings of the imagination, lays bare the order of nature with the power of reason, and even reaches into other people's minds through the gaze and the spoken word. Furthermore, why should the soul be confined to the body when even the body is not confined to itself? So many of the functions which are necessary to having and sustaining organic life occur outside the frontier of the skin—for instance, the purification of drinking water, the replenishing of oxygen in the air, the regulation of temperature, and all the ecological processes which make our planet a life-supporting place.

There is a wonderful passage in Nietzsche's *Beyond Good and Evil* which encapsulates the problem here. First Nietzsche declares that the usual belief in the immortal soul should be rubbished. In his words:

One must also, first of all, give the finishing stroke to that other and more calamitous atomism which Christianity has taught best and longest, the *soul atomism*. Let it be permitted to designate by this expression the belief which regards the soul as something indestructible, eternal, indivisible, as a monad, as an *atomon:* this belief ought to be repelled from science! Between ourselves, it is not at all necessary to get rid of "the soul" at the same time, and thus to renounce one of the most ancient and venerable hypothesis—as happens frequently to clumsy naturalists who can hardly touch on "the soul" without losing it. But the way is open for new versions and refinements of the soul-hypothesis; and such conceptions as "mortal soul" and "soul as subjective multiplicity" and "soul as social structure of the drives and affects" want henceforth to have citizen's rights in science.[189]

Nietzsche's statement here that the 'monad' theory of the soul should be 'repelled from science' means that the idea of the soul should no longer used to explain things.[190] Nevertheless, with some irony, he says we should not abolish the idea of the soul altogether. Instead, we should think of it in new and different ways. But what other ways are there?

In fact there are many. Some ancient European societies thought that spirit was something that had to be developed and expressed over time. Someone's spirit was first of all her particular way of being in the world, the particular ways she moved in it and expressed herself in it. This idea of spirit also included the drive, the strength, the fire, the decisiveness, what the French call *joie de vivre*, which people brought to their way of being in the world. The soul is constantly showing itself, constantly *embodying* itself in so many of the things we do. It comes out in the way we talk when we are passionate about something, or the perseverance and zeal with which we pursue the things that are important to us. We still say of someone who is energetic and determined that he or she is very 'spirited'. Indeed we compare them to animals who resist being tamed, especially to horses that will not be broken for the saddle. And this is asserted to be a *positive* comparison. In this ancient way of thinking, spirit was more like a material force and an immaterial presence at the same time. It was also something you could *see*. It could be observed in the actions, the habits, and the presence of others, and felt in the motions, the drives, the feelings in oneself. For instance, in the *Nibelungenlied*, when Siegfried and his retinue arrive at Worms, the King's uncle, Hagen, is sent to check the newcomers out. He reported that "they must be either princes or princes' envoys, judging by their handsome chargers and splendid clothes, and that whichever land they had left, they were men of spirit."[191] It is this ancient idea which Nietzsche says is the new version of the soul-hypothesis for which the way is open.

Like love, happiness, and beauty, Spirit is represented and expressed in various ways. Beauty can be expressed in painting, music, architecture, and poetry. Love can be expressed in gifts, care and compassion, kind words, helpful actions, and affectionate touching. And happiness can be expressed in smiles and laughter, in an energetic and boisterous demeanour, or a calm and relaxed disposition. Similarly, we can normally tell instantly by looking at someone whether he or she has "got soul". The spirited person has her head up and her eyes forward most of the time. Her walk is relaxed yet confident. She does not dawdle, but neither does she ignore anything interesting that happens to be on the way. She speaks and listens in equal measure. Her dwelling place, whether tidy or cluttered, is comfortable and feels "lived-in". These are all signs that she is open to the world, enthusiastic about participating in it and being alive. For the spirited person is an active person, either physically or mentally, or both. She has a variety of wants and desires, and pursues them vigorously yet intelligently. She takes care of her body, with good food, hygiene, exercise, an attractive appearance, and a confident posture. When relaxing she is not restless, nor troubled by anxiety and wastefulness. Her ability to rest, like her ability to act, is complete. Even if there are things about her life which she would want to change, she feels that the changes she wants to make are not beyond her reach. Overall, she finds that life is desirable: she experiences her life, and her world, and beautiful and good. And this is an experience she both created, and also discovered, within herself. Much of what we mean by the word *spirit* has to do with this experience: and with the alive-ness, drive, spontaneity, readiness for action, and open-ness to the world that this experience produces.

By contrast, the *bereft* person resigns from the world. Her shoulders are stooped and her eyes downcast, as if trying to minimize contact with the world. She finds little in life that is pleasurable or inherently worthwhile. It is doubtful that the bereft person has any long-term, well-thought-out wishes and desires. For although there may be many things she wants, she is often reluctant to exert herself to get them. She is often quick to criticize, and if others act on her complaints she may still be unsatisfied. For it is not just the lack of things she desires that makes her unhappy. It is also a feeling that she has been deliberately denied the things she desires, or even that they have been given to undeserving others. For this reason she may be manipulative, and full of begrudgery. She will often deliberately quell the happiness of others and downplay the importance of their achieve-ments, partly out of resentment, and partly to lower the standards of excellence so that they will fall within her reach. She might present herself to others as a great teacher, counselor, or healer to win the prestige she craves. But she will spend much of her time boasting about being a great teacher or healer, rather than doing any real teaching or healing. In fact it is usually she who needs to be taught, or needs to be healed. Most of the time, when the bereft person participates in the world it is not with spontaneity. Rather, she fulfils her duties or requirements to the minimum level of necessity, or does her utmost to keep up certain appearances, and otherwise settles into a routine of bland ordinariness.

One important difference between these two people is that the spirited person *has more energy* than the bereft person. Having more energy is like having more readiness for life, more passion, more enthusiasm, more desire to do things in the world. It is like possessing a lantern which shines brightly, to see more of the world and to be seen by more things in the world. Spirit, I would like to say, is *life-energy in motion*. Energy is usually defined as the ability to do work, or as that which makes changes happen. Like the traditional notions of spirit, energy stands 'behind' or 'within' things, stored up as reserves of potential or let loose as kinetic forces. Spirit is energy because it is precisely energy that makes life possible— which is what we usually say is the province of spirit as well. Energy *animates* life, that is, energy keeps life in motion, active and engaged, at work or at play. Much of this energy of life is tangible: it comes in the form of food and water, heat, chemical reactions, gravity, and even electricity. Much is also intangible and yet still visible as light, and still audible as sound. It is this energy which is transformed into organic growth, as well as into actions, thoughts, spoken words, choices, and ultimately one's whole way of being in the world. But there is also something intangible about it, which is only 'sensed' or 'felt', more so in the presence of spirited people, that isn't reducible to a scientific force. This dimension of spirit has to do with a kind of *consciousness* that pervades the body and mind, and which manifests as your character, your social presence, your will for the things that are important to you. This energy dwells within each individual person: if it cannot be found within, it will almost certainly never be found without.

In the iconography of the gods, heroes, and saints, this energy is artistically represented as angelic wings, flowing robes, shining haloes and radiating auras of light. It is also what we mean when we speak of a musician who has "got soul". Yet this applies to more than just music. Someone who has "got soul" is someone who has the physical power, the courage, the charisma, the will, the perseverance, the audacity — in short, the energy — to do *any* kind of wonderful and extraordinary thing. Think about Ludwig van Beethoven struggling to compose his music, and even to conduct an orchestra, while stone deaf. Think about Mohammed Ali winning the World Heavyweight Championship in Zaire. Think of Diego Maradonna winning the World Cup for Argentina. Think about Lavoisier and his wife, working together to isolate oxygen in their lab for the first time. Think about the man in Tiennamin Square, China, standing in the way of the tanks lined up in front of him. Think about all the people who danced on top of the Berlin Wall as they pulled it down in 1989. Think of Terry Fox, the long distance runner suffering from cancer, who ran across Canada with an artificial leg to raise money for cancer research. Think of all the firemen who ran toward the World Trade Centre towers after they had been struck by hijacked aircraft. The obvious examples like these are not the only ones. The retired man who volunteers to make the public park into a skating rink each winter, year after year, has it. Nearly everyone who has ever given birth to a child, and raised that child to mature adulthood, has it. Married couples who keep the flame of love alive even to their fiftieth anniversary have it. Visionary scientists and maverick philosophers, working quietly away from the public eye, have it. These people all possessed energy—the energy of life itself—and they possessed it in abundance.

The evidence of this is all around us. When we are celebrating life, affirming our spiritual values, praising our accomplishments, is it not precisely an abundance of energy, a sudden or unexpected out-flowing of energy, which accounts for the festivities? In reference to the world of nature we celebrate the sunrise in the morning, the midwinter solstice in December and the increase of sunlight, the return of flowers and green foliage in the spring, and the harvest of crops in the autumn. In this respect, George Harrison's "Here comes the Sun!" is a distinctly spiritual song. In the social realm we praise the exploits of soldiers returning from battlefields, athletes who win great victories in their sport, successful ventures of exploration or of trade, extraordinary accomplishments in the arts. In our families we praise the coming-of-age of the next generation, school graduations, marriages, and the birth of healthy children. Sometimes we celebrate the death of the elder generations when their lives have been particularly exemplary. The Irish custom of 'waking the dead' is a fine example of this: the family and close friends gather in the house of the deceased for a *ceilidh* (a music and dance party). These are all occasions which from time immemorial have given us cause for celebration. What we are celebrating is the abundance of energy which the occasion has released. We represent this abundance to ourselves as if it were a spiritual blessing, that is, a gift from the gods. We take it as a sign that things are proceeding as they should, and that the world is well. An abundance of energy is the same as an abundance of spirit. Moreover, we normally celebrate this abundance with copious *expenditures* of energy: we dance, sing, feast, make music, and love.

So far I have said that Spirit is the energy of life which manifests primarily in action, and can be more or less, that is, strong in some people and weak in others. The traditional notion of the soul accommodates all these ideas, but strips it of its visibility so as to satisfy a need for the soul to be mysterious, to be just beyond the reach of understanding. The traditional notion is also much easier to mould to suit political agendas, for instance the agenda that the pursuit of political and economic liberation should be discouraged because it constitutes an excessively materialistic attitude about salvation. This is how the Catholic Church condemned Liberation Theology. So if our great teachers are offering us a soul that is ungraspable, invisible, ineffable, and confined to the body, a soul which is immortal but has nothing else going for it, I claim that we should decline the offer. One may as well add, as an afterthought, that it is no great loss; for the notion of the soul I am presenting is able to do much the same work for us that the traditional notion of the spirit is supposed to be able to do. The energy of life is constantly connecting, disconnecting, and reconnecting with other reserves of energy, and so is effectively *one*. This soul is a global animism. Discreet little whirlpools of energy like individual people can participate in this global animism as much, or as little, as they like. Physicists tell us that energy cannot be created nor destroyed, but moves from one transformation-station to another. The process of receiving, transforming, and releasing energy is always ongoing through our life, and continues on after bodily death as the energy dissipates and goes on to other places. That, perhaps, constitutes a form of reincarnation: but I will speak of such things later on. There is something else to look at first.

§ 120. Wonder

While we are defining Spirit as energy in motion, let us not be confined to the human realm. Looking out my window, I can see trees and flowering shrubs growing all along the edge of the back garden. There are birds nesting in the branches, chasing each other through the air, flying around other people's gardens and up over the house. In a neighbour's yard I can see a carpet of ivy covering the wall. A cat is scampering over the top of the wall, on his way to what must be a very serious appointment. There is a rather large insect buzzing up against the window. There is also wind in the air, blowing the clouds from one end of the sky to the other. And blessed sunshine pouring down on my face from on high. Looking out my window, I see an abundance of energy in motion. And that is the same as seeing an abundance of spirit, all over the Earth.

This picture of spirit should not be unfamiliar. Poets and artists have been singing about it for centuries. Here's an excellent example: William Wordsworth's "Tinturn Abbey", written after a week-long country ramble with his sister in the Wye Valley, near Bristol. It is a wonderful expression of that characteristically Romantic near-worship of nature.

> And I have felt
> A presence that disturbs me with the joy
> Of elevated thoughts; a sense sublime
> Of something far more deeply interfused,

Whose dwelling is the light of the setting suns,
And the round ocean and the living air,
And the blue sky, and the mind of man;
A motion and a spirit, that impels
All living things, all objects of all thought,
And rolls through all things. Therefore I am still
A lover of the meadows and the woods,
And mountains, and of all that we behold
From this green Earth...[192]

From the first time that I read this poem it stayed with me, like the memory of an old friend. The spirit that Wordsworth speaks of here is a 'presence' that is 'sensed'; it is something both within himself yet also beyond himself. It dwells in the sunset, the ocean, the sky, and the human mind, which suggests that it is an immanent power, engaged with the world and part of the world, not separated from it like a distant god. Yet it is also a value beyond the self, and therefore something with which one may have a relationship. We are also told that it is a 'motion' that 'impels all living things' and 'all objects of thought', suggesting that it is the animating force behind or within everything. One is also given the impression that this presence is an ever-flowing, ever-green power that is part of, and within, all things, from the silent stones of mountain crags to the inner working of the mind of man. It unites all things and makes them share in a great sacredness. Indeed one is left with a profound image of the beauty and the *divinity* of the Earth.

Wordsworth's poem reminds me of similar statements made by Aboriginal people, where they describe why the Earth is important to them. "When I was ten years of age," said a Siouxan medicine man named Tatanka-ohitika, "I looked at the land and the rivers, the sky above, and the animals around me and could not fail to realise that they were made by some great power."[193] Another Aboriginal man whose words were recorded around 1915 said,

When a man does a piece of work which is admired by all we say that it is wonderful; but when we see the changes of day and night, the sun, moon, and stars in the sky, and the changing seasons upon the earth, with their ripening fruits, anyone must realise that it is the work of some one more powerful than man.[194]

The virtuous response to the Earth, as these speakers seem to imply, is to awaken and sharpen your sense of wonder. This is a complex quality. It implies amazement, and makes one feel as if in the presence of something magical. But it also implies curiousity. An object of wonder may be strange, unexpected, and unfamiliar. But it is also *interesting*. We might be stopped in our tracks by the beauty of what we see, but we also find ourselves wanting to know more. It makes us ask questions, and speculate on possible answers. Thus it has nothing to do with superstitious awe, nor is it the same as humility. Humility *subordinates* he who feels it; wonder *elevates* him. Humility makes you feel you must be silent and pensive. Wonder makes you want to sing. And most importantly, humility can be imposed on you: but Wonder, by contrast, is a quality you have to deliberately cultivate. The unconquerable Immensity of the Earth is a fact that no one can ignore. But the beauty of the Earth, no less a part of its Immensity, is something you have to train yourself to see.

The wonder of the Earth is sometimes best revealed in outdoor sports and other activities where we put the powers of our physical bodies to the test. For the body, like the Earth, is a thing of stone and clay, made of the same material. In the culture of southern Ontario, Canada, where I grew up, there is a widespread belief that everyone should walk the Bruce Trail (an 800-kilometer long hiking trail that roughly follows the Niagara Escarpment), or go canoeing in Algonquin or Temagami, or have some other similar outdoor adventure, at least once in their young lives. The custom is like an unofficial, informal "rite of passage". Indeed parents encourage their children to do this in order to 'build character' and gain 'life experience'. It is not exactly a holiday, nor meant to be 'relaxing'. There can be danger in the form of treacherous ledges, bad weather, encounters with animals. As a rock climber you might find yourself hanging from a cliff side, looking for a handhold and knowing that if you make a mistake you will fall to your death. As a canoeist one might get caught in rapids or strong currents, lose control of one's canoe, and drown. In such situations you have only your own resources to rely on: your own physical strength, reflexes, and psychological discipline. And these situations call for serious choices to be made: the most fundamental of which is the choice to go on or turn back, that is, to persevere or to capitulate. To go on one must have endurance, courage and willpower. The days or even weeks of solitude call for patience and self-awareness, for instance. The practical results of these choices have the effect of revealing what powers, both physical and psychological, you possess. This very often also has the effect of changing what you believe about who you are and what direction your life can take from there. And the successful trek also tends to produce an ability to appreciate natural beauty. People will generate feelings of fondness and love for the landscapes where these personal discoveries took place, and these feelings are often easily widened, to include other landscapes.

Of course, one does not need to be an outdoor adventurer to experience the wonder of the Earth. Forests and trees, hills and lakes, coastlines, and the ever-changing sky, can inspire a feeling of magic and love in nearly anyone, anywhere. Almost a century after Wordsworth, Tolkien expressed his love for the land when he described Frodo's feelings on arrival at Lothlórien, the forest kingdom of the Elves.

It seemed to him that he had stepped through a high window that looked on a vanished world... he saw no colour but those he knew; gold and white and blue and green, but they were fresh and poignant, as if he had at that moment first perceived them and made for them names new and wonderful. (*Fellowship*, pg. 394)

As a child I imagined that the Elora Gorge conservation area, just five minute's walk from my door, was inhabited by Celtic gods and Native animal totems. Although much of the park is made of roads, campsites, pavilions, and other obvious signs of human presence, there were still many corners and crevices where it was easy to perceive the trees and stones as if they properly belonged to an Otherworld. Wonder combines childhood imagination with adult curiousity. It is the ability to see the special magic in things. The same quality of the Earth that presents itself as an Immensity also renders it magical. Its mysteries and hidden places invite us to explore and discover them. Perhaps we would not know and understand the world so well without it. Wonder enables people to see more than they would otherwise see, and so it opens up possibilities and creates choices. And Wonder is also the heart of artistic creativity: without it perhaps there would be no poetry, no music, no storytelling

It must be added that Wonder can suggest certain moral responses. We have a natural feeling of loss, or regret, or even anger and indignation, when the things which inspire our sense of wonder are damaged. The magic of my forest, the Elora Gorge, was diminished when the conservation authority installed a fence along the length of the cliff, to 'protect' park visitors from falling in. And the magic of the Earth is diminished by the loss of resources, the industrial developments, the pollution, and the waste which continues to accumulate every year. From 1975 to 2005, the Earth's mean average temperature increased by an average of 0.2 degrees, which according to NASA scientists is "remarkably rapid". They also claimed that the earth may be warmer now than it has been in the last million years.[195] Continued pollution is changing the chemical composition of the atmosphere, resulting in an increase in the frequency and severity of weather disasters.[196] In February of 2007, the United Nations released the first part of a major four-part study of climate change, contributed to by hundreds of scientists from all over the world. It predicted a possible increase in global temperature by as much as 6.4 degrees by the end of the century, resulting in many more droughts, more destructive storms, increased flooding, loss of food production, the displacement of millions of people, more disease epidemics, and other disasters. The scientists expressed "very high confidence" and "virtual certainty" that these problems were caused by human activity.[197] One need not be a scientist to observe the changes happening to the world, nor must one be a resident in a third world country. 78% of people who responded to a poll conducted by *The Globe and Mail*, Canada's national newspaper, claimed to have seen the signs of global warming first-hand.[198]

To someone who has a mature sense of wonder, climate change is not just a practical problem: it is a moral problem. It is a consequence of the failure to recognise the *authority* of the Earth as both an Immensity, and as our home and place. Worse, possibly, than the lacklustre response to climate change, is the will to deny its reality. Mr. Van Jollisant, chief economist of Chrysler corporation, criticised "quasi-hysterical Europeans" for their "Chicken Little" attitudes towards climate change. At a corporate breakfast during the 2007 Detroit Motor Show, he exclaimed that global warming is a far-off risk of uncertain magnitude. Economists for Ford and General Motors, sitting on the same panel at the same time, did not disagree.[199] A letter written by Mr. Stephen Harper, a few years before he became Prime Minister of Canada, described the Kyoto Accord as a "socialist scheme" designed to suck money from rich countries to poor ones.[200] And oil companies have funded pseudo-science think tanks whose purpose is to plant scepticism about climate change in the mind of the public.[201]

Tolkien delivers an environmental message when he describes the Leave-Taking of the Elves, and the lament of the Ents for the Entwives. He is lamenting the loss of magic and wonder in the landscape. His most vivid symbol of this loss is the transformation of Isengaard, an idyllic arboretum used by Saruman as a kind of headquarters, into a factory for mass-producing weapons of war. His friend and fellow writer C.S. Lewis shared this fear for the future of the English landscape. There is a passage in his science-fiction novel, *That Hideous Strength,* in which a character named Filostrato describes to a young recruit named Mark the future world that he and the corporation he works for is trying to bring about. He compares it to the bleak surface of the Moon:

"...there is cleanness, purity. Thousands of square miles of polished rock, with not one blade of grass, not one fibre of lichen, not one grain of dust. Not even air. Have you thought what it would be like, my friend, if you could walk on that land? No crumbling, no erosion. The peaks of those mountains are real peaks: sharp as needles, they would go through your hand. Cliffs as high as Everest and as straight as the wall of a house. And cast by those cliffs, acres of shadow black as ebony, and in the shadow hundreds of degrees of frost. And then, one step beyond the shadow, light that would pierce your eyeballs like steel and rock that would burn your feet. The temperature is at boiling point. You would die, no? But even then you would not become filth. In a few moments you are a little heap of ash; clean, white powder. And Mark, no wind to blow that powder about. Every grain in the little heap would remain in its place, just where you died, till the end of the world—but that is nonsense. The universe will have no end." (*That Hideous Strength*, pg. 175-6)

This vision of the future is a vision of pure intellectual abstraction, and therefore utterly devoid of organic life. Not even the most basic biological functions exist in it. When Mark expresses horror at the thought, and asks what is to become of humankind, he is told that there will be a race of 'Masters' who will live as disembodied heads, supported by machines.

I wonder how far off from reality this vision is. Not far from my hometown there is a shopping region the size of a small city, with nothing but big-box stores. All the buildings are made of synthetic materials: glass, concrete, plastic, and steel. There are thousands of parking spaces in vast lots, accessible only by multi-lane high density roads designed to accommodate cars, not walkers nor cyclists. There are no houses, churches, schools, sports fields, or green spaces. This is not a special or unique kind of commercial district; in fact it is *typical* of such areas in the region. As far as I am concerned, much of my landscape has been scoured, just as Saruman's Orcs scoured the Shire, to create Filostrato's dead world of 'purity'.

Wonder connects our virtues to the world we live in. It invites us to create a world fit for living the good life. Take a moment now to imagine a place where you can be *yourself* without inhibition. What would it look like? Mine looks like this. I see houses made of stone and brick half-covered in ivy, or of wooden planks painted in a variety of cheerful colours. Each home has a garden in front, and hedgerows define the property lines between them. Each neighbourhood also has its own small park, and is within fifteen minute's walk to a larger park or a nature trail. In the town centre I see a wide open square, with many public monuments and civic buildings: the library, theatre, town hall, post office, train station, and so on. There are open-air cafes in the square, and buskers of every kind: musicians, clowns, acrobats, and singers. There is a Speaker's Corner, where people have a good time arguing with one another. Such public spaces are necessary for democracy. I see no plastic siding on the houses, no cigarette butts on the ground, and definitely no cars! I see a commercial district next to the square, with family owned and operated businesses. I see hand-painted signs over the shop fronts, lit with small scoop lights, never back-lit with neon. There are a few casual traders here too, plying home-made wares from carts or folding tables. I see that most of the food people eat is produced within a few hundred kilometres. I see an ancient forest covering a third of the surrounding landscape. I see farmer's fields bounded with thick and wide hedgerows. I see towns of no more than a few thousand people, and cities of no more than a million. I see history and mythology everywhere, written right on the landscape, and on the hands and faces of the people. And above all, I see *trees*, wonderful tall trees, everywhere.

The good life is a life lived by lights of self-rewarding, excellent qualities of character like honour, courage, friendship, and so on. But the good life does not happen in an abstract, place-less 'nowhere'. It needs a *home:* that is, a place where that kind of aspiration is possible and supported. Therefore it is necessary to imagine a place where you could be completely, perfectly, *finally* happy; and then to do things to make that imagined place a reality. That is a task for which the sense of wonder is absolutely indispensable.

§ 121. Humanity

To the second of the three Immensities I now turn: other people. The ways in which each person is an Immensity to her neighbour tend to isolate people from each other, creating distance, tension, and loneliness. As seen, Lévinas wrote that there is always a deep inequality between people: the other person is a master, a teacher, a figure of authority who demands justice by his very gaze. But to contemplate the Immensity is less than half of the spiritual life. Again, what makes us spiritual is the response. An excellent response to the Immensity of another person closes the distance between people, and brings people together. But the excellent response does this while at the same time acknowledging the uniqueness, autonomy, and distinct *personhood* of others. It does not project on to others a fantasy of who or what you might wish them to be. It accepts others as they are, and doesn't try to change them. Are there any virtues that enable one to do this?

One way to answer this question would be to point to certain psychological dispositions which play an important role in people's social development. For instance, here is British philosopher Jonathan Glover's 'Theory of Moral Resources'.[202] It states that we have three special dispositions within our psychology which generally prevent anti-social behaviour of all kinds, and tend towards cooperation and altruism. The first, Respect, is the deference, the obedience, or at least non-interference, which is offered to people who are deemed to deserve it, for whatever reason. The respect might be grounded in many things: status or accomplishment, membership in some community, or in 'human dignity' or something similarly universal. The second moral resource is called Sympathy. This, he says, is the ability to put oneself in another's shoes. Through Sympathy we become unable to bear the suffering of other people, because we can vicariously feel their weakness and pain as if it is our own. Usually, sympathy is activated by people who are close to us, like family members. But we can also feel sympathy for total strangers, or people who we see only in media reports and will never meet in person. The third is called 'Moral Identity'. It concerns your sense of who you are, and how it is fashioned by what you do and the choices you make, especially as they are repeated over time. Your sense of identity can motivate you to do certain things when they 'fit' with the picture of who you believe yourself to be. And it can make you hesitate before doing something that doesn't fit. Moral identity, Glover says, is the psychological foundation of the virtues. And these three resources taken together, according to him, are the foundation of humanity itself.

But practicing a virtue is not just a matter of doing what we are psycho-logically predisposed to do. A psychological disposition is something we are born with. But a virtue is something to *aspire* to possess. It therefore has to be chosen. It is a wish to do, or to be, something beautiful and good; and it is an arousal of the energy needed to make that wish come true. A virtuous person chooses the excellent, until the habit of choosing the excellent gives her the sense that her life has achieved *eudaimonia*, full human flourishing. This involves the body, the mind, the heart, and the spirit, all together. I therefore ask my question again, but in a slightly different way: How can we respond to the Immensity of other people— with excellence? Are there ways of acknowledging the Immensity of other people while at the same time bringing them closer?

There are: and in general they are the virtues associated with sustaining and enriching human relationships. A close friend of mine recently taught me:

Relationships are living things. They can grow and change over time. They need to be tended and cared for like living things. I see these relationships in my garden, between the plants, the soil, and myself. I see it between people too.[203]

I think this is true of almost all relationships: friends, work colleagues, business partnerships, family members, neighbours, team mates, flowers in your garden, trees in your forest, stars in your sky. I wish only to add that in each case, there will be a number of virtues which are needed to sustain these relationships. And they may vary, depending on the kind of relationship it is. A relationship flourishes best when the virtues needed to sustain and enrich it are the same as the virtues needed to sustain and enrich one's own life. In such good and beautiful relationships, the wish for a good and beautiful life may be realised.

A healthy sense of self-esteem and self-worth, it seems to me, is one of the qualities necessary to sustain good relationships. For if we value our friends' lives as much as we value our own, as the classical and heroic tradition of Virtue understands true friendship, then we must value our own lives most highly, in order to value our friends highly too. In order to have good relationships with others, one must perceive oneself as a good person: one who could contribute positively to the lives of others, and one who is *worthy and deserving of having friends*. Dignity, honour, and self worth have a role here. And these qualities must be discovered on one's own, within oneself. They can not be shown or given to you by others. There is an important place, after all, for Nietzsche's affirmation that the noble soul has reverence for itself.

But that Nietzschean affirmation is not the whole story. The reverence for oneself must extend in an expanding circle to others, if the Immensity of other people is to be responded to with excellence. Some of the qualities needed to sustain good relationships are discovered not within oneself, but at the meeting place between people, that is, in the relationship itself. Friendship, it seems to me, is foremost among them. Aristotle, as already shown, said that friendship is the virtue of people who find in each other a second self. Ricoeur wrote that friendship re-balances the initial inequality that Lévinas claims is always present in any meeting between two people.[204] Friendship closes the distance between people without allowing the one to control or possess the other. It brings people into your world without assimilating them. It creates appreciation for others, without imagining them to be other than what they are. Friendship is not the only quality that can be named here. Generosity, trust, compassion, loyalty, honesty, attention, and the like, are meaningful only in the context of relations with others. We might not know that there is a capacity within us to be generous, trusting, and so on, until we meet another person and find these qualities brought to the surface by a spontaneous human response. And we may not know how these qualities contribute to one's own flourishing, and to that of the relationship, until they are so revealed. In this way the meeting with another person is often an occasion when people discover who they are. It is important to emphasise that these discoveries are made *in a relationship with a friend*. They cannot be made when one enters relationships in order to fulfil some selfish interest. The most significant discovery that friendship makes possible is the discovery that the good and beautiful life is largely a collaborative affair.

Of course, you may always reserve the right to select *who* you will invite into your life. There's no requirement here that you must create strong friendships with absolutely everyone. As mentioned earlier, the best relationships are the ones where the qualities needed to sustain it also promote the individual flourishing of the people involved. A relationship sustained by infatuation, or possessiveness, or lies, for instance, tends to be detrimental to people's flourishing. Sometimes, people are better able to flourish only after certain relationships are let go.

When friendship intensifies to a spiritual level, it becomes *love*. Love is everything that friendship is, but also much more. It is what happens when two friends create the deepest bonds of care, concern, and affection with each other, and allow these bonds to involve nearly every aspect of their being. Love often grows slowly, taking its time. It too is like a living thing. As it grows, each partner's spiritual energy merges with the other, perhaps until there is almost one pool of energy between them. Those who truly love each other share one spirit. When the spirits are brought close this way, everything that a lover does for his beloved becomes an act of love. Even ordinary things, like washing the dishes, become little gifts which reinforce the mutual feeling. Love compels an absolute giving of your whole self: it is almost like a deliberate wish to lose yourself by giving yourself. But in the very act of giving you actually *find* yourself. In this sharing, there is no question of exploitation or inequality. For as love grows, so does trust, care, honesty, affection, generosity, compassion, kindness, and a whole host of other life-affirming qualities. Love can also be defined as *an absolute affirmation of the goodness of the beloved*. This affirmation creates a will to give, to care, and to help, which further unites people. This can be true in all kinds of loves, not only the love of a boyfriend or girlfriend, or a married couple. It is also true of love for parents or siblings, a favourite teacher, a family dog, a town or landscape, and so on. Indeed love may be the paragon of all responses to other people: for a mature lover recognizes the distinctness, the individuality, the Immensity, of the beloved; and that is *precisely* the reason he loves her.

The relationship between friends and lovers is not simply, nor only, that of two people who share values together, or who are 'travelling together through life'. It is also the relationship of two or more people whose life-stories are intertwined. Like the soil of a garden where two trees grow together, storytelling is the soil in which two people grow together. It is a way in which each person's sense of identity is bound up with the identities of other people. It is the medium, the vehicle, even the very fabric, of human relationships. Yet through storytelling we remain ourselves, and our friends remain themselves. There are several reasons why this is so.

First of all, narrative storytelling is a powerful way for people to 'know themselves'. Whenever we tell of what is going on in our lives, where we have been, things we have seen or done, and of plans for the future, we always do so by telling a story. On any given day, most people use a dozen or more stories: they tell anecdotes ("Last night I was at the bus stop when..."), jokes ("A man walked into a bar...") family histories ("When my grandfather was in the war...") bits of public news ("there was a traffic jam on the main road today...") and so on. Sometimes these stories, told in the thick of the everyday, are nothing special in themselves. Even so, the mere act of telling them is an important spiritual act. As Paul Ricoeur wrote, we identify ourselves, or recognise ourselves, in the stories told about our lives.[205] Alasdair MacIntyre wrote that through storytelling we render life intelligible, and at the same time this is possible because human life is naturally structured in a way that lends itself to representation in dramatic narrative.[206] It is through storytelling that life can *make sense*: life as recounted in stories is intelligible, structured, unified, and *one's own*.

Second, as we make choices and decisions, so we become the directors and makers of our lives; so too, we become the authors of our stories. But even so, people are only ever the co-authors of their own stories. For the whole story of anyone's life always includes other people. It is entirely impossible for me to tell the story of my life without also telling part of the story of other people's lives. As MacIntyre wrote,

We are never more (and sometimes less) than the co-authors of our own narratives. Only in fantasy do we live what story we please... We enter upon a stage which we did not design and we find ourselves a part of an action that was not of our own making. Each of us being a main character in his own drama plays subordinate parts in the dramas of others, and each drama constrains the others. [AV pg. 213]

Your story started before you were born, with the story of your parents. As you grow up your story intersects with that of your other relatives, your neighbours, friends, teachers, colleagues, and anyone who made an impact on your life, however small. As people spend more time with each other, and become closer friends or deeper lovers, so do the stories of their lives become inseparable. In this way, when you recognise and identify yourself in the stories you tell of your life, you also recognise that your relationships with others are part of your identity. Insofar as the stories of your friends and lovers are inseparable from your own, so your very identities also intertwine. For your story is inextricably a part of other people's stories, and their stories are inextricably a part of yours. It is not that two people become the same, but that two people find their identities unintelligible without the reference to each other and their relationship together.

Third, narrative storytelling also involves you in the embodied world. For stories do not happen in abstraction: they *take place* somewhere, in a setting, with a background. The story of your life is always inextricably intertwined with the story of your home town, your house, your community, the landscapes where you ran as a child, your nation, even of the Earth itself. For all of your relationships, not just your human relationships, figure into the story of your life. This can support and sustain the sense of wonder: it can render additional significance to the world by involving it in a story which is at the same time the story of you are.

Fourth, and finally, Storytelling also connects you to a future. For on one level, you never know what is going to happen next. There is always an element of surprise. Yet at the same time, storytelling lends a sense of direction, plot, and structure in life, which usually takes the form of an end or a goal which the story is driving to reach. As MacIntyre says:

We live out our lives, both individually and in our relationships with each other, in the light of certain conceptions of a possible shared future, a future in which certain possibilities beckon us forward and others repel us, some seem already foreclosed and others perhaps inevitable. There is no present which is not informed by some image of some future and an image of the future which always presents itself in the form of a *telos*—or of a variety of ends or goals—towards which we are either moving or failing to move in the present... Like characters in a fictional narrative we do not know what will happen next, but nonetheless our lives have a certain form which projects itself towards our future. (*After Virtue* pg. 215-6)

This ties in neatly with Lévinas' observation, seen earlier, that time itself is defined in terms of the presence of other people. The choices we make in response to others, the relationships we create, and so on, open up new possibilities for the future, and move our lives toward new future directions. Indeed, the very point of the Immensity is that there are some choices people make from time to time which takes the story of you life off in a different direction than it would otherwise have gone. Choices made in response to other people are very often choices of this kind.

To sum it up: a good life can be represented as a good story, one which yourself and others find satisfying and enjoyable to live and to tell. So when facing the Immensity, one should make the choice that takes the story of one's life in a good and beautiful direction. The only way to do this, much of the time, is to involve others in the telling. The psychological capacities for respect and sympathy help us to do this, by enabling us reach out to people. But ultimately it is a deliberately chosen excellence which *necessarily* involves other people, like storytelling, friendship, and love, that enriches the story of one's life the most. A virtuous response to the Immensity of other people is a response that creates and sustains friendship and love and other positive relationships. And these relationships, in turn, feed back into your sense of identity and selfhood. The relationships we create with others change the direction of one's life-story, and so change who we are. As the creation of these relationships is a choice, so the response also configures and creates who we are. And as positive relationships contribute to one's own flourishing, so they also contribute to the flourishing of everyone involved. Through one's relationships, flourishing becomes contagious: for when one person flourishes, others do too.

§ 122. Integrity

There is one more kind of Immensity, one last way that the Immensity can appear, for which all that has been said so far is not enough. That Immensity is Death. In death, we face something that is not external to the body and mind, like the world and other people, but internal to one's own being. That is, we face the extinction of one's own being—which makes it no less foreign to one's home world than any other Immensity. When the energy of life dissipates after death, there is no way for anyone to continue to claim that the energy is their own, or that it still 'belongs' to them. It returns to the ecosystem from which it came, to be passed on again to another transformation-station, another form of life. So while this notion of the soul provides for effective immortality, or rather it provides for a kind of reincarnation, it does not provide for the survival of your identity. That energy may be effectively immortal, but personal identity is not. Death is still the great Immensity that it always was.

Certain kinds of changes and transitions can also prepare us for death, for it is possible to think of them as 'little deaths'. There are certain thresholds which each of us must pass through, which allow for no retreat, no stepping back afterwards. Some of them are changes that happen to the body in the course of growing up and growing older. The onset of sexuality and the ability to reproduce, followed swiftly by adulthood and the achievement of the height of our powers, followed again by the slow decline of our powers with old age, are all inevitable and irreversible thresholds of life. They have the effect of rendering a person so changed that it is possible to think of him or her as a different person. In mythology and the symbolism of ritual, death and the passage between different stages of life mutually imply one another. We often take death to be nothing more than one threshold in life among many, and we are taught to face death with similar courage (when we bother to regard it at all). The transitions of life are immensities in their own right. They are limit-situations in the grip of which our lives change. What it is like to experience them is a mystery for someone who has not yet experienced them. But we can have certain expectations based on what we can see of other people who have already made the transition. However much we are changed after we cross each threshold, there will be a continuity between the old self and the new self. We will keep our memories and some of our habits (good and bad!), as well as photographs and diaries and other records. And they shall remain part of the same story, the same personal biography. This enables us to face these transitions with confidence.

Recent Heroic literature reflects this point of view. In the first of the Harry Potter novels, Dumbledore tells Harry that the philosopher's stone, the treasure which enables Nicholas Flamell and his wife to live forever, will be destroyed. Dumbledore explains:

> To one as young as you, I'm sure it seems incredible, but to Nicholas and Perenelle, it really is like going to bed after a very, *very* long day. After all, to the well-organised mind, death is but the next great adventure.[207]

The destruction of the Philosopher's Stone, the treasure which confers immortality, is a great symbol of the end of childhood. Children often believe that they will live forever. (Think of Wordsworth's poem, 'We are Seven', for instance.) The acknowledgement that this is a false belief is a large step out of childhood and into adulthood. So the stone *had* to be destroyed at the end of the story. Its destruction is the symbol of Harry's own advancement to maturity.

Like Nicholas Flamell, Tolkien's Elves are effectively immortal. They can live for thousands of years, and if killed they return to Middle Earth, just as Gandalf returned after his battle with the Balrog. But Tolkien adds that the Elves actually *envy* the race of Men because Men can die. Elves are 'bound to the circles of this world', unable to leave. Certainly, they have found various ways to make their lives worth living and enjoyable.

They are almost constantly singing, for instance. They make their homes into places of great beauty and purity, like Rivendell and Lórien. But by the time the Fellowship meets Galadriel, these magical places are no longer safe. Galadriel, for her part, is growing tired of the world. She made Lórien into "a refuge and an island of peace and beauty, a memorial of ancient days", but now finds herself "filled with regret and misgiving, knowing that the golden dream was hastening to a grey awakening."[208] Most Elves eventually grow *weary* of immortality. They regard the ability to die as a gift. Tolkien's message is that Death is painful and tragic, to be sure, but certainly not evil. One who has had a long and fulfilling life may have reason to welcome death, and treat it as a transition to 'the next great adventure'.

However, the approach of death is not something we can anticipate the same way we can anticipate the stages of life. As Lucretius taught, Death does not 'approach' us as other transitions in life do. Death can be expected, but we do not know exactly *what* to expect. Do not be sidetracked by accounts of near-death experiences or by some popular theology of reincarnation or immortality. We who face the Immensity directly and honestly cannot behave like the orphan peasant children of folk and faerie tales who grow up to find that their true parents are royalty. Death allows no such gratification. The people of Heroic societies had a variety of Otherworlds in their mythology, like Tir Na nOg, Olympus, and Valhalla. But at their highest moments they did not allow their expectations of the after-life get in the way of their virtue. In pursuit of apotheosis, that particularly Heroic form of immortality, they aimed to live lives that would deserve to be remembered. For this purpose they regarded some of their virtues, especially Honour, as more valuable than the preservation of their lives. Honour enables the hero to completely grasp his own death, when the time comes. As an example, consider the words of a Norse warrior named Hamdir, the hero of an Icelandic epic poem called *The Hamdismál*.

We have fought a good fight, and we stand like eagles on a branch on the bodies of Goths struck down by the sword. We have won good repute, whether we die today or tomorrow. No man lives a day beyond the sentence of the fates.[209]

Hamdir's sense of heroic honour gave him something like a victory over fate itself. As he stood on his pile of defeated Goth warriors, only a moment before his own death, he re-affirmed the general Heroic belief that the world is ruled by fate. But one who meets his fate with his honour intact, as Hamdir believed he did, is able to receive and accept that fate on his own terms; and indeed receive it with joy. He may transform the acceptance of his fate into the final flourish that puts an exclamation mark on the story of his rich and satisfying life.

Similar thoughts appear in the works of Classical writers. In his *Meditations*, Marcus Aurelius wrote a great deal about how to respond to death, without falling back on visions of immortality or the afterlife. "Perfection of character is this: to live every day as if it was your last, without frenzy, without apathy, without pretence."[210] This aphorism is probably the most well known of Stoic teachings and in some places it is still popular today. But one might ask, is Marcus Aurelius saying that you should be prepared to leave your life at a moment's notice? I think not: as other remarks in his *Meditations* bear out, his message is also that you should live in such a way that *if* you were to die today, you would not feel your life was wasted or unfinished. The great soul finds his life so fulfilling, so enjoyable, so *complete*, that "Fate does not catch him with his life unfulfilled, as one might speak of an actor leaving the stage before his part is finished and the play is over."[211]

Both Hamdir's last words, and Marcus Aurelius' advice on perfection of character, are ways of affirming the goodness and beauty of life on Earth in the here and now. If you meditated on the thought that you might die tomorrow, you would quickly come to very different conclusions about how to spend your time today. Death forces us to clarify what really matters. The pursuit of money and fame; or petty grievances, gossip, or revenge; or escapist pleasures; or any goal that is unambiguously meaningless would appear hollow, pointless, and *beneath* you to pursue it. You would want to do something to make you feel as if your life had significance. That notion of a significant life, as we have seen, is one of the foundations of the very idea of Virtue itself.

It is hard for me to think of just one single quality that is the specific response to death. It is easier for me to think of several qualities which are manifest *failures* to respond well: morbidity, resignation, willful ignorance, and escapism, for instance. It seems to me that some combination of the Heroic aim for honour, the Aristotelian aim for *eudaimonia*, the Renaissance confidence in humanity, and the creative energy of Romanticism, is called for. Each of them is a distinct yet related way of making our lives self-rewarding in the here and now, as I hope has been shown.

But if pressed to name only one quality, I would choose Integrity. This is a complex quality: it concerns the way in which other qualities hold together over time. It enables you to be *consistent* in the pursuit of your goals. It is never a stand-alone quality; and it is only a good quality if coupled to other good qualities. An idiot, after all, can be consistently idiotic, and one can be a fully integrated asshole. But when coupled with the virtues of humanity and wonder, its place in the good and beautiful life becomes clearer. Integrity is like Honour in that it is related to the preservation of one's values and choices, and the respect one earns from others for doing so. It is like Courage in that it helps keep us on our feet when the winds are blowing us down: winds in the form of emotional upheavals, or peer pressure, public opinion and 'political correctness', for instance. It is like Friendship in that it brings you closer to others, especially those with the same kind of integrity. It is like Pride and Dignity, since the consistency it makes possible is a way of realising one's self-worth. It is like Love in that it helps one to see the goodness and beauty of people and things. If all these qualities can be compared to the flowing of water in a river, Integrity is like the banks and the bed of a river, carved out by the water over many years. It holds the water of your other virtues together, so that they all flow toward a common destination.

Although Integrity cannot be a stand-alone virtue, still there is something noble about it on its own. You find its inherent worth in its implicit connection to death. In his book *The Commissar Returns*, photo archivist David King put together an extraordinary collection of pictures of people who were executed by the Soviet Union's Secret Police, on the orders of Joseph Stalin. Every person photographed in the archive knew he was about to die. Yet it appears from these photos that not one of them was afraid, or regretful. Indeed their expressions were proud and defiant. They were ordinary people: most of them farmers, small business owners, or labourers. It is probable that none of them would fit Aristotle's definition of a Great Soul. Nonetheless, every one of them possessed profound integrity. You can see it in their eyes. They faced their executioner's camera with their dignity intact. That kind of integrity is not something that only special people can have. It is something everyone can find within herself, when the circumstances call for it. By the way, around sixty years later, local people turned those pictures into religious icons in the Eastern Orthodox artistic style. They are on display in a small church near the place where they lived and died. Therefore, it could be said that their integrity was rewarded with apotheosis.

Under most circumstances, integrity depends upon something to look forward to: a person of integrity has a *future* which she wants to realise. She discerns that the narrative of her life is definitely leading her somewhere. This ability to imagine a future, and to pursue it with dedication and perseverance, can enable one to endure just about any hardship or tragedy. The psychologist Viktor Frankl, who was a prisoner in several Nazi concentration camps, wrote of how during his internment he imagined that when the war was over, he would write a book, teach psychology at a university again, and be re-united with his wife. These hopes became his reasons for living. They enabled him to endure disease, malnutrition, overwork, the various abuses from prison guards, and the overall horror of his situation. He also observed how the prisoners who lost hope usually died first. For human beings cannot live without purpose, and without hope. In the case of the people in David King's photo collection, for instance, each prisoner's reason for living may have been to preserve his dignity, and to show a little bit of rebellion. As they still possessed their lives, so they still possessed their responses. That is, they still possessed their ability to choose their response to the situation. To respond as they did, with defiant pride, shows great courage, great independence, great spirit: and also great integrity, to retain these qualities right to the last moment.

What about those who, for whatever reason, are no longer able to imagine a future for themselves? What about those who would prefer to take their own lives rather than continue living with a disease, a disability, a guilty conscience, an unbearable grief, or even an oppressive social order? Alasdair MacIntyre wrote that suicidal people are those who find, not simply that their lives are too painful to continue, but that their lives are unintelligible to them. Similarly, the psychologist Viktor Frankl observed that people contemplate suicide when they feel their lives have lost purpose and meaning. I'd like to add that this unintelligibility may be borne of the absence of something positive to live for. I don't wish to suggest that all suicidal people are simply weak-willed, or that they just lack imagination. I recognise that depression is a medical condition, not a deficiency of character. But I do wish to suggest that an ability to imagine a future, an ability to discern a purpose for one's life, can have a thera-peutic effect on those who find their lives very difficult to bear. It can give them something to do with their lives, and in that way, their lives may become purposeful and meaningful again.

As the quality which gives coherence to the story of one's life, integrity leaves out no part of life. It therefore includes death as part of its consid-eration. Just as Integrity can give one something worth living for, so it can also give one *something worth dying for*. Aristotle wrote that the virtuous person remains true to her values even when there is no material advantage to herself to do so, and even if she may die in the course of upholding them. In his words:

> …it is also true that the virtuous man's conduct is often guided by the interests of his friends and of his country, and that he will if necessary lay down his life in their behalf. For he will surrender wealth and power and all the goods that men struggle to win, if he can secure nobility for himself; since he would prefer an hour of rapture to a long period of mild enjoyment, a year of noble life to many years of

ordinary existence, one great and glorious exploit to many small successes. And this is doubtless the case with those who give their lives for others; thus they choose great nobility for themselves. (*NE* 1169a19)

Remember, Aristotle lived in an age fraught with warfare and violence. Almost everyone could be expected to take up arms to defend the city-state at almost any time. Hence, perhaps, why this passage seems to echo the Heroic idea that a short life of glory is better than a long life of comfort. But Aristotle also asserts a larger point: a virtuous person recognises things that are more important than her own personal survival. Virtuous people 'choose great nobility for themselves', that is, they are prepared to do the right thing because they find it *edifying* and *uplifting* to do it. The virtuous person is so concerned with integrity that she would prefer to give up her life, if the alternative might mean giving up her integrity. J.K. Rowling echoed this idea in *Harry Potter and the Deathly Hallows,* when Dumbledore tells Harry, "the true master does not seek to run away from death. He accepts that he must die, and understands that there are far worse things in the living world than dying."[212]

In the last study I suggested that in storytelling we recognise how are lives are inevitably connected to the lives of others. Here I wish to add that in storytelling the full importance of Integrity can be realised. The integrity of your character, and the plot of the story of your life, correspond to each other. A good story has an intelligible narrative, or in other words a "plot", by which I mean a sense of necessity, coherence, wholeness, and completion. The plot places the events of the story in their proper sequence and "drives" them toward various conclusions. It determines what must be the beginning, middle, and end of the story. Yet this force of narrative necessity does not deprive the characters of their freedom and initiative. For narrative also grants to the characters the power to make choices and begin events. People are still the authors and co-authors of their own stories. This may point the way toward a resolution between free will and destiny; but I'll not explore that possibility here. What I'm suggesting is a little simpler. Perhaps the most visible sign of integrity is a life-story that "makes sense", both to the person living that life, and to others. A life-story with an intelligible narrative may be a life of purpose and meaning. Death is both the end of the story, and at the same time the part of the story where the plot is taken up by others. It is not rigorously excluded from the story: in fact it is an 'integral' part of the story.

§ 123. "Terrible Things, But Great"

So far I have discussed ways of responding to the Immensity that are hopelessly 'moral': they are manifestations of spirit that most people would regard as good and kind, or right and just. What, then, should be said about Mr. Ollivander's words to Harry Potter: that the most evil wizard of the time was in his own twisted way a great man? "He-Who-Must-Not-Be-Named did great things—terrible, yes, but great."[213] Let me therefore re-introduce a problem already treated earlier. Lévinas wrote that the logical beginning-place of ethics is the meeting with the other person. He wrote that others are "masters of justice" whose freedom and identity cannot be grasped or taken away. Yet thieves, murderers, racist bigots, and criminals do not see others (or certain others) that way. At first I dismissed this objection by claiming that it misses the point of Lévinas' theory. We could press the objection further by saying that even a purely theoretical philosophy cannot ignore a practical reality. However, I claim that the philosophical positions being asserted here are *strengthened* by an empirical study of human behaviour.

Here is why. When someone wishes to harm, manipulate, exploit, or victimise someone else, it is normally the case that first he must deprive the victim of her humanity and personhood. First the offender must humiliate and subordinate his victim, in order to silence the claim of humanity created by his victim's presence. If the other person can be thought of as an animal, an inferior creature, or otherwise less than human, then it is easier to nullify the sympathy for his suffering or to ignore the impulse for respect which his presence normally invokes. Offenders are often unable to proceed unless first this act of de-humanisation has been performed. Part of the evil of the kidnapper, the abuser, and the serial killer is not just the cruelty and death he inflicts on his victim but also the way he strips the victim of her standing as a human being. The racist bigot must convince himself that the people he hates are 'inferior', less capable of achievement or even less intelligent, more prone to wastefulness or crime, or even incapable of feeling pain. Soldiers must convince themselves that their enemies are 'targets' rather than people. For example, a Soviet soldier who had fought in Afghanistan told a reporter, "To kill or not to kill? That's a post-war question... The Afghans weren't people to us." [214] Sometimes an offender must strip himself of his own humanity as well, for instance by imagining himself to be something fantastic, stronger or smarter than other men, favoured by destiny or even by God. Only then is he able to ignore the call of the other person. But even the worst career criminals and killers cannot live without the acknowledgement and response of the people around them. Most commit acts of cruelty and barbarism only in rare moments. Afterwards they are likely to do something self-consciously mundane, like watch television or feed the dog, as if to restore themselves to normal. The rest of the time, criminals look for respect and acknowledgement from others the same way we all do. They look for that acknowledgement even from those whom they terrorize—that is, they look for it in the form of fear and submission.

A friend of mine from Northern Ireland confided in me something which serves as an excellent, albeit unnerving, example of this. He described how the sectarian views which his father impressed upon him from a young age, as well as news of atrocities committed during the Troubles as they happened, affected his view of people. Each story of an arson attack or an act of vandalism on a house or neighbourhood of his community, or a punishment-beating or a murder perpetrated by someone from the other community, made him think of the members of the other community as less and less like human beings. "I couldn't see them as people anymore, because they had done these things," my friend told me. "It made me want to do something worse back to them. But now, looking back, I hate myself for thinking it." Note the expression of what Glover called Moral Identity in my friend's last remark. It is an account of how this attitude not only affected his view of other people, but also his view of himself: he saw himself becoming someone he did not want to be. In fact he added, much to my surprise, "I was becoming my father". This observation about his own character motivated him to change his life.

Selfhood is a precious and beautiful thing; an Immensity in its own right. But it is also very fragile. There are people whose sense of who they are is built around irrational or inhuman concepts such as blind obedience, closed-minded tribalism, or pride for the capacity to be cruel. Certain political programmes have deliberately worked on changing people's sense of self, in order to secure people's loyalty and to make the functionaries of the system capable of carrying out its programme. As Glover explains, "Part of the Maoist project [of the Chinese Communist Revolution] was the deliberate construction of a new moral identity. To do this it was necessary to destroy people's previous sense of who they were and to make sure there was no room for it to grow back".[215] Similarly, Soviet communists attempted to *reduce* the vocabulary in official dictionaries, in order to control the people's ability to express themselves. By controlling what people can think and speak, it becomes harder for certain habits and commitments to be expressed, and so harder for the sense of selfhood that those actions represent to take hold. A people whose language has been controlled are more likely to be loyal and less likely to posses the imagination to rebel. This explains why George Orwell elaborated at length about language and "Newspeak" in his classic novel of political totalitarianism, "1984". The corporate brand-name logo and the advertising jingle serve that purpose in capitalist societies. It is distinct from the state-produced propaganda of communist societies only in that it is produced spontaneously by the private sector, whose interest is the acquisition of wealth. But its effect is the same: loyalty to a corporate brand (if not to a nation-state). This illustrates two things: not only the power of the resource of moral identity, but also the important need to cultivate the other resources to counter-balance that power when the moral identity comes under attack or is shaped into something monstrous.

Likewise, Glover observed that direct face to face contact is what often triggers the human responses, even though they may have been hardened by conditioning. Here is an outstanding example from Glover's collection:

In 1985, in the old apartheid South Africa, there was a demonstration in Durban. The police attacked the demonstrators with customary violence. One policeman chased a black woman, obviously intending to beat her with his club. As she ran, her shoe slipped off. The brutal policeman was also a well-brought-up young Afrikaner, who knew that when a woman loses her shoe you pick it up for her. Their eyes met as he handed her the shoe. He then left her, since clubbing was no longer an option.[216]

The act of picking up the shoe, and the direct eye contact, served to trigger in the policeman the breakthrough of normal human responses. As I interpret it, this is the breakthrough of the energy of spirit which is the same for all of us and which tends to bring people together.

There is something in every living thing that connects us to other people, and to the world, and makes us unable to live without them. There is something within each of us, a drive or force in human psychology, which cannot help but feel respect for others, feel compassion and sympathy for them, and indeed feel pride and self-esteem for being someone who does well. When we see the autonomy of the other person, revealed to us by the gaze and the voice, we feel we must respond to that autonomy, at least to acknowledge it, and we find it hard to do otherwise. This has nothing to do with submission and obedience. If that were so, we would be unable to respond: we would feel the call but would know not what to do. Rather, it has to do with who we are and how we live. It is this human spirit which enables us to respond to the Immensity with initiative and with confidence.

But the objection that the argument is "unrealistic" can take another form. Nietzsche, the philosopher whose remarks on spirit were found to be illuminating earlier, in some ways argues for a link between greatness of spirit, and the capacity for cruelty. Here, for instance, he describes this link as if it was a fact of history and of nature:

Let us admit to ourselves, without trying to be considerate, how every higher culture on earth has so far *begun*. Human beings whose nature was still natural, barbarians in every terrible sense of the word, men of prey who were still in possession of unbroken strength of will and lust for power, hurled themselves upon weaker, more civilised, more peaceful races, perhaps traders or cattle raisers, or upon mellow old cultures whose last vitality was even then flaring up in splendid fireworks of spirit and corruption. In the beginning, the noble caste was always the barbarian caste: their predominance did not lie mainly in physical strength but in strength of the soul—they were more *whole* human beings (which means, at every level, "more whole beasts").[217]

It would be all to easy to dismiss Nietzsche's point of view as that of an ignorant egotist. But his point is precisely that greatness of soul is not a matter of good or evil: greatness of soul is beyond such assessments. And this he asserts to be a factual observation, not a normative moral claim. But Nietzsche's other teaching is that since not everyone possesses a great soul, there will inevitably be something like a class division between those who have one and those who don't. Those who have one, in his mind, are justified in manipulating and exploiting those who don't, in order to continue to raise themselves up. *That* is the really disturbing part of his philosophy: that is the part which produced the Second World War.

As stated, the distinction between those who possess more spirit and those who possess less is mainly a matter of what they do. It is therefore an ethical category—it concerns how people choose how they will act, and how they will live. But it is not a principle of distinguishing right and wrong choices, nor is it a principle of distinguishing good and evil. Therefore nothing in this principle logically implies that the spirited person is sweet and kind. Indeed the things that have been said about Spirit so far can support the claim that someone who is consistently hard or vindictive is not necessarily lacking in Spirit. I have defined Spirit as the energy which leads us up to the threshold of the Immensity and carries us across. It is connected to physical powers like strength and courage, and to psychological instincts like sympathy and respect. But it can also be connected to viciousness, coldness, and even self-destructiveness. The world's best known tyrants and dictators were cruel, ambitious, hard, egotistical, and violent, but not necessarily lacking in spirit: perhaps they were able to inspire the loyalty and obedience of their supporters precisely because of the greatness of their spirit. If you find the idea that some people have more spirit than others hard to accept, then the idea that corrupt or evil people may have great spirit will be downright blasphemous.

The response to this claim, which meets it at its own level, is as follows. Nietzsche said we should be 'hard' and 'honest' when investigating human psychology, and he believed that if we were hard and honest, we would find the Will to Power. But we also find strong empirical evidence to support the notion of humanity. Glover's 'moral psychology' shows that the moral responses are very much a natural and normal part of human life. Furthermore, the Nietzschean project of self-creation can have an extraordinary de-humanising effect. Someone who directs his life according to his conception of the Will to Power ends up cutting himself off from human contact. Love and companionship is impossible for him, because he refuses to take anyone as his equal, except only temporarily. He repudiates the claims others may make upon him to come to their aid. Yet he also cannot reach out to others in times of his own need, for that would make him feel dependant and weak. But as Aristotle observed, we are all social beings, and no one can live without others. Someone who has no need for human company is "either too bad or too good, either subhuman or superhuman". (*Politics* 1253a1.)

Someone whose spirit manifests as cruelty and hardness, I'd like to say, effectively digs up his own root. This is a reason why one should not wish to become a Nietzschean *Ubermensch*. But it is not, I am almost reluctant to say, a way of denying the greatness and the spirit of the *Ubermensch*. I do not have a reply to this final form of the old objection. It is as much a part of the 'other side' of Virtue as any of the Heroic and Classical qualities. While this conclusion may be repugnant to some, it is at least honest (in the Nietzschean sense!). Popular opinion may hold that evil people possess corrupted spirits, or are lacking in spirit altogether. But it is not the job of a philosopher to put a stamp of professional approval on popular opinion. We lovers of the Immensity are not interested in finding new clothes for old emperors. The most I can say here is that there are some manifestations of greatness that are *not* to be emulated as role-models. And that the ability to recognise greatness wherever it is found, even in evil people, may be a defence against evil. It may help us to understand and respect the power of spirit, and help us to direct its kinetic momentum toward more praiseworthy goals.

§ 124. The Worthwhile Life

Some problems in human life are universal. Wherever we are, we must deal with the situation of our bodies and bodily needs, and the problem of how to fulfil those needs in whatever environment we live in. We are dealing with the way the world is always moving, changing, and transforming from one condition to another, as predictably and yet as unpredictably as the weather. We are struggling with social problems of all kinds, from economic uncertainty and political conflict, to the innovations of culture with their liberal champions and conservative critics. Alongside these are the problems of a person's internal life, arising in one's relation to herself, as in the questions of meaning, belonging, and purpose. And finally, we are faced with death, the most total of all transformations. No matter what the challenge, adversity, or situation, it seems to spiral into one of three basic themes, which I have called Immensities: the Earth, Other People, and Death.

Ancient heroic societies, on encountering these problems, responded by upholding models of excellent human beings, who by their heroism managed to 'overcome' fate. The worthwhile life, in the Heroic world-view, was a life worthy of being emulated by others, and worthy of having its story told by future generations. With their gods living in the natural world and in human relations, they could regard such things as sacred. Even while understanding such things as sources of trouble and uncertainty, they could regard them as having religious significance. They could find inspiration in fertile soil and the crops which grow there; mighty trees and romantic landscapes; the ordered movements of the sun, moon, and stars; good food and drink and music and storytelling in the feasting hall with friends and family; physical activities like athletics, hunting, working, fighting, dancing, and lovemaking; the beauty of music and poetry; material craftsmanship of high quality; and especially in noble attributes of personality like courage, honour, friendship, trust, generosity, justice, and the like. The worthwhile life, to them, was a matter of enjoying the good things in life, sustainably, deliberately, and completely, *notwithstanding the fates*, which rendered all such things precarious.

We, today, are facing the same Immensities. For us, too, the place where our lives are called into question is, at the same time, the place where we try to find a life worth living. I have described some of the things which we have in us that enable us to respond to the Immensity: Spirit, Wonder, Humanity, Integrity. Is there a special unifying quality which holds them all together? Is there a 'meta-virtue' which enables us to tell the difference between a good response to the Immensity, and a poor one? What is the major difference between a virtue and a vice? This is the last major unresolved question of this study.

Aristotle gives us a simple and elegant answer. A virtue is a quality of character that is necessary for success in the pursuit of *eudaimonia*, which is happiness, flourishing, a good and beautiful destiny. As the translation of the original Greek word for Virtue, *arete*, suggests, a virtue is an excellence in the service of that pursuit. It is a predisposition to act in a way that is fitting, noble, even beautiful. A virtue, he concludes, benefit she who possesses it. Furthermore it is a quality which, when called upon, can be measured by the Doctrine of the Mean. It is neither too much of what is called for, nor too little; it responds neither excessively nor insufficiently. But I claim there is more to it than that. I'd like to suggest that the Immensity adds four things to the understanding of virtue.

The first is the idea that the engine of virtue is Spirit. The Immensity calls to you from across the threshold, but it is not the Immensity itself which causes you to cross it. The Immensity presents you with questions to answer, and problems to solve, not laws to obey. It is a presence or a reality which calls for choices to be made, especially choices which would launch one's life forward in new or different directions than it would otherwise have gone. Spirit is what enables us to make those choices. Virtue is the result of those choices: or more to the point, it is the result of habitually choosing excellence in response to such situations. A virtue is like a circuit or a channel for the energy of one's spirit. The exercise of a virtue gets the energies of life flowing, both in oneself and in the things of the world around you. My first definition of a worthwhile life, therefore, is a life of aroused energy. However, as we have seen, Spirit is not, by itself, purely and perfectly 'good'. It can produce both heroes and monsters. It can lead to both excellence and to wickedness. The arousal of spirit is always a game played with fire.

The second addition to our knowledge of virtue and excellence is that human flourishing emerges from a constructive *dialogue* with the Immensity: and by 'dialogue' I mean an exchange of "two words" (*dia-logos*), an inquiring word spoken by one partner in a conversation, and an answering word spoken by the other. The Immensity is just such an enquiring word: it is a *question*. It asks, Who are you? What are you going to do? Where will you go from here? The Immensity does not provide a ready-made package of meaning, just on its own, for us to receive. And we are not passive recipients of its message. Neither do we create meaning in our lives *ex nihilo*, 'out of nothing', with some monumental Nietzschean act of egotistical will. Rather, a meaningful, worthwhile life emerges from the on-going dialogue with the Immensity. It evolves out of the very tension and strangeness inherent with any situation that calls one's life into question. The worthwhile life, with this second understanding, is a life spent in fruitful conversation with the Immensity.

This leads to the third thing that the understanding of the Immensity adds to our knowledge of virtue. It provides a new means to tell the difference between a good response and a poor one. An excellent response *affirms a positive reason beyond the self to live*. An excellent response affirms something to care about, a future to look forward to, a reason to act, a reason not to give up. And it affirms something that will be signif-icant to other people and to the world too, not just to one's own self. An Excellent response is one which finds the beauty, the wonder, the magic, the *meaning* of events in her life. It thereby affirms the goodness and beauty of both the Immensity itself, and she who answers its call. A reason to live, a worthwhile life, and a knowledge of oneself, all mutually imply each other. In the finding of any one of these three things, the other two soon appear. The worthwhile life, in this third way, is a life of purpose. It is a life with something worthwhile to do.

The virtues, then, can be defined as the qualities of character one needs to arouse the energy of life, use that energy to have a fruitful dialogue with the Immensity, and to find in the conversation something positive and valuable to live for. A virtue is a way to affirm the goodness of life. The creation of a life worth living, and a world worth living in, is the virtuous person's reward.

This may seem to merely repeat what Aristotle said, that the virtues benefit the possessor. But this understanding of virtue asserts something a little larger. The virtues, as habitual responses to ethically challenging situations, also configure you, define you, and shape you. They help you to both discover and also create your identity. Without them, not only would you miss the benefit they provide, but you would also be a different person. The biography of your life would take a different direction, and the known limits of your powers and potentials would be different. Aristotle wrote that we become virtuous or un-virtuous through our "transactions with our fellow-men." I'm asserting something wider: a transaction with *any* circumstance that calls your life into question is the occasion for becoming virtuous. The Excellent response is distinguished from the poor response in that excellence transforms the appearance of the Immensity into a revelation of meaning. In so doing, excellence also transforms she who responds into a more complete human being, more in possession of herself, more in command of who she is. Much of the time, the Immensity calls for the same virtues in response to its presence: we are called upon to be courageous, hopeful, trusting, generous, just, and so on. The right way to apply these virtues may differ from time to time and place to place. But the excellent response is always the same, in principle. It is the response which finds in the situation a way to affirm that life, one's own as well as that of other people and the natural world, is beautiful and good.

In saying this, I do not mean something abstract. Life is not an abstraction. Life is flesh and blood and bone. Life is green foliage and summer breezes, and also cold winter winds and sharp jagged rocks. Life is force and motion, always on the go, always in transition. Life is challenge, hardship, and unavoidable tragedy. Life is passion, love, desire, anger, bliss, pain, and fire. Life is thought and reason, and brave imagination. Life is foolishness, stupidity, and making mistakes. Life is death, sometimes. Life is experienced directly, through the senses, and grasped directly with the hand. In all these things, life is energy in motion; life is full of spirit. All of this must be affirmed as good, one way or another, in order to find purpose and meaning, and ultimately happiness. A virtue is a means to do exactly that. Like Frodo and Sam crossing the plain of Gorgoroth, the virtuous person looks up once in a while, and finds a star. She understands that life can be meaningful under any circumstances.

Similarly, the meaning of life is not an abstraction. It is something tangible, something one can see, something one can grasp. Yet like life itself, it too is always on the move. The meaning of life is *any given person's reason for living, at any given moment*. It might be to care for children, to run a small business, to write a symphony, to build a house, to complete a university degree. It might involve campaigning for social justice, or environmental protection, or some other important cause. It might involve being a good carpenter, a good musician, a good boyfriend or girlfriend. There can be many meanings for life, many reasons for living. You can have more than one at the same time. And they don't all have to be monumental. One's reasons for living can be very simple. But generally speaking, a reason to live is a practical accomplishment of some kind which one is aiming for in the world. It is a material or social or other circumstance that one is looking forward to, and in various ways trying to create in the present. It is not just a matter of changing one's attitude, for the conversation with the Immensity is not a purely internal dialogue. It is also a dialogue carried out in the world, through one's words, actions, and choices. For it is what we *do*, more than anything else, that creates a worthwhile life.

It may seem that this conception of the meaning of life, as something personal and flexible, is potentially arbitrary. Someone's reason for living might be to spread terror and pain. But I believe this can not be the case, because while a reason for living is found within yourself, still it is not created out of nothing. Charles Taylor observed that if choice, and only choice, confers value and significance upon the things we choose, then there will be a subjective arbitrariness involved, and ultimately our choices would be insignificant. As he argues, individual choices can only gain significance against a 'backdrop' or 'horizon' of meaning, supplied by things of value that transcend the self. The alternative view, that the things we choose are valuable simply because we have chosen them, is a circular argument: its logic fails on its own terms.[218] I do think each person's reason to live is her own. However, I also think it emerges primarily from an engagement with the firestorm of life, where problems are responded to, choices are made, possibilities imagined, relationships created, powers and potentials put to the test, and new self-discoveries thereby made. There is nothing arbitrary, relativist, or circular about this. Everyone's life is inevitably bound up with the lives of other people, the natural world, the accidents of fortune, and the transience of existence. All these things figure into of everyone's life story irrevocably. A spirited person responds to all these things in a life-affirming way. And in that response, she may find within herself a revelation of self-knowledge, and purpose, and happiness.

The fourth contribution that the Immensity makes to Virtue is a means to separate good responses from poor ones, and virtues from vices. In principle there are two kinds of poor responses to the Immensity. One is the *wretched* response. This is the response that fails to affirm anything good in one's life or the world. The wretched person is like the bereft person described earlier. He recognises the occasions when his life is called into question, but he responds with passive resignation, bland banality, or even morbidity. He not only fails to flourish as completely as he could, but he ends up dwelling on the things that make him miserable, and so perpetuates his misery. Such a life probably requires less exertion, less work, less *spirit*. Therefore it may be an easy life. But I think that no one would call such a life worthwhile.

The other form of un-excellent response to the Immensity is the *vicious* response. A true vice, it seems to me, is not simply a poor response to the Immensity. It is a refusal to respond at all. It is a disposition to ignore the call of the Immensity, to deliberately block it out of your world, to wilfully deny its presence. A truly vicious act is one which does not allow the dialogue with the Immensity to take place. Against the Earth, the vicious person thinks nothing of urban sprawl, pollution, and destructive forms of waste disposal or resource development. He may even deny the reality global warming and climate change, as some major corporate interests have done. Against other people, the vicious person is predisposed to cheating, stealing, lying, selfishness, and exploitation. An act of murder, singled out by Lévinas as the essence of injustice, eliminates the very possibility of dialogue with the victim. For once the victim is dead he can no longer speak. Something similar may be said of sexual violence, race prejudice, extreme religious fundamentalism, and various forms of domination and oppression. They all refuse to recognise that the other person is one who could be a partner in a dialogue. Against death, the vicious person acts as if he believes himself to be immortal. He takes unnecessary risks while driving his car, for instance, because he assumes that fatal accidents only happen to other people. He might continue doing the things of ignorant childhood well into middle age, or later: spreading malicious gossip, for instance, or playing unkind practical jokes. He might undergo unnecessary and expensive cosmetic surgery to preserve the appearance of youth. He might prefer to prolong someone's suffering from an untreatable disease or injury, rather than let go, if that is what the patient wishes to do. Such a person may not be lacking in spirit. But he ends up cutting himself off from the possibilities for self-discovery and life-enjoyment which the Immensity offers. His choices, therefore, are not just harmful to himself or others, but contrary to his own flourishing.

Choices like that are also ultimately futile. The presence of the Earth, other people, and death, are fundamental facts of life. To reject them is to declare war against reality. And this is a war that no one can win. This gives us the non-arbitrary, non-subjective 'background' against which responses to the Immensity can find their significance. But as we lovers of the Immensity know, even if you *do* respond to the Immensity, and respond with excellence, you still can't win. The world will always be larger than your ability to grasp; other people will never go away; and no matter what you do, you will still die. But one who engages the Immensity in a fruitful dialogue soon discovers reasons why her life is worthwhile *nonetheless*. She is thus able to *use* the meeting with the Immensity to affirm a reason for living. She can thus *enjoy* the meeting fully and completely. The Earth becomes the field and stage of life, a place to call home, and the wellspring of all that is beautiful and wondrous. Other people become friends, helpers, collaborators, and lovers. We can create permanent relations with others, such as by starting families and communities. We become able to receive even the criticism of others as something useful. Death, the final Immensity, becomes the impetus for creating a sense of purpose and meaning beyond the self, that is, the impetus for finding a reason to live which is above narrow self-interest. In the mind of a fully heroic and civilised person, death is not evil. And just as the excellent response affirms something to live for, so it can also affirm something to die for. The virtuous person accepts that death is a part of life, and that a good death can be an integral part of a good life.

This gives us a way to confirm the ancient picture of the worthwhile life. From the Heroic world, the *Hávamál* says:

All undone is no one, though at death's door he lie:
Some with good sons are blessed,
And some with kinsmen, or with coffers full,
And some with deeds well-done.[219]

'Deeds well done' are deeds that are fitting, effective, complete, honourable, noble, and beautiful: in a word, *excellent*. Notice how this stroph of the *Hávamál* associates excellence closely with social relations, family and friends, just as much as with 'coffers full' of material wealth. Integrity is implied by the 'death's door' perspective. If you knew you were about to die, or if you imagined yourself on your deathbed and looking back on your life, Integrity would tell you whether your reasons for living were consistent, sound, and life-affirming. And a strong notion of meaning is also implied by the claim that a life which possesses these blessings is 'not undone', that is, not wasted nor unfinished, but fulfilling and complete. As 'deeds well done' is the last line of the stroph, I think it is therefore accorded extra emphasis. The bounties of the embodied world, like feasting, sex, music, and art, are all rendered meaningful when they are involved with excellent deeds. The same goes for the development of personal powers and talents, like courage, and various rational qualities like prudence or temperance to regulate their use. Similarly, we could add to the list any number of activities which require, or produce, an arousal of spirit, and which direct that spirit to life-affirming ends. Literature, philosophy, the theatre, gourmet cooking, sports and athletics, scientific enquiry, social activism, even gardening, can all be included here. The worthwhile life is an active life. It is characterised by the feeling that the world offers itself to you as a place where your purposes may be fulfilled. Or, perhaps, the world appears as a place which has *its own* purposes which are being fulfilled in *you*. For that is how we often experience it. A good dialogue with the Immensity tends to arouse the feeling of being alive, being whole, being most fully *ourselves*. Indeed, happiness itself is the feeling that life is beautiful and good.

§ 125. The Messenger.

May I add one last thing, at this final hour? Many writers who contributed to our understanding of the Virtues also offered 'tests', that is, thought-experiments by which you can evaluate the worth of your own life. J.K. Rowling's Mirror of Erised is one of them. So is Tolkien's Ring of Power, especially on the occasion when someone is tempted to use it, or to take it from someone else. I've a test like this of my own, that shall take the form of a question, as well as an imaginary circumstance in which this question is asked. Take a relaxing breath or two before reading on.

Imagine that you are at home alone, preparing for bed. Then a messenger appears in your room, and says to you: 'Every part of your life, as you have lived it until this moment, has been prepared for you right from the beginning. The many millions of events, all the accidents and coincidences that had to happen so that you could be standing here, were all planned from the very start. For nothing in this universe is random, and nothing is caused by blind chance. Ancient chains of cause-and-effect, set in motion before the Earth was born, have now reached their conclusion in you, in this moment. Therefore this world has been prepared as the field and the stage of your life. Since the world was made especially for you, therefore *your experience of life* shall stand as the paragon of all experiences. And every measure has been taken to ensure that the quality of your life becomes the most beautiful, most fulfilling, most near to the divine, that any human life can be. The very *purpose* of civilisation and history has been all along to produce the experience of life that you are having right now. Your life shall henceforth stand as the greatest achievement of any God or mortal man, the exemplar of all pleasure and worth, the model of the highest happiness that anyone anywhere can achieve. In this way the purpose and destiny of the world, the very *meaning* of the world, has been fulfilled in you. And henceforth all people shall look to you as their model.'

Well, how would you respond? Would you say, 'No, that can't be right! My life is tired, dull, and weary! God help me, I am a fast-food clerk living in a smelly basement apartment with lousy plumbing and a landlord who hates me. All I do for fun is watch reality television and drink bad beer. No, my experience of life cannot serve as the paragon of the world. I cannot abide the thought that a wasteful, despairing, wretched, and banal kind of life like mine is a model of perfection. Surely the world can do better!'

The idea that the highest experience of life might be misery and frustration, or even grey mediocrity, should be thoroughly repugnant. Who would *aspire* to a life of dusty cellars and overcast skies? Who would call it *the highest possible human experience*? Only a soul almost entirely bereft of its energy would answer thus. If you find yourself answering the messenger like this, then let her serve as an initiator; let her message motivate you to change your life.

There must be someone who could answer the messenger by saying 'How wonderfully lucky, how extraordinarily, obscenely lucky, that I should be living the highest life a human being can live! And how great the responsibility, knowing it will be a model for others to follow. But I am up for it; I am the lucky one; I shall show the world what a good and beautiful destiny looks like. And I am grateful that this new work shall take no extra effort on my part, for I have already done it. Your news has only made it better.'

But even this spirited person would be partly wrong. Luck has very little to do with it. The worthwhile life is a gift the Virtuous person gives to herself. The creation of *eudaimonia*, the good and beautiful destiny, begins when you declare that your life *shall* be meaningful and worthwhile. It begins in the pursuit of a life that *could* stand as a model for others, and perhaps *ought* to be remembered by future generations. It begins with the realisation that the Messenger's story can only be true for you if it is also true for everyone and everything else. For they too are also products of the same forces in history, and the same inevitability. This idea can summon and stir up the sense of wonder. Not cold duty, but beauty; not naïve benevolence, but excellence, should be our aims here. Such are the qualities of the kind of person who could answer the messenger in a life-affirming way.

Put out the candle now, and close the window. For a moment before doing anything, be still and at rest. In your sleep tonight, let these thoughts drift in your dreams. And when the morning comes and the sun awakens, thank the messenger for her glorious good news.

BIBLIOGRAPHY

Aristotle, *The Nicomachean Ethics* trans. H. Rackham (Ware, Hertfordshire, UK: Wordsworth Classics, 1996)

Aristotle, *The Politics* trans. T.A. Sinclair, rev. Trevor Saunders (London: Penguin, 1981)

Bloom, *The Closing of the American Mind* (New York: Touchstone / Simon & Shuster, 1987)

Boethius, *The Consolation of Philosophy* trans. V. E. Watts (Penguin, 1969)

Carpenter, H. (ed). *The Letters of J.R.R. Tolkien* (Boston: Houghton Mifflin, 1981)

Casey, *Pagan Virtue: An Essay in Ethics* (Clarendon Press, Oxford UK, 1990)

Cicero, *On the Good Life* trans. M. Grant (London: Penguin, 1971)

Clare Boss, ed. *A Treasury of Irish Myth, Legend, and Folklore* (New York USA: Gramercy / Crown Publishers, 1986)

Curd & McKirahan, eds. *A Presocratics Reader: Selected Fragments and Testimonia* (Indianapolis USA: Hackett, 1996) pp. 36-7.

Dante, *Divine Comedy* (New York: Washington Square Press, 1968)

Dickens, *A Tale of Two Cities*, (New York, Dover Publications, 1999)

Euripides, *The Baccae* trans. M. Cacoyannis (New York: Meridian, 1987)

Firstbrook, P. *Surviving the Iron Age*, (London UK: BBC Worldwide, 2001)

Glover, J. *Humanity: A Moral History of the 20th Century* (New Haven: Yale University Press, 1999)

Glover, Jonathan. *Humanity: A Moral History of the 20th Century* (New Haven USA and London UK: Yale University Press, 1999)

Godwin, J. *The Pagan Dream of the Renaissance* (Boston: Weiser Books, 2005)

Goethe, *Selected Poetry* ed. & trans. By David Luke (Penguin, 1999)

Gregory, *Gods and Fighting Men* (Gerards Cross, Buckinghamshire, UK: Colin Smythe, 1970 [first published 1904])

Hamilton, E. *The Greek Way to Western Civilisation* (New York USA: Norton & Co., 1942)

Harries, Karsten. *The Ethical Function of Architecture* (Cambridge Massachusetts, and London UK: MIT Press, 2000)

Harris, M. *Our Kind: The Evolution of Life and Culture* (New York: Harper Perennial, 1989)

Herodotus, *The Histories* trans. A. de Sélincourt (Penguin, 1954)

Homer, *The Illiad* trans. Robert Fagels (Penguin, 1990)

Kahn, Charles. *The Art and thought of Heraclitus* (Cambridge UK: Cambridge University Press, 1979)

Kant, Immanuel *Groundwork of the Metaphysics of Morals* trans. H. J. Paton (New York USA: Harper Torchbooks, 1964)

Kant, *On History* ed. Lewis White Beck, (New York USA: Bobbs-Merrill, 1963)

Lévinas, E. *Time and the Other: And Additional Essays* trans. R. Cohen (Pittsburgh, USA: Duquesne University Press, 1987)

Lévinas, *Totality and Infinity: An Essay on Exteriority* trans. Alphonso Lingis (Pittsburgh: Duquesne University Press, 1969)

Machiavelli, *The Prince* trans. G. Bull (London: Penguin, 1999)

MacIntyre, Alasdair *After Virtue* 2nd Edition (London UK: Duckworth, 1895)

MacIntyre, Alasdair. *Whose Justice? Which Rationality?* (London: Duckworth, 1988)

Marcus Aurelius, *Meditations* trans. M. Hammond (Penguin, 2006)

McLuhan, T.C. *Touch the Earth: A Self-Portrait of Indian Existence* (New York USA: Promontory Press, 1971)

N. K. Sandars, trans. *The Epic of Gilgamesh* (Penguin, 1960) pg. 69.

Nietzsche, *Beyond Good and Evil* trans. W. Kaufmann (New York: Vintage, 1989)

Nietzsche, *The Antichrist*, trans. H.L. Mencken (Costa Mesa, California, USA: Noontide Press, 1980)

Nietzsche, *The Gay Science* trans. W. Kaufmann (New York: Vintage, 1974)

Ó h-Ógáin, Dáithí *The Sacred Isle: Belief and Religion in Pre-*

Christian Ireland (Wilton, Cork, Ireland: Collins Press, 1999)

Perkins, ed. *English Romantic Writers* (New York: Harcourt Brace & World, 1967)

Pico della Mirandola, *Oration on the Dignity of Man* (Chicago: Regnery Gateway, 1956)

Plato, *The Trial and Death of Socrates* trans. G.M.A. Grube (Indianapolis: Hackett, 1975)

Plutarch, *The Rise and Fall of Athens: Nine Greek Lives* trans. I. Scott-Kilvert (London: Penguin, 1960)

Ricoeur, Paul. *Figuring the Sacred* (Minneapolis: Fortress Press, 1995)

Ricoeur, Paul. *Oneself as Another* trans. Kathleen Blamey (University of Chicago Press, 1992)

Ricoeur, Paul. *Time and Narrative* Vol.1, trans. K. McLaughlin and D. Pellauer (University of Chicago Press, 1984)

Rousseau, J. J. *The Confessions*, (Penguin, 1966 [first published 1782])

Rowling, J.K. *Harry Potter and the Philosopher's Stone* (London: Bloomsbury / Vancouver, BC, Canada: Raincoast Books, 1997)

Rowling, J.K. *Harry Potter and the Goblet of Fire* (London: Bloomsbury / Vancouver, BC, Canada: Raincoast Books, 2000)

Rowling, J.K. *Harry Potter and the Half Blood Prince* (London: Bloomsbury / Vancouver, BC, Canada: Raincoast Books, 2005)

Rowling, J.K. *Harry Potter and the Deathly Hallows* (London: Bloomsbury / Vancouver, BC, Canada: Raincoast Books, 2007)

Schopenhauer, *The World as Will and Representation* Vol. 1. (New York: Dover, 1969)

Shakespeare, *Macbeth* (Penguin, 2005)

Shipley, J. *Dictionary of Word Origins* (New York: Philosophical Library, 1945)

Sturlson, Snorri. *The Prose Edda* trans. J. Byock (Penguin, 2005)

Tacitus, *Germanica* trans. H. Mattingly (Penguin, 1970)

Taylor, Charles. *The Malaise of Modernity* (Toronto: CBC Massey Lectures / Concord, Ontario, Canada: House of Anansi Press, 1991)

Tolkien, JRR. *The Fellowship of the Ring, The Two Towers*, and *The Return of the King* (London: Unwin, 1982 [first published 1954-5])

Tolkien, JRR. *The Hobbit* (London: Harper Collins, 1996 [first published 1937])

Tolkien, JRR. *Unfinished Tales of Númenor and Middle-Earth* (Boston: Houghton Mifflin, 1980)

Turville-Petre, G. *The Heroic Age of Scandinavia* (London UK: Hutchinson's University Press, 1951)

Twenge, *Generation Me: Why Today's Young Americans are More Confident, Assertive, Entitled – and More Miserable than Ever Before* (Free Press, 2007)

United Nations Intergovernmental Panel on Climate Change, Working Group I, *Climate Change 2007: The Physical Science Basis: Summary for Policy Makers* (Geneva, Switzerland: IPCC Secretariat, 2007)

Watling, E.F. (trans.) *The Theban Plays* (Penguin, 1974)

Wittgenstein, L. *Tractatus Logico-Philosophicus* trans. D.F. Pears & B.F. McGuinness (London: Routledge, 1974)

Yeats, W.B. *Collected Poems* (London: Picador Classics, 1990 [first published 1933])

—- *The Instructions of King Cormac Mac Airt* trans. Kuno Meyer (Dublin: Royal Irish Academy, 1909; Todd Lecture Series, vol. XV)

—- *The Nibelungenlied* trans. A.T. Hatto (Penguin, 2004)

—- *The Orkneyinga Saga* trans. Pálson & Edwards. (Penguin, 1981)

—- *The Poetic Edda* 2nd edition, trans. Lee M. Hollander (U. of Texas Press, 1962 / 2004))

—- *The Táin* trans. T. Kinsella (Oxford UK: Oxford University Press, 1970)

—- *Audacht Morainn* trans. F. Kelly (Dublin Ireland: Institute for Advanced Studies, 1976)

Bede, *The Ecclesiastical History of the English People* trans. Leo Sherley-Price (London UK: Penguin, 1955)

Bede, *The Ecclesiastical History of the English People* trans. Leo Sherley-Price, rev. R.E. Latham (Penguin, 1990)

—- *Beowulf* Dual Language Edition, trans. Howell D. Chickering (Anchor Books, Toronto Canada, 1977)

NOTES

[1] Taylor, *The Malaise of Modernity*, pg. 14.

[2] C.f. Twenge, *Generation Me*; Alexandra Shimo, "The Underachievers" *The Globe and Mail* 13 January 2007; Janet Hamlin, "College students think they're so special" *The Associated Press* 27 February 2007.

[3] Bloom, *The Closing of the American Mind*, pg. 84

[4] Robert Sibley, "Coolness as Self-Defence" *The Ottawa Citizen* 23 December 2006, pg. B2.

[5] Taylor, *The Malaise of Modernity*, pg. 14.

[6] Tacitus, *Germania*, 7 (pg. 107)

[7] Tacitus, *Germania*, § 8 (pg. 10)

[8] C.f. Harries, *The Ethical Function of Architecture*, pg. 137.

[9] Bede, *The Ecclesiastical History of the English People* II.13, pp. 129-30.

[10] *Beowulf*, XVI.1060 (pg. 109)

[11] *Beowulf*, VI.455 (p.g 75).

[12] Curd & McKirahan, eds. *A Presocratics Reader: Selected Fragments and Testimonia* pp. 36-7.

[13] McLuhan, *Touch the Earth*, pg. 12.

[14] Herodotus, *The Histories* pg. 78.

[15] *Hávamál* §47 (pg. 21)

[16] N. K. Sandars, trans. *The Epic of Gilgamesh* pg. 69.

[17] Gregory, *Gods and Fighting Men*, pg. 29.

[18] *Illiad*, Bk. 23, 100-110 (pg. 562)

[19] Kinsella, trans. *The Tain* pg. 197.

[20] "Another one of the common axes of criticism of the contemporary culture of authenticity is that it encourages a purely personal under-standing of self-fulfillment, thus making various associations and communities in which the person enters purely instrumental in their significance. At the broader social level, this is antithetical to any strong commitment to a community. In particular, it makes political citizenship, with its sense of duty and allegiance to political society, more and more marginal. On the more intimate level, it fosters a view of relationships in which these ought

to serve personal fulfillment. The relationship is secondary to the self-realisation of the partners." Taylor, *The Malaise of Modernity*, pg. 43.

[21] "Friends whose affection is based on utility do not love each other in themselves, but in so far as some benefit accrues to them from each other... And therefore these friendships are based on an accident, since the friend is not loved for being what he is, but as affording some benefit or pleasure as the case may be. Consequently friendships of this kind are easily broken off." Aristotle, *NE* 8.iii.1, 1156a14 (pg. 207-8)

[22] *NE* 8.iii.6, 1156b9 (pg. 208)

[23] *NE* 8. iv.6, 1157b1 (pg. 211)

[24] *NE* 8.1.1, 1155a2 (pg. 205)

[25] MacIntyre, *After Virtue*, pg. 123-4.

[26] MacIntyre, *Whose Justice? Which Rationality?* pg. 20. The passage continues as follows: "And since what is required of one in one's role is to give what is due to those others occupying roles that stand in determinate relation to one's own, king to kinsman or subject, swineherd to master or fellow servant, wife to husband and other kin, host to stranger, and so on, there is not the same contrast between what is to one's own interest and what is to the interest of others as that which is conveyed by modern uses of 'self-interest' and cognate terms." (pg. 20)

[27] Taylor, *The Malaise of Modernity*, pg. 39, emphasis his.

[28] As Aristotle says, "If then the great-souled man claims and is worthy of great things, greatness of soul must be concerned with some one object especially. 'Worthy' is a term of relation: it denotes having a claim to goods external to oneself. Now the greatest external good we should assume to be the thing which we offer as a tribute to the gods, and which is most coveted by men of high station, and is the prize awarded for the noblest of deeds; and such a thing is honour, for honour is clearly the greatest of external goods. Therefore the great-souled man is he who has the right disposition in relation to honours and disgraces. And even without argument it is evident that honour is the object with which the great souled are concerned, since it is honour above all else which great men claim and deserve." *NE* 4.iii.9, 1123b15 (pg. 94)

[29] *Illiad*, 6.522-5 (pg. 210)

[30] *Beowulf*, XXII.1529. (pg. 137).

[31] *Beowulf*, XXXIX.2890. (pg. 223).

[32] Casey, *Pagan Virtue*, pg. 77.

[33] Casey, *Pagan Virtue*, pg. 74.

[34] Tacitus, *Germania*, § 19 (pg. 118)

[35] Fergus Kelly, trans. *Testament of Morann* § 55-6, pg. 17.

[36] *The Instructions of King Cormac Mac Airt* § 29, pg. 45.

[37] Casey, *Pagan Virtue*, pg. 83.

[38] Tacitus, *Germania*, 14 (pg. 113)

[39] *Beowulf* O.20-25 (pg. 49)

[40] Tacitus, *Germania*, § 21 (pg. 119)

[41] Tacitus, *Germania*, § 11 (pg. 111)

[42] *Hávamál* § 2, (pg. 15)

[43] *Hávamál* § 48 (pg., 21)

[44] *Beowulf*, 0.1-3 (pg. 49)

[45] *Beowulf*, XIX.572 (pg. 83).

[46] *Orkneyinga Saga,* pg. 80-82.

[47] Bede, *Ecclesiastical History of the English People*, bk.1, ch.7 (pg. 52.)

[48] *Orkneyinga Saga* pg. 60.

[49] Kinsella, trans. *Táin Bo Cuailnge*, pg. 60.

[50] Aeschylus, *Agamemnon*, 1132; cited in Hamilton, *The Greek Way*, pg. 23.

[51] Sophocles, *Oedipus Rex* in E.F. Watling, trans. *The Theban Plays* pg. 52.

[52] Homer, *Illiad*, XII, 243.

[53] *Illiad*, 21.119-128 (pg. 523-4.)

[54] Lévinas, *Time and the Other*, pg. 73.

[55] Gregory, *Cuchullain of Muirthemney* in *A Treasury of Irish Myth, Legend, and Folklore* pg. 684.

[56] Lévinas, *Time and the Other*, pg. 50.

[57] *Beowulf*, 35, 2518-2537. (pg. 201).

[58] *Beowulf*, 35, 2587. (pg. 205).

[59] Tacitus, *Germania* § 19 (pg. 117)

[60] In case the reader has recently lost a loved one, let me please clarify that

I am *not* suggesting you should follow Deirdre's lead!

[61] Tacitus, *Agricola*, § 16 (pg. 66)

[62] Tacitus, *Germania*, § 18 (pg. 116)

[63] § 71, *Havamal*, pg. 24.

[64] Firstbrook, *Surviving the Iron Age*, pg. 167.

[65] Firstbrook, *Surviving the Iron Age*, pg. 180.

[66] Firstbrook, *Surviving the Iron Age*, pg. 175

[67] Firstbrook, *Surviving the Iron Age*, pg. 177

[68] "...the notion that what is obligatory on all—moral goodness—might be possible only for people favoured by fortune, or much easier for them, will strike many of us as a sort of scandal. If moral goodness is our supreme obligation, then to be morally good must be in the power of everyone, and not only, or especially, of those with special skills, or kindly feelings, or exceptional intelligence, or luck in other ways." Casey, *Pagan Virtue* pg. 202

[69] "Other traits generally attributed to the great-souled man are a slow gait, a deep voice, and a deliberate utterance; to speak in shrill tones and walk fast denotes an excitable and nervous temperament..." (*NE* 4.iii.35)

[70] Tacitus, *Germania*, § 6 (pg. 106-7)

[71] cited in Ó h-Ógáin, *The Sacred Isle*, pg. 99.

[72] Sturlson, *The Prose Edda*, pg. 12.

[73] *Beowulf*, XIV.954. (pg. 103).

[74] *Beowulf*, XVIII.1221 (pg. 119)

[75] Gregory, *Cu Chullain of Muirthemney*, in Clare Boss, ed. *A Treasury of Irish Myth* pg. 356

[76] *Illiad*, 9,.497-505 (pg. 265)

[77] *Hávamál, or The Sayings of Hár,* § 76, pg. 25.

[78] Caroline Wyatt, "Thor Searches for Odin" *BBC World News*, 26 May 2001; Alasdair Doyle, "Norse God Odin was Once A Real King" *Reuters* 3 December 2001.

[79] Sturluson, *The Prose Edda* pg. 6.

[80] Marcus Aurelius, *Meditations*, VII.55 (pg. 66)

[81] Cicero, *Discussions at Tusculim*, bk. 5 (pg. 84-5)

[82] *ibid*, bk. 5, (pg. 85)

[83] Boethius, *The Consolation of Philosophy* pg. 55-6.

[84] Cicero, *On Duties* II (*On the Good Life*, pg. 127

[85] *ibid.* pg. 129

[86] Lucretius, *On the Nature of Things* cited in Solomon & Murphy, *What is Justice?* pg. 78.

[87] *ibid*, pg. 78.

[88] Plutarch, *The Rise and Fall of Athens*, pg. 46.

[89] Plutarch, *The Rise and Fall of Athens* pg. 48, 49.

[90] *A Presocratics Reader*, pg. 30.

[91] Cicero, *Discussions at Tusculum*, bk. 5. (pg. 53)

[92] *A Presocratics Reader*, pg. 30.

[93] I should clarify, however, that Heraclitus, and the author of St. John's Gospel, lived a few hundred years apart. Heraclitus lived around the 5th century BCE, and the unknown author of the fourth gospel was writing around the year 90 CE—some sixty years after Jesus was crucified. Heraclitus' books were still available at that time, which we know because they were being quoted favourably by Stoic philosophers including Marcus Aurelius. So it is very likely that the author of St. John's Gospel had read Heraclitus, although absolute certainty may be impossible to obtain.

[94] Plato, *Apology*, 29a.

[95] Plato, *Apology*, 28b.

[96] Boethius recounted a story which reflects this change in the meaning of honour. "A certain man once made a virulent attack on another man for falsely assuming the title of philosopher more in order to satisfy his overweening pride than to practice virtue, and added that he would accept that the title was justified if the man could suffer attacks upon him with patience and composure. For a time he did assume patience and after accepting the insults asked with a sneer whether the other now agreed he was a philosopher. 'I would', came the reply, 'if you had not spoken'.". Boethius, *Consolation of Philosophy*, II (pg. 75)

[97] Fragment CXIV (Kahn); 119 (Diels); 94 (Marcovich). The translation used here is Kahn, *The Art and thought of Heraclitus*, pg. 80-1. Kahn translates *ethos* as 'custom, habit', and in the context of this fragment as

"the customary pattern of choice and behaviour distinctive of an individual or a given type". Pg. 335, fn. 376. According to translator and editor Charles Kahn, this fragment is best interpreted as saying that: "...a man's own character, not some external power, assigns to him the quality of his life, his fortune for good or ill. His lot is determined by the kind of person he is, by the kind of choices he habitually makes, and by the psychophysical consequences they entail or to which they correspond." Kahn, *The Art and Thought of Heraclitus*, pg. 261.

[98] 'Kalon', also appears in Aristotle's *Rhetoric* (136a33) where it is translated as "the praiseworthy good in itself" or as "the pleasant because of good", and in the *Topics* (145a22) as "the fitting".

[99] Kant, *Critique of Practical Reason* 5:128, pg. 107.

[100] C.f. MacIntyre, *Whose Justice? Which Rationality?* Pg. 97.

[101] MacIntyre, *Whose Justice? Which Rationality?* Pg. 98.

[102] *Havamal*, § 12, pg. 16.

[103] *Havamal,* § 20, pg. 17.

[104] M. Cacoyannis, trans. Euripides, *The Baccae* pg. 81-2.

[105] *Ibid*, pg. 19.

[106] Tacitus, *Agricola*, § 21 (pg. 73)

[107] § 70, *Njail's Saga*, trans. M. Magnusson and H. Pálsson. (London: Penguin, 1960) pg. 159.

[108] Ricoeur, *Oneself as Another* pg. 198

[109] "The activity of God, which is transcendent in blessedness, is the activity of contemplation; and therefore among human activities that which is most akin to the divine activity of contemplation will be the greatest source of happiness." (*NE* 1178b20)

[110] *Consolation*, II (pg. 67)

[111] Boethius, *The Consolation of Philosophy*, pg. 102.

[112] c.f. *The Politics*, 1331a30

[113] Cicero, *Discussions at Tusculum*, in *On the Good Life*, pg. 114.

[114] "Theology, seeing us from afar hastening to draw close to her, will call out: 'Come to me you who are spent in labour and I will restore you; come to me and I will give you the peace which the world and nature cannot give'". (*Oration* pg. 21)

[115] "And they paid me a greater tribute still, by taking me into their company, where I was the sixth in order of importance." (1:4, pg. 18)

[116] Godwin, *The Pagan Dream of the Renaissance*, pg. 6.

[117] Godwin, *The Pagan Dream of the Renaissance*, pg.2

[118] Cicero, *On Duties* II (*On the Good Life*, pg. 131.)

[119] "The prince must nonetheless make himself feared in such a way that, if he is not loved, at least he escapes being hated." (XVII, pg. 97)

[120] The president's words were broadcast on a television interview on NBC. When asked "Can we win?" the war on terror, Bush said, "I don't think you can win it. But I think you can create conditions so that the — those who use terror as a tool are — less acceptable in parts of the world." (See also: "Prez on war against Terror: "I don't think you can win it" *The Associated Press* 30 August 2004.) The following day he had to backtrack, saying that "we will win" but "not in the usual way", and that "we may never sit at a peace table" with the enemy.

[121] "Dan Balz and Shailagh Murray, "Lieberman Defeated in Democratic Primary" *The Washington Post / Associated Press* 9 August 2005.

[122] Cited in Glover, *Humanity*, pg. 250.

[123] Cicero, *On Duties* II (*On the Good Life*, pg. 132.)

[124] *Macbeth*, Act 5 scene 5, lines 19-28.

[125] *Macbeth* Act 5 scene 5, lines 46-52.

[126] *Macbeth* Act 5, scene 8, lines 31-4

[127] Groundwork, pg. 96.

[128] Kant, *On History*, pg. 21.

[129] *Urfaust*, in Goethe, *Selected Poetry*, pp. 15-16

[130] Goethe, *The Sorrows of Young Werther*, pg. 30.

[131] Goethe, *The Sorrows of Young Werther*, pg. 60.

[132] J.J. Rousseau, *The Confessions*, pg. 167.

[133] Goethe, *The Sorrows of Young Werther*, pg. 30.

[134] Goethe was dismayed, therefore, that the book apparently triggered an outbreak of suicides. Hundreds of young men and women, following Werther as their model, threw themselves into the throes of romantic love, and shot themselves when that love went unrequited. Some even wore the same blue and yellow suit that Werther was wearing. Goethe felt that they

had missed the point of his novel.

[135] Berlin, "The Essence of European Romanticism" in The Power of Ideas, pg. 204.

[136] Nietzsche, *Beyond Good and Evil*, § 225, pg. 154.

[137] Nietzsche, *Beyond Good and Evil*, § 225, pg. 154; emphasis his.

[138] Nietzsche, *Beyond Good and Evil*, § 259, pg. 203.

[139] "'Freedom of the will'—that is the expression for the complex state of delight of the person exercising volition, who commands and at the same time identifies himself with the executor of the order—who, as such, enjoys also the triumph over obstacles, but thinks within himself that it was really his will itself that overcame them. In this way the person exercising volition adds the feelings of delight of his successful executive instruments, the useful "under-wills" or under-souls—indeed, our body is but a social structure composed of many souls—to his feelings of delight as a commander." Nietzsche, Beyond Good and Evil, pg. 26.

[140] Nietzsche, *Beyond Good and Evil*, § 258, pg. 202.

[141] Nietzsche, *Beyond Good and Evil*, § 201, pg. 114.

[142] Nietzsche, *Beyond Good and Evil*, § 214, pg. 145.

[143] Nietzsche, *Beyond Good and Evil*, § 260, pg. 205

[144] Nietzsche, *Beyond Good and Evil*, § 227, pg. 155.

[145] Nietzsche, *Beyond Good and Evil*, § 259, pg. 204.

[146] "We must become *physicists* in order to be able to be *creators* in this sense—while hitherto all valuations and ideals have been based on *ignorance* of physics or were constructed so as to *contradict* it. Therefore: long live physics! And even more so that which *compels* us to turn to physics—our honesty!" *The Gay Science* § 336, pg. 266.

[147] Nietzsche, *Beyond Good and Evil*, § 227, pg. 155, emphasis his.

[148] Nietzsche, *Beyond Good and Evil*, § 257, pg. 201.

[149] Nietzsche, *The Antichrist* §2 / pg. 43, emphasis his.

[150] Nietzsche, *Beyond Good and Evil*, §153 / pg. 90.

[151] Nietzsche, *Beyond Good and Evil*, §164 / pg. 91

[152] Nietzsche, *Beyond Good and Evil* §287 / pg. 228.

[153] Nietzsche, *Beyond Good and Evil* §265 / pg. 215, emphasis his.

[154] In the Foreword which Tolkien wrote for later editions of *The Lord of*

the Rings, he indicated that the book was not to be read as an allegory. "As for any inner meaning or 'message', it has in the intention of the author none. It is neither allegorical nor topical." *Fellowship*, pg. 11.

[155] Carpenter, ed. *The Letters of J.R.R. Tolkien*, pg. 194.

[156] Two Towers, pg. 202 (my edition)

[157] Rowling, *Harry Potter and the Goblet of Fire*, pg. 456

[158] *ibid*. pg. 614-5.

[159] *Ibid*. pg. 627-8.

[160] Rowling, *Harry Potter and the Philosopher's Stone*, pg. 213.

[161] *Ibid*, pg. 214.

[162] Rowling, *Harry Potter and the Half-Blood Prince*, pg. 479

[163] c.f. *Harry Potter and the Deathly Hallows* pp. 559-562.

[164] c.f. *Harry Potter and the Half Blood Prince*. pp. 242-260

[165] The first writer to use the word 'Immensity' in the way I wish to use it was William Butler Yeats, although he uses it in a different context. It appears in his preface to Lady Augusta Gregory's Gods and Fighting Men (first published 1902). Here are his words: "When we have drunk the cold cup of the moon's intoxication, we thirst for something beyond ourselves, and the mind flows outward to a natural Immensity; but if we have drunk from the hot cup of the sun, our own fullness awakens, we desire little, for wherever we go our heart goes too; and if any ask what music is the sweetest, we can but answer, as Finn answered, 'what happens'." (pg. 18.) The word was also used in this way by an old Irish seannachie who was interviewed in a documentary film about Irish folk-religion which I saw when I was very small. I regret I can no longer recall the name of the film. The seannachie was describing how he occasionally greets people by asking, 'What way are you?' The kind of answer he was looking for was an answer that describes the spiritual significance that the person attributes to her life. When a journalist asked how the seannachie himself would answer his own question, he said, 'I am the way of a man who staggers between the immensities'. The journalist asked, 'What are the immensities?' The seannachie answered, 'Birth and death.'

[166] Ricoeur, *Time and Narrative*, vol.1, pg. 52.

[167] Nietzsche, *The Gay Science*, § 125 (pg. 181)

[168] Aristotle, *Politics*, VIII, 1239a29.

[169] Yeats, "Brown Penny" (circa 1910) in *Collected Poems* pg. 110.

[170] Ricoeur, *Oneself as Another*, pg. 150.

[171] Wittgenstein, "Proposition 1", Tractatus Logico-Philosophicus.

[172] Sturlson, *The Prose Edda* pg. 3-4.

[173] Lucretius, *The Nature of Things* cited in Solomon & Murphy, What is Justice? Pg. 75-6.

[174] Ricoeur, *Figuring the Sacred* pp. 52-3.

[175] "Unnatural Disasters" *The Guardian* 15 October 2003.

[176] Dickens, *A Tale of Two Cities*, pg. 8

[177] Lévinas, *Totality and Infinity*, pg. 73.

[178] Lévinas, *Time and the Other*, pg. 75.

[179] Lévinas, *Time and the Other*, pg. 82

[180] "Anticipation of the future and projection of the future, sanctioned as essential to time by all theories from Bergson to Sartre, are but the present of the future and not the authentic future; the future is what is not grasped, [it is] what befalls us and lays hold of us. The other is the future. The very relationship with the other is the relationship with the future." Lévinas, *Time and the Other*, pg. 76-7.

[181] Lévinas, *Totality and Infinity*, pg. 85.

[182] Harris, *Our Kind*, pg. 406.

[183] Maureen Dowd, "Powell without Picasso" *The New York Times* 4 February 2003.

[184] J. Gibson, private communication, 3 September 2006.

[185] Andrew Duffy, "Triage in the Death Zone", *The Ottawa Citizen* 30 July 2006, pp.B3

[186] Duffy, *ibid*, pg. B3.

[187] Ricoeur, *Figuring the Sacred*, pg. 51.

[188] Harris, *Our Kind*, pg. 400.

[189] Nietzsche, *Beyond Good and Evil*, § 12, pg. 20.

[190] The German word *Wissenshaft*, here translated as 'science', can also mean any kind of careful and deliberate intellectual activity. Thus it can include philosophical discourse, literary or artistic interpretation, and not just the sciences. A better translation of *wissenshaft*, in my view, would be

a compound word like 'wisdom-craft'.

[191] *Nibelungenlied* ch III (pg. 27)

[192] Perkins, ed. *English Romantic Writers*, pg. 210

[193] McLuhan, *Touch the Earth*, pg. 16.

[194] McLuhan, *Touch the Earth*, pg. 39.

[195] Hilary Osborne, "Earth's temperature is dangerously high, NASA scientists warn" *The Guardian* 26 September 2006

[196] "Report: Climate Change causing jump in natural disasters" *Reuters* 29 September 2000

[197] United Nations Intergovernmental Panel on Climate Change, Working Group I, *Climate Change 2007: The Physical Science Basis: Summary for Policy Makers* (Geneva, Switzerland: IPCC Secretariat, 2007)

[198] Martin Mittelstaed, "Welcome to the New Climate" *The Globe and Mail,* 27 January 2007.

[199] Steve Shifferes, "Chrysler Questions Climate Change" *BBC News* 10 January 2007.

[200] "Kyoto letter has come back to haunt Harper, Liberal MP's say" *CBC News* 27 January 2007.

[201] David Adam, "Oil Firms Fund Climate Change Denial" *The Guardian* 27 January 2005.

[202] C.f. Glover, *Humanity*, pp. 22-30.

[203] L. Jackson, private communication, 9 July 2007.

[204] C.f. Ricoeur, *Oneself as Another*, pp. 188-194.

[205] "The narrative constructs the identity of the character, what can be called his or her narrative identity, in constructing that of the story told. It is the identity of the story that makes the identity of the character." Ricoeur, *Oneself as Another*, pg. 147-8.

[206] "...we render the actions of others intelligible in this way because action itself has a basically historical character. It is because we all live out narratives in our lives and because we understand our own lives in terms of the narratives that we live out that the form of narrative is appropriate for understanding the actions of others." (MacIntyre, *After Virtue*, pg. 211-2).

[207] Rowling, *Harry Potter and the Philosopher's Stone*, pg. 297

[208] "The History of Galadriel and Celeborn" in Tolkien, *Unfinished Tales* pg. 251.

[209] *Hamdismál*, cited in Turville-Petre, *The Heroic Age of Scandinavia* pg. 32.

[210] *Meditations* 7.69 (pg. 69)

[211] Marcus Aurelius, *Meditations*, 3.8, pg. 20

[212] J.K. Rowling, *Harry Potter and the Deathly Hallows*, pg. 577.

[213] Rowling, *Harry Potter and the Philosopher's Stone* pg. 85

[214] Glover, *Humanity*, pg. 49.

[215] Glover, *Humanity*, pg. 296.

[216] Glover, *Humanity*, pg. 38.

[217] Nietzsche, *Beyond Good and Evil*, pg. 201-2.

[218] C.f. "Sources of Authenticity" in Taylor, *The Malaise of Modernity*, pg. 31-41.

[219] *Hávamál* §69 (pg. 24)

BOOKS

O is a symbol of the world, of oneness and unity. In different cultures it also means the "eye," symbolizing knowledge and insight. We aim to publish books that are accessible, constructive and that challenge accepted opinion, both that of academia and the "moral majority."

Our books are available in all good English language bookstores worldwide. If you don't see the book on the shelves ask the bookstore to order it for you, quoting the ISBN number and title. Alternatively you can order online (all major online retail sites carry our titles) or contact the distributor in the relevant country, listed on the copyright page.

See our website **www.o-books.net** for a full list of over 500 titles, growing by 100 a year.

And tune in to myspiritradio.com for our book review radio show, hosted by June-Elleni Laine, where you can listen to the authors discussing their books.

MySpiritRadio

A Pagan Testament
The literary heritage of the world's oldest new religion
Brendan Myers

A remarkable resource for anyone following the Wicca/Pagan path. It gives an insight equally into wiccan philosophy, as well as history and practise. We highly recommend it. A useful book for the individual witch; but an essential book on any covens bookshelf.
Janet Farrar and **Gavin Bone**, authors of *A Witches Bible, The Witches Goddess, Progressive Witchcraft*

9781846941290 320pp **£11.99 $24.95**

Shamanic Reiki
Expanded Ways of Workling with Universal Life Force Energy
Llyn Roberts and Robert Levy

The alchemy of shamanism and Reiki is nothing less than pure gold in the hands of Llyn Roberts and Robert Levy. Shamanic Reiki brings the concept of energy healing to a whole new level. More than a how-to-book, it speaks to the health of the human spirit, a journey we must all complete.
Brian Luke Seaward, Ph.D., author of *Stand Like Mountain, Flow Like Water, Quiet Mind, Fearless Heart*

9781846940378 208pp **£9.99 $19.95**

The Last of the Shor Shamans
Alexander and Luba Arbachakov

The publication of Alexander and Luba Arbachakov's 2004 study of Shamanism in their own community in Siberia is an important addition to the study of the anthropology and sociology of the peoples of Russia. Joanna Dobson's excellent English translation of the Arbachakov's work brings to a wider international audience a fascinating glimpse into the rapidly disappearing traditional world of the Shor Mountain people. That the few and very elderly Shortsi Shamans were willing to share their beliefs and experiences with the Arbachakov's has enabled us all to peer into this mysterious and mystic world.
Frederick Lundahl, retired American Diplomat and specialist on Central Asia

9781846941276 96pp **£9.99 $19.95**

The Way Beyond the Shaman
Birthing a New Earth Consciousness
Barry Cottrell

"The Way Beyond The Shaman" is a call for sanity in a world unhinged, and a template for regaining a sacred regard for our only home. This is a superb work, an inspired vision by a master artist and wordsmith.
Larry Dossey, MD, author of *The Extraordinary Power Of Ordinary Things*

9781846941214 208pp **£11.99 $24.95**

Celtic Wheel of the Year, The
Celtic and Christian Seasonal Prayers
Tess Ward

This book is highly recommended. It will make a perfect gift at any time of the year. There is no better way to conclude than by quoting the cover endorsement by Diarmuid O'Murchu MSC, "Tess Ward writes like a mystic. A gem for all seasons!" It is a gem indeed.
Revd. John Churcher, Progressive Christian Network

1905047959 304pp **£11.99 $21.95**

Healing Power of Celtic Plants
Angela Paine

She writes about her herbs with such a passion, as if she has sat all day and all night and conversed with each one, and then told its story herein. She has hand picked each one and talks of its personality, its chemistry, magic, how to take it, when not to take it! These herbs and plants are of this land, grown out of our heritage, our blood and sadly almost forgotten. I love this book and the author. It's a great book to dip into.
Trish Fraser, Druid Network

1905047622 304pp **£16.99 $29.95**

Tales of the Celtic Bards
Claire Hamilton

An original and compelling retelling of some wonderful stories by an accomplished mistress of the bardic art. Unusual and refreshing, the book provides within its covers the variety and colour of a complete bardic festival.
Ronald Hutton, Professor of History, University of Bristol

9781846941016 320pp **£12.99 $24.95**

Living With Honour
A Pagan Ethics
Emma Restall Orr

This is an excellent pioneering work, erudite, courageous and imaginative, that provides a new kind of ethics, linked to a newly appeared complex of religions, which are founded on some very old human truths.
Professor Ronald Hutton, world expert on paganism and author of *The Triumph of the Moon*

9781846940941 368pp **£11.99 $24.95**

Maiden, Mother, Crone
Claire Hamilton

Conjures the ancient Celtic Triple goddess in rich first-person narratives that bring their journeys to life. The greatest gift offered is Hamilton's personification of the goddesses' experience of pain, ecstasy and transformation. She brings these goddesses to life in such a powerful way that readers will recognize remnants of this heritage in today's culture.
SageWoman

1905047398 240pp **£12.99 $24.95**

Medicine Dance
One woman's healing journey into the world of Native...
Marsha Scarbrough

Beautifully told, breathtakingly honest, clear as a diamond and potentially transformative.
Marian Van Eyk McCain, author of *Transformation Through Menopause*
9781846940484 208pp **£9.99 $16.95**

Savage Breast
Tim Ward

An epic, elegant, scholarly search for the goddess, weaving together travel, Greek mythology, and personal autobiographic relationships into a remarkable exploration of the Western World's culture and sexual history. It is also entertainingly human, as we listen and learn from this accomplished person and the challenging mate he wooed. If you ever travel to

Greece, take "Savage Breast" along with you.
Harold Schulman, Professor of Gynaecology at Winthrop University Hospital, and author of *An Intimate History of the Vagina*

1905047584 400pp **£12.99 $19.95**

The Heart of All Knowing
Awakening Your Inner Seer
Barbara Meiklejohn-Free

A 'spell' binding trip back in time. It's a rediscovery of things we already knew deep down in our collective consciousness. A simple-to-understand, enjoyable journey that wakes you up to all that was and all that will be.
Becky Walsh LBC 97.3 Radio

9781846940705 176pp **£9.99 $24.95**

Crystal Prescriptions
Judy Hall

Another potential best-seller from Judy Hall. This handy little book is packed as tight as a pill-bottle with crystal remedies for ailments. It is written in an easy-to-understand style, so if you are not a virtuoso with your Vanadinite, it will guide you. If you love crystals and want to make the best use of them, it is worth investing in this book as a complete reference to their healing qualities.
Vision

1905047401 172pp **£7.99 $15.95**

Passage to Freedom
A Path to Enlightenment
Dawn Mellowship

"Passage to Freedom" is an inspiring title that combines a spiritual treasure trove of wisdom with practical exercises accessible to all of us for use in our daily lives. Illustrated throughout with clear instructions, the information and inspiration emanating from Dawn Mellowship is a major achievement and will certainly help all readers gain insight into the way through and around life's problems, worries, and our own emotional, spiritual and physical difficulties.
Sandra Goodman PhD, Editor and Director, Positive Health

9781846940781 272pp **£9.99 $22.95**

The Good Remembering
A Message for our Times
Llyn Roberts

Llyn's work changed my life. "The Good Remembering" is the most important book I've ever read.
John Perkins, NY Times best selling author of *Confessions of an Economic Hit Man*

1846940389 196pp **£7.99 $16.95**